The SHERLOCK HOLMES COMPLETE PUZZLE COLLECTION

THIS IS A CARLTON BOOK

Published by Carlton Books Ltd
20 Mortimer Street
London W1T 3JW

A CIP catalogue for this book is available from the British Library.

ISBN 978-1-78097-960-1

Editorial: Matt Lowing and Chris Mitchell
Text and puzzles: Tim Dedopulos
Design manager: Stephen Cary
Picture research: Steve Behan
Puzzle checker: Richard Cater
Production: Lisa French

Content previously published as *The Sherlock Holmes Puzzle Collection* and *The Sherlock Holmes Puzzle Collection: The Lost Cases*

The publishers would like to thank Mary Evans Picture Library for their kind permission to reproduce the pictures in this book.

Every effort has been made to acknowledge correctly and contact the source and/or copyright holder of each picture and Carlton Books Limited apologizes for any unintentional errors or omissions, which will be corrected in future editions of this book.

Printed in Dubai

10 9 8 7 6 5 4 3 2

The SHERLOCK HOLMES COMPLETE PUZZLE COLLECTION

Dr John Watson

Over 200 devilishly
difficult mysteries, inspired
by the world's
greatest detective

CARLTON
BOOKS

Contents

ELEMENTARY

STRAIGHTFORWARD

CUNNING

7

FIENDISH

Introduction

THE NAME OF MY DEAR FRIEND and companion Mr. Sherlock Holmes is familiar to all who possess any interest whatsoever in the field of criminal investigation. Indeed, there are some weeks where it hardly seems possible to pick up a newspaper without seeing his name splashed luridly across the front page. Unlike so many, however, his renown is justly deserved – not for nothing has he frequently been heralded as England's greatest detective, living or dead. Personally, I suspect that his abilities are unmatched anywhere in the world at this time.

I myself have been fortunate enough to share in Holmes' extraordinary adventures, and if I have been unable to rival his insight, I have consoled myself by acting as his de facto chronicler. I also flatter myself a little with the notion that I have, betimes, provided some little warmth of human companionship. We have spent many years, on and off, sharing rooms at 221b Baker Street, and I like to think that the experience has enriched both our existences. My name, though it is of little matter, is John Watson, and I am by profession a doctor.

My dear friend has long had a passionate ambition to improve the minds of humanity. He has often talked about writing a book that will help to instil the habits which he considers so absolutely vital to the art of deduction. Such a tome would be a revolutionary step in the history of mankind, and would most certainly address observation, logical analysis, criminal behaviour, scientific and mathematical knowledge, clear thinking, and much more besides. Alas, it has yet to materialise, for the world is full of villainy, and Sherlock Holmes is ever drawn to the solution of very real problems.

But over the course of our adventures, Holmes has never given up on the cause of improving my modest faculties. On innumerable occasions, he has presented me with opportunities to engage my mind, and solve some problem or other which to him is perfectly clear from the information already available. These trials have sometimes been quite taxing, and have not always come at a welcome moment, but I have engaged in all of them to the very best of my abilities. To do otherwise would be to dishonour the very generous gift my friend is making me in devoting time to my analytical improvement.

In truth, I do believe that his ministrations have indeed helped. I consider myself to be more aware than I was in my youth, and less prone to hasty assessments and faulty conclusions. If I have gained any greater talent in these areas, it is entirely thanks to the efforts that my friend has exerted on my behalf, for it is most certainly not an area for which I am naturally disposed. Give me a sickly patient, and I feel absolutely confident of swiftly arriving at the appropriate diagnosis and, to the limits provided by medical science, of attaining a successful recovery for the poor unfortunate. But my mind does not turn naturally to criminality, violence or deception. If this were a perfect world, then we would all co-exist in genial and honourable honesty, and I would be perfectly suited for the same. Alas, that is far from the case, and my dear friend is far better adapted to the murky undertows of the real world than I.

Still, as I have already attested, Holmes' little trials have had a beneficial effect even on me. For one who is more readily disposed to such efforts, the results may well be commensurately powerful. Thus, I have taken the liberty of assembling this collection.

Working assiduously from my notes, I have compiled well over two hundred of the puzzles that Holmes has set me over the years. I have been assiduous in ensuring that I have described the situation as I first encountered it, with all pertinent information reproduced. The answers are as detailed as I can usefully make them. Some I managed to answer successfully myself; for others, I have reproduced Holmes' explanations as accurately as my notes permit.

To improve the accessibility a little, I have attempted to order the trials into approximate groupings of difficulty – *elementary*, *straightforward*, *cunning* and *fiendish*, to be exact. Holmes has a devious mind, and there were times when he was entirely determined to baffle me, whilst on other occasions, the problems were simple enough to serve as illustrative examples of certain principles. I believe that I have broadly succeeded in classifying the difficulty of his riddles, but I beg your indulgence in so uncertain a matter. Every question is easy, if you know the answer, and the opposite holds equally true.

It is my fervent hope that you will find this little volume enlightening and amusingly diverting. If it may prove to sharpen your deductive sense a little, that would be all the vindication that I could ever possibly wish; all the credit for such improvement would be due Holmes himself. I, as always, am content to be just the scribe. I have taken every effort to ensure that the problems are all amenable to fair solution, but if by some remote happenchance that should prove not the case, it must be clear that the blame lies entirely on my shoulders, and that none should devolve to my dear companion.

My friends, it is with very real pleasure that I present to you this volume of the puzzles of Mr. Sherlock Holmes.

I remain, as always, your servant,

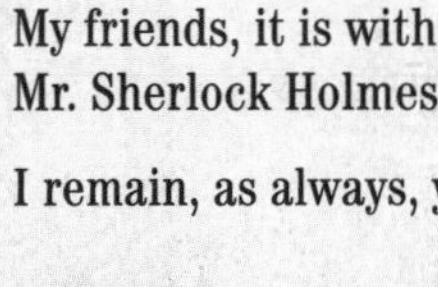

Dr John H. Watson.

PART ONE

ELEMENTARY

A Matter of Identity

As we were walking through Regent's Park one afternoon, on our way to St. John's Wood, Holmes drew my attention to a pair of young women engaged in earnest conversation with a somewhat older man.

"Observe those ladies, Watson. What can you tell me about them?"

I studied them closely. They were as alike as peas in a pod, identical in facial structure, deportment, dress and coiffure. I said as much to my companion, and asserted that they surely had to be twins.

"Indeed?" Holmes looked amused. "For a fact, I can tell you that Louise and Lisa Barnes share the same mother, the same father, and the same precise day of birth, but I'm afraid you are utterly wrong. They are most certainly not twins."

Can you explain?

❋ Solution on page 273 ❋

A Difficult Age

"Logic is paramount, Watson." Sherlock Holmes was in a thoughtful mood, pacing slowly up and down the length of the sitting room, pipe firmly in hand. "The better able you are to pick apart a problem in your mind and evaluate all of the ramifications it encompasses, the stronger will be your deductive reasoning."

"Of course," I said.

"So, then. Let us say that I know of a particular fellow. Today is a singular occasion, for two days ago, he was 25 years of age, but next year, he will be 28.

How is such a thing possible?"

✱ Solution on page 274 ✱

15

The First Curiosity

Holmes has on occasion extolled the virtues of absurdity as a way of breaking free of the confines of regimented thinking. "Watson," he told me once, "the ridiculous is one of the best methods to shatter the iron confines of pedestrian thought."

With that in mind, he engaged in a programme of springing baffling and sometimes ludicrous problems on me at moments when I least expected them.

The first caught me completely unawares.

"I have considered commissioning a house with windows facing south on all four sides," Holmes declared, to my amazement. "Do you think this is a good idea?"

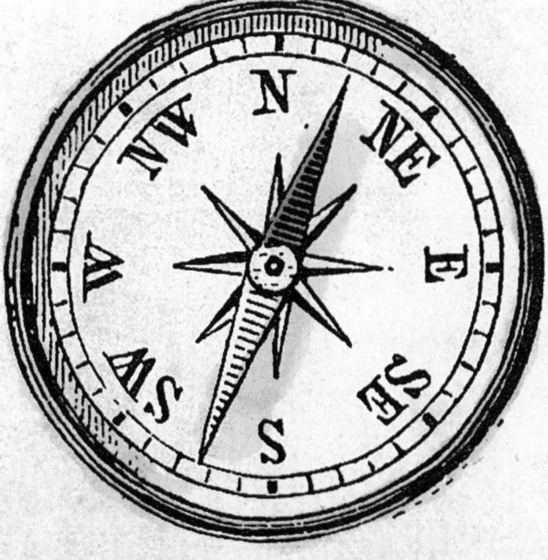

❋ Solution on page 274 ❋

16

Rabbit Race

"Did you ever engage in a rabbit race?" Holmes' rather peculiar question brought me up short, and I stopped in the street to stare at him. "Why do you ask?"

"I was considering an illustrative question for you, my dear Watson," he said, "such matters can be somewhat revealing."

I shrugged. "Pray continue, if my lack of the requisite experience does not invalidate the problem."

"Not in the least, the problem is quite elementary. Imagine then, if you will, a pair of quite companionable rabbits of long-standing familiarity to each other. Instructed to race for the amusement of children, they are happy enough to amble along at the same speed, keeping each other company and, inevitably, yielding a dead heat."

"That seems plausible enough," I ventured.

"After the race, one of the judges notes that the first half and second half were run in the same time, and that the last quarter lasted as long as the penultimate. If the first three quarters took 6¾ minutes, how long was the entire race?"

❋ Solution on page 275 ❋

The Barrel

“Come Watson,” said Holmes. “Let’s test your mental musculature with a simple challenge.”

“Very well,” I replied.

“Imagine you are faced with a sizeable, open-topped barrel of water,” Holmes instructed me. “You know that it is close to being half-full, but you do not know whether it is exactly so, or more or less. With no instrument available with which to measure the depth of the water, can you devise a means to ascertain its state?”

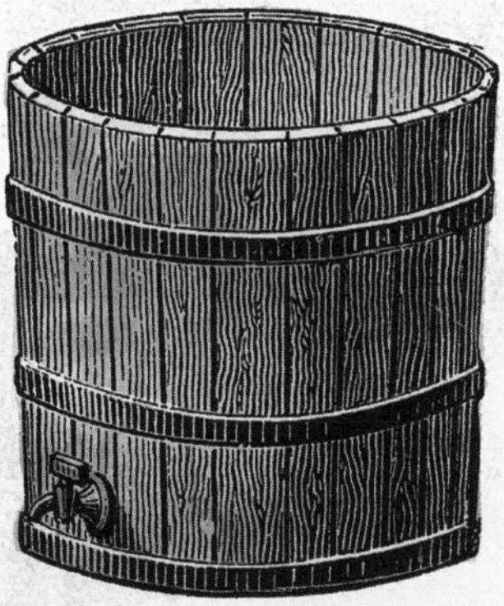

❋ Solution on page 275 ❋

The First Mental Trial

"My dear Watson, a keen mind must be able to follow a thread of logic through convoluted labyrinths at which even an Ariadne would quail."

"I dare say that's true," said I. "Do I assume that means you have some trial for me?"

"I couldn't say," replied Holmes, "but if you did, that assumption would be well founded."

"Very well," I said. "Pray, go ahead."

"This should prove a gentle warm-up. There is something you own that it is yours, and always has been. Despite this, all your friends use it, whilst you yourself rarely get to make use of it at all. What am I talking about?"

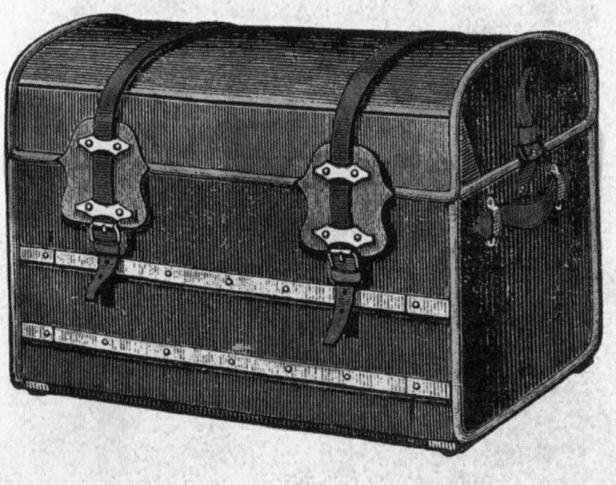

❋ Solution on page 276 ❋

Elementary Geometry

One morning, as we were heading into South London, Holmes said to me, "A grasp of elementary geometry is a powerful weapon in the fight against crime."

I admitted that this sounded like sage advice, given the occasional need to apprehend villains by the swiftest route.

"There are other purposes as well," Holmes admonished.

"Of course," I said.

"So here is a basic little matter for you. Assume you are a villain, robbing a warehouse near a straight stretch of the river. Your plan is to carry your goods to the riverside, where a confederate is waiting with a small boat, and then have him sail off casually while you make your way back to a cab, waiting at the entrance to the dock. Obviously you need to make sure that your total route is the shortest possible, as every second may count. How would you go about calculating the precise location of the boat along the river-bank?"

Solution on page 276

The First Literal Oddity

As you must be aware, with this volume in your hands, I have some very meagre scrapings of ability in the weaving of sentences. I hesitate to call my facility, such as it is, a talent, but I hope I have managed to document my friend's extraordinary adventures in an amusing manner.

In amongst his efforts at improving my very basic skills of deduction and investigation, Holmes from time to time would challenge my linguistic facility. Whilst this was undoubtedly a change of pace from some of his little challenges, he none the less managed to ensure that his wordplay provided me with a genuine test. These trials of his may be diverting to you, and are offered in that spirit.

I was minding my own business one morning, munching on a piece of Mrs. Hudson's toast, when Holmes suddenly barked "Honorificabilitudinitatibus!"

I managed to splutter "I beg your pardon?"

"Honorificabilitudinitatibus, Watson. 'Of honour', more familiarly. You may place some blame for its inclusion in the canon of English at the feet of Master Shakespeare. Or if that monstrosity is not to your taste, how about 'unimaginatively', 'verisimilitudes', or 'parasitological'?

"I don't follow you," I said.

"What do those words have in common, man?
It should be simplicity itself for a fellow of your abilities."

❋ Solution on page 277 ❋

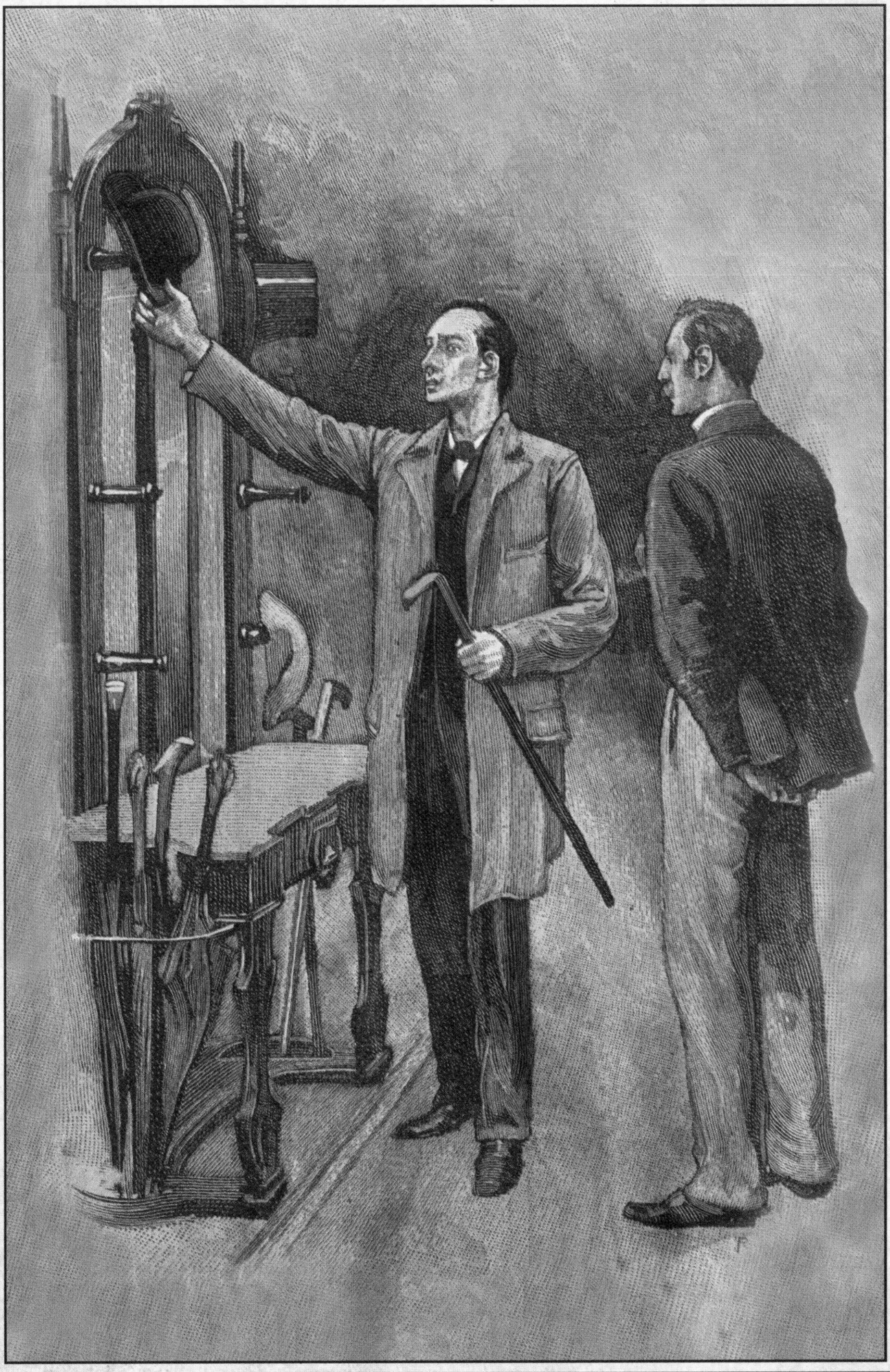

The Meal

There was one occasion where I did manage to stump the great Sherlock Holmes with a puzzle that vexed him most mightily. The problem is simple. A woman presented a man with some food. He duly ate it. As a direct and absolute consequence of eating it, he died. If he had not eaten it, his death would have been averted.

As I explained in response to Holmes' terse questioning, the food was perfectly pleasant. It was not in the least bit toxic or deleterious, nor did it convey any disease or ailment. It was not stolen, or subject to mistaken identity, and no-one later came looking for it. The man consumed the food successfully, without any discomfort, and with no obstruction of the air passages. In fact, he enjoyed it, and his death was greatly delayed. Never the less, the food he consumed on that specific occasion was solely responsible for his demise.

Can you see the answer that even the world's greatest detective could not?

❋ Solution on page 277 ❋

Regent Street

As we were travelling along Regent Street one evening, Holmes paused to engage a painter who, with his mate, was just finishing up the work of renewing the lamp posts along the street.

Holmes quickly ascertained that the men had been apportioned the east and west sides of the street. One had arrived early, and made a start, but had picked the wrong side. His companion arrived after three posts had been completed, and the chap moved back to start on the correct side. We caught them as they were finishing, and to help speed the process up, the tardier man had switched to his mate's side at the end, and painted six posts for him.

Thus completed, the men were idly curious as to which had painted the more posts, the early fellow or the tardy one, and by how many. They confirmed that there were the same number of posts on both sides

Holmes declared the matter elementary, and indicated I should explain. What would your answer have been?

❋ Solution on page 278 ❋

Rider

"Allow me to vex you with a little question about a horseback journey," Holmes said to me.

"I am not a comfortable rider these days," I said.

"That is of no matter. It will not affect your appreciation of the question."

I nodded. "Very well."

"On a journey in the country, you travel to your destination at a reasonably sprightly 12 miles per hour. On the return, you set a more modest pace, in deference to your steed's exertions, and manage just 8 miles per hour. What is your average speed for the journey?"

Solution on page 279

25

The Second Mental Trial

"I am going out for a while, Watson."
"I trust you will have a congenial time," I replied.

"I feel it can be made more profitable by the combination of a little business with a little mental work on your part," Holmes told me.

"Oh?"

"I will cheerfully buy you a cup of tea if you meet me on the corner of the Strand at a precise time."

"And when is that?"

"That should be an elementary matter for you to deduce, my friend. Three hours before the meeting time is as long after three in the morning as it is in advance of three in the afternoon. Will I see you there?"

I assured him that he would. Could you have done the same?

Solution on page 279

The Gang

One evening, after Sherlock Holmes and myself had provided some assistance to Scotland Yard on a matter of some delicacy, Inspector Lestrade took the opportunity to challenge my companion with what he hoped would prove a vexatious riddle. His hopes were unfounded of course, but I'm sure that comes as no surprise.

"I was at a break-in yesterday, Mr. Holmes," began the Inspector. "Nasty business. A group of burly young men apprehended a man and his wife outside their home, and forcibly restrained them there. Meanwhile, two of their number kicked the door straight off its hinges and charged in there. They came out a few minutes later with the couple's most precious treasure. Then, to top it all off, rather than scarpering like your usual villain would, they handed their loot over to the weeping wife, and went about their business. I saw the whole thing, but I didn't make even a single arrest. What do you make of that?"

✱ Solution on page 280 ✱

The First Portmanteau

"Observation, analysis, deduction." Holmes punctuated each word with a brisk rap on the arm of his chair. "These are the cornerstones of the art of investigation. I want you to study this little arrangement I've had drawn, Watson."

I agreed to do so of course, but confessed a certain bemusement as to what I was looking for. I have copied it for you, of course.

"It is a visual portmanteau, old chap. The image contains a number of clues referring to a rather well-known spot in London. Different elements of the picture show different aspects of the location, and in combination, there is only one place on Earth where it could possibly be. You should be able to identify it rather easily, I think."

I looked again, and you know, Holmes was right. There was only one place the image could refer to. Do you know where?

✱ Solution on page 280 ✱

The Third Mental Trial

"My dear Watson, will you understand my meaning when I inform you that an entirely hypothetical acquaintance of mine, Alfie, told me about a bus journey he had recently made."

"I see," I said. "This is by way of a puzzle."

"Quite so. Alfie told me that his bus was quite busy, and he was initially unable to seat himself. His fortunes changed at the half-way mark however, and he finally got the chance to take the weight off his feet. When he had just one half as far to go again to his destination as the distance for which he had been seated, an infirm gentleman boarded the bus, and Alfie generously gave up his place for the man. At the end of his journey, he decided to calculate the proportion for which he had managed to avoid standing. Can you tell me what it was?"

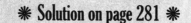

Solution on page 281

Catford

"I heard of a schoolmistress, down in Catford, with a rather peculiar morning ceremonial," Holmes told me.

"The mind boggles," I replied. Catford can be a queer place, although it is rightly famed for its historic curry house.

"It is her habit," he continued, "to start the school day with a series of polite bows. Each boy must bow to each other boy, and then to each girl, and then to the teacher. Likewise, each girl must bow to each other girl, and then to each boy, and then to the teacher. The whole process requires 900 obeisances. If I tell you that there are twice as many girls in the school as boys, you will undoubtedly be able to tell me how many boys there are there."

"Undoubtedly," I replied drily.

Can you solve the issue?

❋ Solution on page 281 ❋

30

The Second Curiosity

I was reading some patient notes one evening. I was quite absorbed, so when Holmes said, "I believe there to be a place that is located between England and France, yet is further from England than France actually is."

"Great heavens!" I exclaimed, startled out of my contemplation.

"Not quite," Holmes remarked wryly. "Care to make a more terrestrial guess?"

✻ Solution on page 282 ✻

Trains

"You know how important it can be to have a clear impression of the way that trains perform in this day and age, Watson. Entire cases can hang on it."

I agreed whole-heartedly.

"A sense of timing in these matters is highly desirable. So pray, consider this little matter. Two trains start on a journey at the same moment, each headed to the origin point of the other, via parallel tracks. When they pass each other, the slower still has four hours to travel to its destination, whilst the faster has just one hour still to go. How many times faster is the one going than the other?"

❋ Solution on page 282 ❋

Gloucester

We were investigating a matter concerning a Gloucester cattle-man, a nasty storm, and some peculiar stone shards. One of the elements of the case involved the degree to which the fellow was watering his 'honest' milk.

A maid, tired of her employer, was able to inform us of the procedure. He started with two kegs, one – the smaller – of milk, and the other of water.

He then manipulated the milk as follows. First, he poured enough water into the smaller keg to double the contents. Then he poured back enough of the mix into the larger keg to in turn double its contents. Finally, he poured liquid from the larger keg into the smaller until both held the same volume.

Then he sent the larger keg to London, as the finished product.
Can you say what amount of the final blend was actually milk?

✱ Solution on page 283 ✱

Wiggins

On one memorable morning, young Wiggins, the lead scamp of Holmes' Baker Street Irregulars, put a poser to me after completing some small errand for his master. It is my suspicion that secretly he wanted to put the question to Holmes himself, but either lacked the nerve, or feared that it would be too trivial a matter for the great man.

If the latter, then he made his choice wisely.

"Here guv'nor," Wiggins said to me, "I've got a little riddle. What do you say we wager a farthing on your being able to solve it."

"Is that so? A farthing. Very well. What will you give me if I have the answer?"

"A smile," said the little rascal. "Surely you wouldn't take money from one such as myself, Doctor."

"Very well," I said. "I enjoy a challenge."

"You won't regret it, sir. So, tell me, what occurs once in June, once in July, and twice in August?"

My first thought was the full moon, but I quickly discarded that as not being the case in this year. "Hmm," I said. I could see Holmes' eyes glittering with amusement, but he said nothing, and left the matter to me to resolve.

✷ Solution on page 283 ✷

To Catch a Thief

One night in Deptford, we were waiting in a house for a burglar to attend. The man appeared as expected, but managed to turn heel and flee. Holmes shot after him as swiftly as possible.

He returned after a short space, with the burglar in tow. I enquired as to how difficult it had proven to catch the fellow.

"It was a simple matter," Holmes replied. "By the time I left the house, he had a 27-step lead, and he was taking eight steps to my five. It would have been bleak, save for the fact that he is a short man, and two of my strides were worth five of his. In fact, from that, you should be able to tell me how many strides I required to apprehend the scoundrel."

❋ Solution on page 284 ❋

The Second Literal Oddity

I was reading quietly one evening in Baker Street when Holmes put down his violin and turned to me.

"I have another little lexical trial for you, if you are of a mind to accept," said he.

"Of course," I replied.

"Capital. Ponder then upon the words 'cabbaged' and 'fabaceae', the latter being of leguminous fame. What oddness do they share, and why might I remark upon it?"

Solution on page 284

Cheapside

We were engaged on some business on Cheapside one afternoon when Holmes turned to me.

"Answer me something, Watson," he said.

"Of course," I replied.

"If there is a fellow whose mother is my mother's mother-in-law, then who is he to me?"

It occurred to me that Holmes must have been talking to Mrs. Hudson again.
I put this to him, and he did not deny it, but required an answer none the less. Can you reckon it out?

✱ Solution on page 285 ✱

The Third Curiosity

"Quick, Watson!" Holmes passed me a small pad and a pencil. "Write down the numeric figures for twelve thousand, twelve hundred and twelve pounds!"

I paused, momentarily confounded. "What?"

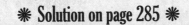

✻ Solution on page 285 ✻

Swinging Pendulums

"I have a little physical science question in mind for you, Watson."

I nodded. "I'll do my best," I said.

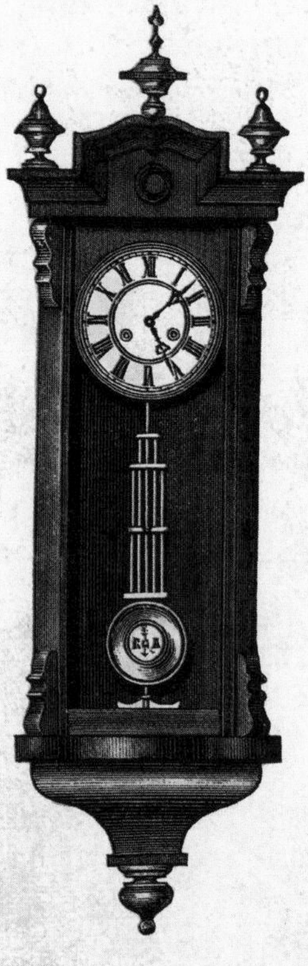

"Imagine a vacuum jar with a pair of pendulums suspended inside. They are identical, the same size bob, of the same material, at the end of the same length of string. Set them swinging together – with a careful shake, perhaps – and they will move identically, as you would expect."

"Indeed," I said, "I'm glad to hear it, for I would have been stymied were it not the case."

"Now, if you let out the string slightly on one of them, it will slow that bob down, so that the elongated one falls behind the swing of the other."

"Very well," I said.

"What do you think would happen if instead of lengthening the string, I changed one of the bobs for a substantially lighter material?"

✱ Solution on page 286 ✱

An Issue of Age

Holmes and I were taking luncheon when he offered me a test of my ingenuity to season the meal. I accepted, and he posited the following rather remarkable case.

"Let us say that there is a married couple. The wife is younger than the husband, and it so happens that her age is equal to the digits of his age reversed. Given that the difference in their ages is equal to exactly an eleventh of their sum, can you tell me how old the lady is?"

❋ Solution on page 286 ❋

The Board

Holmes informed me that the senior management of one of the larger London banks had suffered something of a split over a matter of a slightly risky investment policy. Despite a group meeting to attempt some sort of arbitration over the debate, the situation became heated, and a substantial chunk of the attendees marched out in high dudgeon.

"If the chairman had gone with the rebels," Holmes noted, "A full two thirds of the meeting would have left. But on the other hand, had he been able to persuade his putative allies, his deputy and the financial officer, to remain, the departees would have made up just one half of the group."

"I see," I said.

"Quite so," he replied. "Can you then tell me how many men were at the meeting?"

✻ Solution on page 287 ✻

Almonds

After one particularly successful mission on the part of the Baker Street Irregulars, in addition to paying the three boys involved the agreed-upon bonus, he also gave them a very large bag of sugared almonds, boasting 840 sweets in total.

The boys decided to share the sweets exactly on the basis of their ages, which totalled 28. For every seven sweets that the eldest took, the one in the middle took six; for every four that the one in the middle claimed, the youngest got three.

Can you tell how old the boys were?

Solution on page 287

On the Strand

During *The Nasty Affair of the Highwayman's Daughter*, Mr Sherlock Holmes and I found ourselves in a luxurious room on the third floor of a hotel on the Strand. The woman in question – I hesitate to describe her as a lady – was as black-hearted as any I've encountered. We were holed up in Room 303, Holmes cunningly disguised as a Keralan fakir. Our quarry was next door, with some of her next targets. We were preparing to apprehend her when, sadly, events overtook us.

There was a shriek from Room 304, and then a woman's voice shouting "No, Hugo! Don't shoot! *No!*" This was followed by a loud gunshot.

We immediately made a dash for 304. The door was unlocked, and we burst in. I'm not ashamed to say that I had my revolver in my hand. Inside, we found a grim scene. The highwayman's daughter lay dead on the floor. At the far end of the room clustered three people, all white-faced, in clear shock. The gun lay at their feet, where it had clearly been dropped by nerveless hands.

Holmes took one look at the group, and said, "Obviously a teacher, a tailor and a lawyer," indicating each in turn. "Watson, restrain the..."

"Lawyer," I said, seizing the unique chance to stick my oar in.

"Clearly," Holmes said, with just the faintest hint of irritation. But how did I of all people know which was the guilty party?

✱ Solution on page 288 ✱

Granddad

You might be interested in this minor follow-up to *The Nasty Affair of the Highwayman's Daughter*. A day later, Holmes and I were back in our lodgings at 221b Baker Street, and I was writing up my notes on the case. Holmes sat there thoughtfully for a period of time, puffing his pipe, whilst I scratched away with my pen.

Eventually, he turned to me. "Her father was quite old, you know," he said.

It seemed an odd point for Holmes to make. "Oh?" I replied.

He nodded. "Older than her grandfather, in fact."

"What?"

He arched an eyebrow at my reaction.

Whatever did he mean?

✻ Solution on page 288 ✻

Hookland

Holmes and I found ourselves in rural Hookland one Tuesday afternoon, some miles east of Coreham, just in sight of Eden Tor. Holmes had taken on the guise of a local farmer, in order to better observe the movements of Major C. L. Nolan. We were standing at a fence, looking over the estates that Nolan was currently visiting, when a genuine local approached us. Holmes turned and leaned back against the fence to watch the newcomer approach, elbows resting behind him on the top strut.

The fellow came to about ten feet away, and stopped.

“Yalreet, boi?” said Holmes conversationally.

“Yalreet,” replied the farmer. “Ow’s yur mools?”

Holmes scratched his chin thoughtfully. “Li’l buggers is ’ow.”

The pair of them continued in this fashion for some time, before the fellow lolloped off again, apparently satisfied as to our bona fides. Once he’d gone, Holmes explained that they’d been talking about moles.

“Our visitor claimed to have caught an entire nest of moles this morning,” Holmes told me. “He furthermore suggested that five of them were completely blind in the right eye, four blind in the left, three sighted in the left eye, two sighted in the right, and one sighted in both. I told him the least number of moles that could be, which is when he nodded and left.”

“So you weren’t discussing Potemkin after all, then?” I muttered.

How many moles did the farmer catch?

❋ Solution on page 288 ❋

The Watchmen

Holmes and I had cause to observe a warehouse near Wapping Docks during the adventure of the frightened carpenter. A rather expensive necklace had been stolen and we had been charged with its safe return. The warehouse was guarded by a pair of rough-looking men with a little sentry post. Every hour on the hour, one of them would start off on a complex route around the grounds, winding in and out of stacks of pallets at a constant pace, returning finally to the post 45 minutes later.

The men took it in turns to make their round, and the route that they took was always the same, but sometimes they progressed in a clockwise manner, heading left from the hut, and sometimes anticlockwise, heading right. This choice appeared to be settled, as far as we could tell, by the toss of a coin.

"If I were going to assault this place," Holmes said, after some hours of observation, "I know when I'd choose. The guard is in the same spot at a specific time every hour. That's when I'd strike."

"How can you possibly know that?" I protested. "You don't know which way the fellow is going to head."

"It's obvious," Holmes said.

How?

✵ Solution on page 289 ✵

The Prison

"You are incarcerated, Watson," Holmes told me one morning over my kippers.

"I am?"

"Indeed so. In some backwater town in Albania, say."

"How unfortunate," I replied. "Their prison cook seems quite satisfactory, however."

"Luckily for you, the prison warden is a megalomaniac with an obsession for mathematical riddles."

"Sounds all too plausible, old chap."

"You are offered a chance," Holmes continued loftily. "Your door contains a combination lock with five dials, each numbered 0 to 9. You may serve out your time peacefully, or you may tell the guard your guess for how many possible combinations there are for your lock. If your guess is correct within five per cent, you will be set free. If it is wrong, you will be put to death. What do you do?"

What I actually did was eat some more kipper, and ponder permutations. How many combinations do you think there are for the lock?

✱ Solution on page 289 ✱

48

The First Wordknot

As I was going through some medical textbooks one afternoon, hoping to confirm a diagnostic suspicion regarding a patient, Holmes accosted me bearing a slip of paper.

"Here," he told me urgently. "Take this."

I glanced at the paper. It bore the following message:

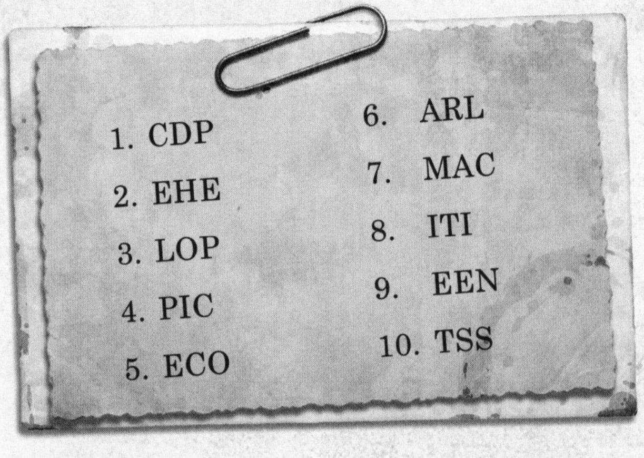
1. CDP
2. EHE
3. LOP
4. PIC
5. ECO
6. ARL
7. MAC
8. ITI
9. EEN
10. TSS

"What is it, Holmes? Some sort of devilish cipher?"

"Not too devilish, I trust," he told me. "There are three ten-letter words on this note. The first line bears their initial letters, the second their second letters, and so on, until the tenth line, which bears their final letters. However, on each line, the three letters are jumbled around. The words are linked by a loose theme. Can you find them?"

The penny dropped. "This is a test?"

"Obviously."

Can you find the three words?

Solution on page 290

49

Whisky

I took a sip from my glass of whisky, and relaxed back into the armchair, enjoying the warmth of the merry fireplace in front of us. "This is excellent, Holmes."

He nodded. "As it should be, at seven shillings."

I winced. "Can you get anything back for the empty bottle?"

"Yes, the brandy is worth 80 pence more than the glass."

There are, of course, twelve pence to the shilling. How much was the bottle worth?

❋ Solution on page 290 ❋

Cousin Tracy

Having befuddled me with her candle purchases, Mrs Hudson proceeded to recount a lengthy and somewhat muddled story regarding her cousin Tracy, and Tracy's husband Albert. As best I could ascertain, both Tracy and Albert were on their second marriages, having lost their earlier spouses to illness, or possibly misadventure.

Clearly this shared loss proved a bond for the couple. The family now stretched to nine children in total, quite the brood. There was a certain amount of tension between his children, her children, and their children, and their shenanigans appeared to be the foundation of the anecdote.

From what I could glean from the mess of names and dates, Tracy and Albert each had six children whom they could call their own in a biological sense. Mrs Hudson neglected to specify how many had been born from the happy couple's union, and Holmes was quick to inform me that I ought to be able to work it out for myself.

Can you say how many were children of both Tracy and Albert?

✻ Solution on page 291 ✻

Trilogy

Mrs Hudson's final shot, after well over a quarter of an hour of the most baffling details of her cousin Tracy's extended family, was the strange fate of a loosely-related in-law. Cousin Tracy's husband's brother's cousin-in-law's father, to be precise. This worthy, whose name I didn't catch, had apparently served in the Zulu war of '79. He had been exposed to some horrifying brutalities whilst out there, and on his return, was never quite the same.

Some years later, as Mrs Hudson would have it, the former soldier was at his parish church with wife and child, as was usual on a Sunday. On this ill-fated occasion, he dozen off quietly, falling into a terrible nightmare about being captured by the Zulus with the rest of his brigade. The Zulus began decapitating their prisoners one by one. In the dream, he was about to meet the same fate when his wife, realizing her husband was asleep, tapped him on the back of the neck with her fan to wake him up. The sudden shock overwhelmed his already-stressed system, and he immediately dropped stone dead.

This was the point at which Holmes rose from his seat and politely but forcefully thanked Mrs Hudson for breakfast, and ushered her out of our rooms. Closing the door behind her, Holmes muttered, "Blatant piffle!" He then stalked off in high dudgeon, and moments later the sounds of aggrieved violin-playing filled the air.

Why did Holmes disbelieve Mrs Hudson?

✻ Solution on page 291 ✻

The Candles

"There's something wrong with that new candle-boy," Mrs Hudson observed one morning, when she arrived to remove our breakfast things. "He absolutely refuses to deliver normal-sized boxes of candles."

Holmes sat up, evidently curious. "How so, Mrs Hudson?"

"He says he's only got six sizes of box, and he's not breaking them for nobody. It wouldn't be so bad if his boxes weren't so stupid."

"Oh?" I asked, now intrigued despite myself.

She nodded, clearly irritated just by the thought of it. "His boxes come in lots of sixteen, seventeen, twenty-three, twenty-four, thirty-nine, and forty candles. That's all. They're all the same size. It's ridiculous. He says I have to make an order for specific amounts of the various boxes."

I smiled at her sympathetically. "And how many candles do you normally order, my dear lady?"

"One hundred," she said. "We go through them like nobody's business. I don't dare order them now, though."

Holmes snorted and sagged back into his chair, which I took to mean the end of his interest in the matter.

Could Mrs Hudson get her candles, and if so, what would she have to order?

✻ Solution on page 292 ✻

TO
LET

Buckets

I was cleaning my pipe one evening, with my revolver shortly to follow, when Holmes appeared in my peripheral vision and placed a big metal bucket in front of me with a loud clang. I startled, turning to look at him as I pulled backwards.

"Water," Holmes declared.

"I'm fine for the moment, thanks," I told him as patiently as I was able.

"You misunderstand," he said.

I nodded glumly. "I dare say I do."

"Two identical buckets, filled to the precise brim with water." He paused. "Pray engage your imagination. This empty one is by way of illustration."

"Done," I said. "Although I dare say I could have managed the feat without a real-world model."

"Reassuring to hear," Holmes said. "Now, one of the buckets has a large chunk of wood floating in it. The precise shape does not matter."

"Very well."

"Which of your two buckets weighs more, the one with the wood, or the one without?"

What do you think?

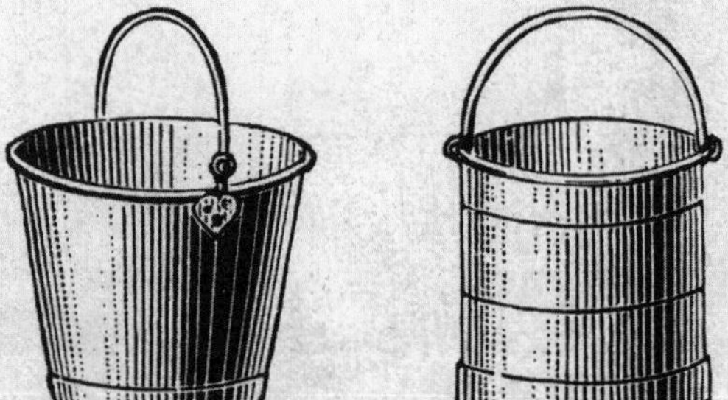

✱ Solution on page 292 ✱

The Maddened Miller

One of the odder features of *The Adventure of the Wandering Bishops* was a peculiarly enraged Hookland miller. The source of his ire was, we eventually discovered, an altercation between his wife and her sister, which disrupted certain plans he had regarding the purchase of a large quantity of land. But that really is by the by.

Holmes, still in his farmer's disguise, had approached the miller with several sacks of grain, purchased earlier in return for a dozen chickens. The miller's usual tariff was one tenth part of the flour he produced for any given customer. Holmes, of course, was only too happy to pay this trifling price.

When the work was done, we found ourselves in possession of a bushel of freshly ground flour. The less said about that, the better. But my question is this. How much flour did the enraged miller claim?

Solution on page 292

The First Camouflage

I remember the day clearly, even now. It was late October, a Friday. We had finished luncheon a short while before, and I was sitting in a pleasant state of post-prandial sleepiness. I was on the verge of nodding off when Holmes loudly called out, "I've got four words for you, Watson."

I think I managed some groan of mild protest, which Holmes duly ignored.

"Elephantine. Beechwood. Bugleweed. Stepmother."

"And?" I asked.

"Each word contains a smaller word, well camouflaged within its parent. What is the common theme uniting the four smaller words?"

It was definitely not the way that I'd fondly imagined my afternoon progressing. Can you find the solution?

❋ Solution on page 293 ❋

Fabulous

"Hubris, Watson, is one of the very heights of folly. To become so swollen with arrogance that one assumes oneself infallible – and to act or, more pertinently, fail to act as a result of that arrogance – why, that is the cause of inevitable disaster."

"Is that so?" I asked, somewhat confused.

Holmes waved a newspaper at me. "Some buffoon of a runner was so overconfident about his opponent that he opened himself to utter ridicule. According to this piece, our fellow gave his inferior rival a head-start equal to one-eighth of the length of the course. Now, they started at opposite ends for some reason, and after his late start, the superior runner ambled along with colossal contempt for his opponent. He got a nasty shock when, at just one-sixth of the way along the course, he met his rival coming the other way. He lost, of course." Holmes paused, and a glint appeared in his eye.

"Quite so," I said swiftly.

"Maybe you can tell me, old chap, how many times the buffoon would have had to increase his speed in order to win the race? Round to the nearest whole number, and let's assume that the slower man maintains the same speed throughout."

What do you think?

Solution on page 293

Out East

Whilst doing some research during *The Nasty Affair of the Highwayman's Daughter*, I stumbled across an interesting little snippet of fact about her father's home country. It was a small, mountainous state in eastern Europe of no great political or cultural distinction, with a reputation for sullen bloodthirstiness amongst its menfolk. No great surprise, given the context in which I was examining it.

Be that as it may, the discovery I made was that in the preceding year, some 1.4 per cent of the country's women as compared to 2.1 per cent of the men had married spouses of the same nationality.

I announced this to Holmes, who immediately challenged me to deduce the comparative percentage of women in that place.

What do you think?

✵ Solution on page 294 ✵

The Suicide

Inspector Lestrade of Scotland Yard was a small, lean man with a strong hint of ferret in his ancestry. Whilst his approach to crime was wholly pedestrian, he was nevertheless a tireless servant of the law. Holmes and I worked with him a number of times to bring villains to justice. Despite having received ample evidence of Holmes's brilliance however, he somehow maintained an intrinsic faith in his own opinion when it differed. So I was utterly unsurprised, during *The Adventure of the Impossible Gecko*, when he dismissed Holmes's first analysis out of hand.

"Look, Holmes, I understand that your client fears foul play. But it's a suicide, clear and simple. There's nothing here to suggest otherwise." Lestrade gestured around the study we were in. "The only thing we've moved is the deceased."

It was a dim little room, lined with book-filled cases and dominated by a leather-topped oak desk and the chair that went with it. In the centre of the desk sat a pill bottle, completely empty. The remaining couple of pills lay next to it, big white oblong things about the same size as the tip of my little finger. The rest of the bottle – twenty pills or more – had gone into our client's uncle the night before. The only other thing in the room was a sheet of financial projections, which appeared utterly dire.

"My point precisely," Holmes said, with a hint of asperity. "Surely even you, Inspector, can see that suicide is highly unlikely at the very least."

He was right, of course. Can you see what he'd spotted?

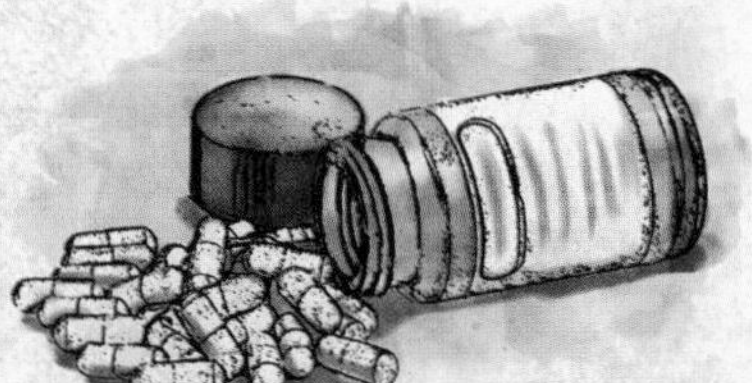

✵ Solution on page 294 ✵

Scarves

One blustery autumn afternoon, Holmes and I were walking along the Marylebone road, past Madame Tussaud's museum of wax figures. I was struggling somewhat to keep my hat in place when a particularly savage gust whipped it straight off my head. As I stooped to retrieve it, I noticed that a lady in front of us had likewise lost her scarf, which went tumbling away down the pavement.

Holmes had noticed the errant scarf as well, and turned to me with a calculating look. "Indulge me a moment, Watson, and picture that the street was significantly more crowded, and that there were a dozen ladies who found themselves suddenly without their scarves. For that matter, let's also imagine that young Wiggins was nearby, had gathered up all the scarves, and was handing them back at random to the ladies, in hope of a penny or two for his speedy service."

Wiggins was the spokesman and putative leader of the Baker Street Irregulars, a gaggle of urchins that Holmes often recruited when in need of extra eyes or hands.

"It doesn't seem impossible," I allowed, although knowing the lad, I very much doubted he'd be quite so careless as to return the scarves randomly.

"Well, then," Holmes said, "can you calculate the probability of just eleven of the ladies receiving their correct scarves?"

To my mild surprise, I realized that I could. Can you?

✻ Solution on page 294 ✻

Joe

"I asked my nephew Joseph how old he was last Saturday," Mrs Hudson declared, having brought up some hot tea one afternoon. "You'll never believe what he told me, Doctor Watson."

"I'm sure I shall," I reassured her. "I trust you implicitly, my dear lady."

She gave me a queer look, before continuing. "He told me, bold as brass, that three years ago he'd been seven times as old as his sister Ruthie. Then he added that two years ago, he'd been four times her age, and one year ago, just three times her age. After that outburst, he sat back and beamed at me. Well, I'm sure you'll have no trouble figuring out their ages, a learned man like yourself, but it wasn't what I was expecting, not at all." She beamed at me in turn.

Fortunately, long association with Sherlock Holmes had hardened me to this sort of challenge, and I was able to respond. Can you calculate the answer?

✻ Solution on page 295 ✻

The Wenns

Holmes and I were lurking outside a small hotel named The Wenns in the quiet fenland town of King's Lynn. It was perhaps one of the less diverting ways of spending a Monday evening, but we were hot on the heels of the frightened carpenter's brother-in-law, whom Holmes needed to observe in the wild, as it were. The little marketplace was quaint enough, to be sure, but as the evening dragged on, I confess I was becoming rather bored.

Catching my mood, Holmes decided to give my mind something to chew on, by way of a distraction from the drizzle. "You'll have observed that the bar in there is quite crowded, Watson."

"Quite so," I replied. "Warm and dry too, no doubt."

"Indubitably. Still, let us pretend that each of the patrons has a different number of penny coins in his possession, and that there are more patrons by number than any single one of them has pennies."

There was a pause whilst I untangled this, and then I nodded.

"Now, if I tell you that none of the patrons possesses exactly 33 pennies, can you tell me how many patrons there are at most?"

"I'm sure I can, in theory at least," I replied.

"Then please do so," he said.

What is the correct answer?

❋ Solution on page 295 ❋

Maida Vale

During *The Adventure of the Maida Vale Baker*, Holmes tasked Wiggins and the Irregulars with observing both the baker, Gerry by name, and his dissolute cousin, James. Caution was strictly advised, as both men were prone to a certain lamentable rashness.

When Wiggins returned to 221b, he reported that Gerry had left the bakery at 9am sharp, and set off up Watling Street at a leisurely two miles an hour. An hour later, James had followed in his cousin's footsteps, but walking more briskly, at four miles an hour, and with a lovely Irish setter in tow.

The dog had immediately dashed off after the baker, and according to Wiggins's intelligence, had no sooner caught up to Gerry than it turned around and ran back to James. It then proceeded to continue running back and forth between the men – at an even ten miles per hour – until James had caught up with Gerry, at which point all three stopped entirely.

We made sense of it all in the end, but how far did the dog run?

❋ Solution on page 296 ❋

Sheep

The thorny particulars of the inheritability of sheep became a pressing concern for Holmes and myself during the frankly rather peculiar *Adventure of the Raven Child*, which unfolded largely in the mountains of Gwynedd. A landowner with a heroic combined flock of sheep had died in bizarre circumstances after spending a night alone at the top of Cader Idris – a feat said by the locals to turn you into either a poet or a madman. As if there were a difference.

Anyhow, for the purposes of this volume, I shall spare you the convoluted details, and instead focus on the practical issue of sheep herds. The landowner's sons, David, Idris, and Caradog, all inherited a portion of their father's herd, along with the lands and tenant shepherds required to support the sheep. David, as the eldest, received twenty percent more sheep than Idris, and twenty five per cent more sheep than Caradog, the youngest brother.

If I tell you that Idris received precisely one thousand sheep, can you tell me how many Caradog inherited?

⁕ Solution on page 296 ⁕

65

The Second Wordknot

If I recall correctly – and I am reasonably sure that I do – I was engaged in the precarious business of attempting to butter a very hot crumpet when Holmes presented me with my second wordknot. It was some weeks since I'd wrestled with the first of its kind, but the simple principle of untangling three loosely associated ten-letter words was still reasonably fresh.

"You recall, I assume, that the first letter of each word is on the first line, the second letter of each on the second line, and so on?"

I assured Holmes that I so recalled, and with that he left me to it.

1. ART
2. HOQ
3. UOU
4. RAD
5. MOM
6. AAL
7. LIR
8. TII
9. NEN
10. EES

Can you untangle the knot?

✻ Solution on page 297 ✻

The Partner

Much of the nastiness surrounding *The Adventure of the Maida Vale Baker* was rooted in his business affairs. It is often the case, I have found, that the trust one places in family and friends is misplaced when it comes to affairs of the wallet. The baker, Gerry, and his cousin James had been partners in the bakery since the beginning. James provided the capital, whilst Gerry did the work and ran the business. Once the basic investment capital had been repaid, they settled on an agreement whereby Gerry owned one and a half times as much of the business as James did.

Matters did not start to get complicated until a new arrival appeared on the scene. Mr Andreas was a contact of James, a friend of a friend. A gentleman of Greek extraction, he was possessed of a certain presence that warned the discerning onlooker not to trifle with him. Sadly, neither James nor Gerry apparently had sufficient discernment.

The deal they struck was that Mr Andreas would pay the handsome sum of £1,000, and each of the three partners would then hold a one-third stake in the business. Matters quickly became unseemly.

What would have been the most equitable distribution of the money, £1,000?

✱ Solution on page 297 ✱

Fruity

On occasion, Mrs Hudson enjoyed presenting Holmes with some small test of ingenuity, if for no other satisfaction than to take a perverse pride in how rapidly he was able to respond. Sometimes, Holmes would pass the onus of response to me, either because he deemed the matter beneath his weighty appraisal, or because of his ongoing attempts to improve my logical processes. Mrs Hudson seemed scarcely less pleased on those occasions. I assume that whatever she lost by way of Holmes's rapier mind, she made up for by watching me fumble around trying to best her.

One morning, before I'd even been able to take a cup of tea, one such conundrum winged its way towards me. I pulled myself together, looked up from my cup, and said, "I'm sorry, Mrs Hudson, could you repeat that?"

"Of course, Doctor," she replied. "I was weighing the fruit earlier, for a crumble, and it hit me. One apple and six plums were the same weight as my one pear, while all three apples and the pear were the same weight as ten plums. So I was wondering, how many plums do you think would match the weight of the pear?"

"Thank you," I said, and took a long, slow drink of tea.

What do you think the answer is?

✻ Solution on page 298 ✻

Hands

We were introduced to an inordinately large number of people during *The Adventure of the Frightened Carpenter*. At one point, it was starting to feel as if I was going to have to personally shake hands with everybody in London. Given that several of them had insisted on attempting to crush my hand to pulp as part of the process, I was rapidly tiring of the whole affair, and made some throwaway remark to Holmes to that effect.

"Don't disparage the humble handshake, Watson," Holmes told me. "It's a vital part of the social glue that holds the city together, no matter how tiresome it might prove on occasion. Consider yourself grateful that we are not in a culture where a crushing grip is the standard of politesse."

"Oh, I am," I assured him.

"Here's a little something to take your mind off your manual weariness. Do you imagine that there are an odd or even number of people who have themselves shaken hands with an odd number of people?"

Can you deduce an answer?

✱ Solution on page 298 ✱

A Sense of Urgency

Holmes inevitably seized a moment when I was at my most distracted before springing his little tests and puzzles upon me. I asked him about this once, and his reply was something to the effect that observation and deduction were frequently required at times when the pressure was greatest. By interrupting me when my mind was elsewhere, he hoped to strengthen my logical faculties to work under duress. I could see the sense in it, but it was often damnably inconvenient.

I was in the middle of making notes upon an intriguing yet highly convoluted article in *The Lancet* when Holmes dashed over with a scrap of paper and thrust it under my nose. He even made his voice sound concerned. "Quick, Watson! Hurry! What's the answer?"

The paper bore this inscription:

10*9*8*7*6*5*4*3*2*1*0*–1*–2=X

What's X?

Solution on page 299

Hot and Cold

Sherlock and I were taking tea one chilly January morning when he looked up from studying his cup, to turn his attention to the frosty window. "We place a kettle or a pot on top of the hob in order to heat up. In earlier times, people hung their cauldrons and kettles over fireplaces. Not right in the middle of them, but over them."

"Quite so," I agreed. "More convenient or more effective. Or both."

"Both," he agreed. "But imagine for a moment that you have a cube of metal, say, that you wish to cool, and a block of ice that you have to keep intact. How would you arrange the two for greatest efficiency?

"Well, I'd..." I trailed off, to think about the matter.

What is the best option?

Solution on page 299

On the Buses

During *The Affair of the Frightened Carpenter*, Holmes had cause to invest some time into studying the movements of a fellow named Sam Smith. It left Holmes somewhat waspish, because it transpired that Smith was in the frugal habit of travelling by bus to his appointments, and walking back from them on foot.

On the second day, the combined travel time was precisely eight hours. Holmes also had to spend 90 minutes loitering outside a lumber merchant's depot, but that's by the by. Given that the bus managed an average of 9 mph, and Smith's walking rate was a third of that, how far did Holmes have to walk while trailing the man?

❋ Solution on page 300 ❋

Hookland Knights

A lead followed during *The Adventure of the Wandering Bishops* brought us to a rather unusual under-chapel below the streets of Weychester. Three sarcophagi carved to look like armoured crusader knights dominated a small room off the main chapel.

Beneath the feet of each knight was a set of finely carved numbers. On the first was the group 30, 68, 89. On the second, the numbers 18, 23, 42. The third bore the numbers 11, 41, 74.

At the end of the small room, the wall held a dozen carved stone heads in a straight line across its middle. Each of the heads was clearly modelled after a different individual. Every face bore an expression of unsettling glee, however. It was most unpleasant. Above the heads was painted the number 16, in white, a good foot high.

"Clearly, a reference to..." Holmes stopped mid-sentence. "Watson, this should exercise you. Which knight is that painted number pointing us to?"

✱ Solution on page 300 ✱

The Third Wordknot

Holmes's third wordknot came to me as we sat down to suffer through a thoroughly uninspired performance of an already lacklustre operetta. Normally you would never have found either of us within 50 feet of such a performance, but Holmes was on the trail of a decrepit raven-seller, and, well, there we were. I was actually glad of the distraction his puzzle afforded me, even though the unfortunate wailings made it difficult to concentrate.

The letters from which I had to disentangle three related ten-letter words, one letter each per line, were:

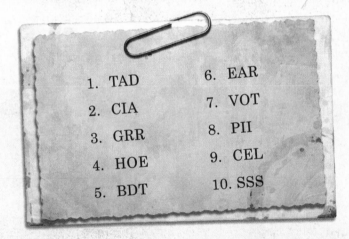

1. TAD
2. CIA
3. GRR
4. HOE
5. BDT
6. EAR
7. VOT
8. PII
9. CEL
10. SSS

Can you work out what the words were?

✻ Solution on page 301 ✻

The Painting

A fellow came to me once looking to sell a rather handsome portrait that had been in his family for some time. This was nothing to do with a case of Holmes'. He was a patient of mine at my practice, and had noticed that I had a selection of artworks adorning the walls of my office and treatment room.

Whilst the picture was undeniably attractive, his asking price was not – £640. Well, half a year's income is a ludicrous amount of money for a piece of art, so of course I declined pleasantly. Two weeks later he was back, and had dropped his asking price to a "mere" £400. Once again, I conveyed my regrets. After two more weeks, he returned, utterly unabashed, and offered me the piece for £250. On his second visit after that, I finally gave in and purchased the piece.

To the nearest whole pound, how much did I pay?

✱ Solution on page 301 ✱

Daniel

I was reading the newspaper one afternoon when a rather grizzly little news story caught my eye. It concerned the unfortunate fate of one Daniel Boutros, the son of a rather wealthy shipping broker.

Young Mr Boutros had been to Essex on a climbing trip with a companion. Despite being generally considered skilled at the sport, something had gone wrong, and he had fallen from the top of an escarpment. His friend Alan Dickey, the lead climber, had already reached the top and was belaying Boutros from up there when the rope failed.

This was, of course, very sad, but what startled me were the florid lengths to which the newspaper reporter went in describing the scene. Several paragraphs were devoted in their entirety to poor Boutros's body, and the way it lay shattered over the mounds of coiled rope at the foot of the cliff. The friend, Dickey, was said to be in shock.

I mentioned the piece to Holmes, who grunted noncommittally. After a moment, he asked if there was any mention of a frayed rope-end. I scanned through, and sure enough, the reporter did mention frayed pieces of unwound rope.

"It's still murder," Holmes said.

Can you see why he came to that conclusion?

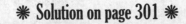

❋ Solution on page 301 ❋

PART TWO

STRAIGHTFORWARD

❋❋

Water into Wine

"Here is a little question for you, Watson." I indicated my readiness to engage my brain.

"I take two wine glasses, one twice the size of the other. I fill the smaller half-way, and the larger just to one third. Then I fill the remaining space in both glasses with water."

"I'm glad this is a theoretical issue," I noted.

"If I then pour both glasses into a previously empty pitcher," Holmes continued, "can you tell me what proportion of the resulting liquid is wine?"

✻ Solution on page 303 ✻

Alby

"It's like this, Mr. Holmes," said the redoubtable Mrs. Hudson one morning.

"My cousin Alby works at the Millwall Iron Works. He's a supervisor, as it happens. Every morning at 8 o'clock sharp, he makes his way down the stairs. When he gets to his destination a little afterwards, he brews himself a cup of tea, and then settles down with the morning papers. There's a boy who sells them just on the corner by the main gate of the works. I know for a fact that he hardly manages to get half-way through the paper before he's sound asleep, and he remains flat out for the next eight hours. Judgement Day itself would have a hard timing waking our Alby. Yet even so, management are very happy with his performance and the amount of work he puts in. How do you think that can be?"

❋ Solution on page 304 ❋

The Third Literal Oddity

"Consider the humble goatgrass, Watson." Holmes was pacing back and forth in a thoughtful manner, and these were his first words for some time. I looked at him curiously.

"Aegilops is the genus. Bears a striking similarity to winter wheat. Or if Aegilops isn't to your fancy, then how about 'billowy', or 'ghosty'? For that matter, let us not forget 'spoonfeed'."

The penny dropped. "One of your word-plays."

"English is a marvellously eccentric language," Holmes said, by way of agreement.

What is curious about the words he mentioned?

Solution on page 304

The Time

Holmes and myself were making our way back to Baker Street after a disappointingly fruitless day when a fellow across the street hailed us somewhat abruptly.

"You! I say, you, in the odd hat! Tell me the time!"

Holmes looked over at him. "If you add a quarter of the time from midday up to now to half the time remaining from now to midday on the morrow, you will have the precisely correct time."

"I say," the man said, more quietly, and walked on.

Do you know what time it was?

❋ Solution on page 305 ❋

The Fourth Curiosity

I was engaged in the perusal of an entertaining volume when Holmes startled me somewhat by suddenly pushing my book down.

"Tell me, my dear Watson. By what part does four fourths exceed three fourths?"

"A fourth," I replied irritably.

Holmes looked at me quizzically. "Really?"

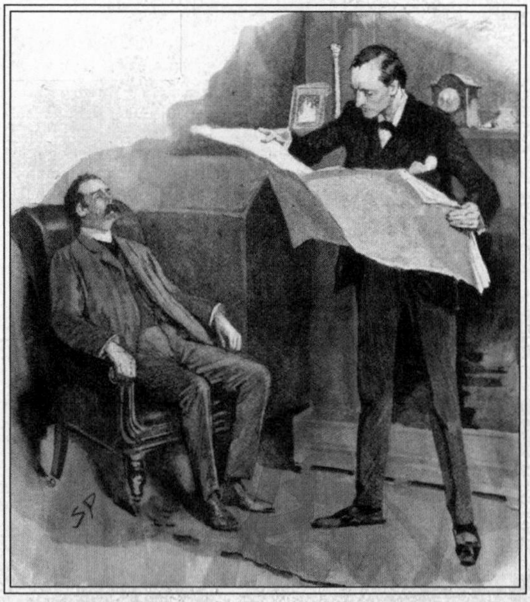

✱ Solution on page 305 ✱

A Very Hudson Christmas

Mrs Hudson brought another matter of her confusing relations to Holmes and myself one December evening, more out of a desire to provide us with a little vexatious entertainment I think than out of any genuine uncertainty on her part.

"Gentlemen," she said, "I am hosting a gathering of some of my family this year. In addition to myself, I shall be entertaining two grandparents, four parents, one father-in-law, one mother-in-law, one brother, two sisters, four children, two sons,two daughters, three grandchildren, and not least, one daughter-in-law. Fortunately, there are no brothers-in-law to deal with. I'm curious as to how many places I need set."

"You'll need a mighty table, Mrs Hudson," said I.

"Not necessarily," Holmes declared.

What is the least number of people that may be involved?

✱ Solution on page 306 ✱

Drifts

One snowy morning in January, Holmes paused in the street to bring a curious fact to my attention. Strong winds had driven the snow into drifts along the side of the pavement, but as he pointed out, there was a proportionately far greater deposit of snow against the side of the nearby telegraph pole than there was against the side of the house which lay some dozen or so yards beyond it.

It would have seemed to me that the opposite really ought to have been the case, but after a little thought I was able to demonstrate to Holmes that I could fathom the answer to his satisfaction. What was it?

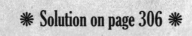

✻ Solution on page 306 ✻

The Fourth Mental Trial

"I was talking to my hypothetical acquaintance Alfie earlier," Holmes said.

I declared that this statement appeared to herald another mental test.

"Indeed. I enquired as to Alfie's age. He, in turn, informed me that in six years time, he would be one and a quarter times the age that he was four years ago."

"I suppose you want me to tell you his age."

"Please do," said Holmes.

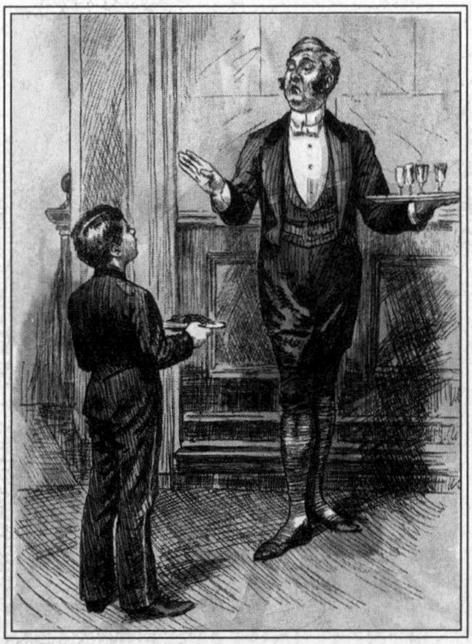

✳ Solution on page 307 ✳

Suffolk

"I want you to give some thought to three villages in Suffolk, Watson."

I was getting used to Holmes' trials by this point. "Real ones?"

"Real enough, although I am taking flagrant liberties with their actual geography. Consider Crowfield, Hemingstone and Gosbeck."

"They have suitably resonant names."

"Quite. So. Let us say that Hemingstone is directly south of Crowfield, and is connected by a straight road. Gosbeck is off to the east, some 12 miles as the raven flies from the Hemingstone-Crowfield road, and closer to Hemingstone than it is to Crowfield. It is your intention to travel from Hemingstone to Crowfield, but by a slight mishap, you discover that you have instead taken the route via Gosbeck. The roads are equally straight. On arriving at your destination, you discover that the route you used is 35 miles long. How many extra miles did your route take you?"

✻ Solution on page 307 ✻

The Fire

"Ah, here's a diverting little question for you, Watson."

"You are trapped in a small, unkempt valley. It is just a few hundred yards in length, less than that in width, and surrounded almost entirely by stern cliffs that defeat your ability to climb. Some blackguard, who means you ill, has lit a fire at the far end, and the prevailing wind is blowing it straight up the valley towards you. Shelter is not an option. There is no source of water. You have only your usual accoutrements – pocket watch, pistol, notepad, pencil, pipe, tobacco and matches. Can you formulate a plan that will prevent you from being roasted alive?"

✹ Solution on page 308 ✹

Modesty

"I was faced with a modest young lady the other day," Holmes said to me. "She was chary of confessing her true age."

"As many women are," I noted.

"Quite so. I was reasonably persuasive on the matter however, and finally got her to admit that she was the eldest of fifteen children, each born with a year and a half between them. When she confessed that her age was eight times that of the youngest of her siblings, I knew at once how old she was."

How old was she?

Solution on page 308

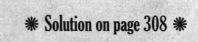

The Seventh Sword

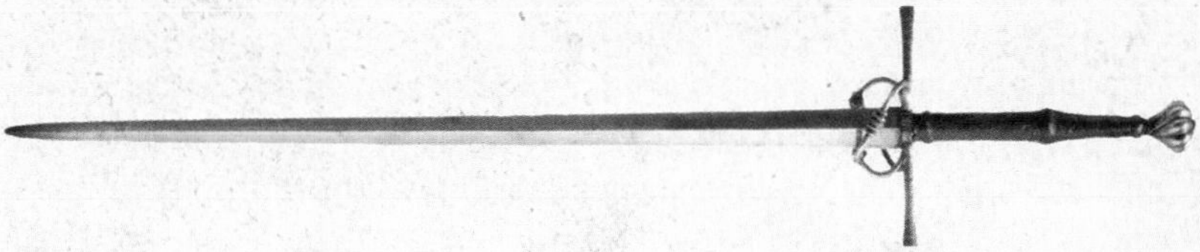

A priceless sword with associations to Mary, Queen of Scots had been stolen from an estate, and Holmes had agreed to lend his services in the matter. The local constabulary was making much of the thief's escape, and sought to ascertain which of the nearby villages was the closest – Shenstone, Rushock or Chaddesley.

The sword's custodian expressed his opinion that it seemed as if all three were as far away as each other, although he had never actually attempted to measure the distances involved. The sergeant maintained that the exact distance was important to know.

It was known that the distance from Shenstone to Chaddesley was one and a half miles, from Shenstone to Rushock was one and three tenths miles, and from Rushock to Chaddesley was one and two fifths miles.

Can you discern the distance from the estate to the villages?

✱ Solution on page 309 ✱

The House

On one occasion which you may recall if you have seen some of my other notes, Sherlock Holmes and I encountered a young woman with a most peculiar problem. She had been picked over scores of other candidates for a position as a nanny just outside Winchester. The one immutable requirement was that she cut her hair to a particular style. She was paid at an exorbitantly generous rate, and given the most eccentric duties.

Her housework was far lighter than any girl would have suspected. Indeed, she was completely barred from one of the areas of the house. So her domestic work was light at best. On top of that, the child of the family was of an age where he barely seemed to need much supervision. In fact, he clearly resented the intrusion. There were times however when she was required to don particular outfits of clothes, sit in precise locations within the house, and engage in various social pursuits. At these times, the father and mother of the house were sociable and jolly. Outside of these times, they were far less engaged.

As if that was not enough to deal with, the house also had a persistent observer, a small fellow who seemed to hang about watching intently at all sorts of queer hours. Strange noises were heard inside the building from time to time as well. The young woman grew increasingly disturbed with the oddness of her situation, and turned to Holmes for an explanation. He was able to provide one almost immediately.

Can you?

❋ Solution on page 309 ❋

The Wood Merchant

Late last August, a curious little incident occurred in Torquay, and an innocent man very nearly found himself the unfortunate victim of a miscarriage of justice. Over the course of one weekend, three local businesses were burgled of a substantial sum of valuables. A number of witnesses reported catching glimpses of a suspicious figure – a distinctive looking man, tall, muscular and well tanned, with a prominent nose and a great big bushy beard.

Local police suspected that the beard was a disguise, and after some diligent searching, they located a straight razor and a mound of facial hair in a quiet nook not far from the rear of one of the burglary sites. Suspicion fell on a local wood merchant, who was undeniably tall, tanned, muscular, clean-shaven and nasally endowed; furthermore, the fellow made deliveries of firewood to all three of the businesses. He had been out of the town over that weekend, and therefore had no plausible alibi.

It was the man himself who made contact with Holmes, laying out the above details and begging for aid in clearing his name. Holmes didn't feel any need to take the case on, but he did send the chap a brief note pointing out one salient fact. This alone was sufficient for the fellow to persuade the police to discount him entirely, as his effusive letter of thanks later attested.

Can you think what Holmes told the chap?

✻ Solution on page 310 ✻

The Dark Marriage

Holmes waved his newspaper at me one morning. "There is a curious tangle in the announcements today, my friend."

"Is that so?" I asked.

"We have here the announcement of a recently deceased fellow who, so it says, married the sister of his widow."

"What the devil? He married his widow's sister?"

"Quite so," Holmes replied. "It appears to be perfectly accurate."

How is it possible, given that it is not possible for the dead to marry?

✱ Solution on page 310 ✱

The Fourth Literal Oddity

"Time to exercise your writerly mind again, my friend. Turn your thoughts to the words 'scraunched' and 'strengthed'. The former means 'to have made a crunching noise', as if one had walked on gravel; the latter is long out of use, but means, as might be surmised, 'to summon ones strength'. Whilst you are contemplating these singular words, you may also like to think on their counterpart 'Io'. She was a legendary priestess, one of Zeus' many ill-fated conquests in the Greek mythologies."

I confess that I did not reply to Holmes, having been already distracted by the challenge. What do you make of it?

✱ Solution on page 311 ✱

95

Port and Brandy

"Answer me this," Holmes said to me one evening, as we were relaxing after dinner. "The decanter of port and the decanter of brandy over there are both around half full. Let us assume, for the sake of convenience, that they contain identical measures of liquid. Now, imagine I were to pour off a shot of port, and exactly decant it into the brandy jar. I then follow this action by shaking the brandy to mix the blend, and pour off a second shot, of the mix this time. I finish up by tipping the mixed shot back into the port."

"Sounds like a devilish mess," I said.

"Actually, an even blend of the two is quite remarkably potable. But that is by the by. Do you suppose there is now more port in the brandy, or more brandy in the port?"

Solution on page 312

The Fifth Mental Trial

"I was with Wiggins earlier," Holmes told me. "He and a couple of the other irregulars had it in mind to buy a rather attractive ball to play knock-about with. The trouble was that the thing cost 18 pence, and they had only 15 pence between them, all in farthings. They asked for a little assistance. I informed them that if they had sixty farthings between themselves, I had exactly three coins less in my pocket than the average number of coins possessed by the four of us. If they could tell me how many coins I had, I'd pass them a thruppenny bit."

"Did they manage it?"

"Oh yes, Wiggins is a sharp little scamp. Could you have done the same?"

Solution on page 313

Stamina

During my military training in India, we were frequently sent on punishing missions to build up our stamina for when we saw actual service in Afghanistan. Those were challenging times, but the sense of accomplishment from getting through the various trials really drove one to excel. As you might imagine, our instructors encouraged us to our best efforts through a system of minor rewards and other inducements.

One particular afternoon still stands out in my memory. We had been sent on a twenty-mile hike through the variable local terrain, leaving shortly before the scorching local noon, with no supplies save a half-pint canteen of water. Our instructions were to make our way round a specific route without stopping for rest or forage; the first man back would win himself lighter duties for the following day. I was stronger then, and put in what I thought was a good showing. By the end of the course, I was as thirsty as a bull, staggering from the heat, caked in dust and grime.

As I arrived, I saw that at least one other chap had narrowly beaten me in. He was in a dreadful state, collapsed on the ground panting, drenched in sweat. Our sergeant was clearly waiting for him to catch his breath. He gave him a few moments, and then proceeded to roundly curse the fellow for a shirker and a cheat, and assigned him to latrine work for the next three days. Then he turned to me, and despite my sudden concerns, told me I was the fourth in, and to go refresh myself.

Holmes understood the sergeant's reaction immediately, of course. Do you?

✷ Solution on page 313 ✷

The Fifth Curiosity

"I've had word," Holmes told me over breakfast, "of a fellow who has turned up some curious coins in his allotment."

"Fortunate for him."

"I dare say," Holmes replied. "He reports that one of the coins is dated as far back as 51 B.C., while another is clearly marked 'Henry I'. What do you make of it?"

✻ Solution on page 314 ✻

The Shoreditch Bank Job

"I have a little puzzle that ought to appeal to you, Watson."

I allowed that it was a distinct possibility, and encouraged Sherlock Holmes to go ahead.

"A couple of fellows who are... familiar to me were, last month, discussing the best way to break into a particular bank in Shoreditch. I know for a fact that they even enticed a local constable into entering their discussions, and clearing up some of their uncertainties for them. He was fully aware of what they were about; the bank, of course, had absolutely no idea, and so far as I know, still has no clue regarding their identities. Last week their plans bore fruit, and brought them a substantial sum of money. They duly gave a modest percentage of it to the constable who had been so helpful."

"My word! Have you informed the authorities?"

"I have not, my friend. None of the conspirators has done anything the least bit wrong."

Can you deduce what Holmes was talking about?

❋ Solution on page 315 ❋

The Second Portmanteau

"Watson, are you in the mood for something of a challenge?"

Holmes seemed in high spirits, and was clutching a document of some sort. I allowed that I was game for whatever he happened to have in mind.

"Capital," Holmes said. "You will recall the portmanteau image I brought to your attention some time ago, of course."

"Indeed," I replied. "A composite picture in which each element was a clue to the identity of a certain spot within London."

"Quite. I have another for you, almost as straightforward as the last. In the spirit of fairness however, I must confess that the location is actually slightly outside of London, on this occasion."

So saying, he handed me the sheet of paper he bore. I have duplicated it for your attention. Can you deduce where it points to?

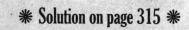

❋ Solution on page 315 ❋

102

The Day of the Book

It was April 23rd, and I was gazing idly out of the window of 221b at the preponderance of St. George's Cross flags which had appeared in celebration of our patron.

"He was from Palestine, you know." Holmes had followed my gaze, and my train of thought.

"Indeed," I said.

"He is much beloved in Catalonia too – where it is traditional to give a book, and a rose. An interesting feature, given that it is also the anniversary of the deaths of both Shakespeare and Cervantes. In fact, they died in the same year too, 1616. It would have been a bleak day for literature... if they had not passed away more than a week apart, that is."

Can you explain this odd statement?

Solution on page 316

The Cross of St. George

"While we are considering St. George," Holmes said, "I have a little matter for you to wrestle with concerning his flag."

"Oh, really?"

"In shape a centrally placed and evenly sized cross of red against a white field, it is possible – desirable, even – to so balance the size of the cross so that the red fabric occupies exactly the same area of the flag as the white fabric. Let us suggest a flag that is four feet wide and three feet high. How wide should the arm of the cross be?"

❋ Solution on page 317 ❋

The Somewhat Crooked Butler

"Consider a somewhat crooked butler, Watson.".

I found that image to fit well within my experience, and said so.

"Quite so. This fellow has been drawing off his master's ale. Let us say he fills a generous jug from a ten-gallon keg, and replaces the missing volume with water. Some time later, he repeats the exact procedure. After he has done so, he discovers that the keg now contains a blend of exactly half ale and half water, not unlike that in some pubs of my acquaintance. How large is his jug?"

❋ Solution on page 317 ❋

C

One morning, Holmes handed me the following enigmatic message on a piece of paper:

1 2 3 4 5 6 7 8 9 = 100

I looked it over, and asked if it were perhaps some sort of code.

"Not in the least, my dear Watson," came the reply. "It is a mathematical riddle for you. There are several ways to add mathematical operators to this list of numbers to ensure that the statement becomes mathematically accurate. The easiest, for example, is to turn the line into 1+2+3+4+5+6+7+ (8x9). That solution requires nine separate mathematical operators however – one multiplication sign, seven addition signs, and one pair of brackets."

"I see," I managed.

"Permitting yourself just the previously mentioned operators and, additionally, the minus sign and the division sign, what is the least number of operators you can use that still has the sum make sense? You cannot move numbers around at all, but you may combine adjacent numbers into a single value, so that 1 and 2 become 12; this does not cost you an operator."

Can you find the answer?

❋ Solution on page 318 ❋

The Hudson Clan

"Can you sort out a little matter of kinship for me, Mr. Holmes?" Mrs. Hudson had just brought up the morning's post.

Holmes looked up at her with a distracted glance. "I dare say so, Mrs Hudson. What appears to be the problem."

"Well," she said, "I've been trying to figure it out. If Sally Shaw is my third cousin once removed, on my mother's side – which she is – then what relation is her grandmother to my son?"

A knotty problem. Can you find an answer?

✱ Solution on page 319 ✱

Cousin Jennifer

One evening recently, after our housekeeper Mrs. Hudson had brought us a pot of tea, she turned to Sherlock Holmes with an uncharacteristically mischievous smile. "I have a little poser that I fancy might amuse you for a moment or two, Mr. Holmes, if you care to hear it."

Sherlock arched an eyebrow. "Go ahead, by all means."

"Well then Mr. Holmes, the long and the short of it is that my cousin Jennifer just got out of London Hospital on Whitechapel Road. She'd been there for a week, and her with nothing wrong with herself whatsoever. No illness, no injury, no mental problems, nothing. Not a word of complaint from her, before, during or after. But they kept her in for a whole week, and wouldn't let her do a single thing for herself. Why, they wouldn't even let her touch a knife or a fork. And to cap it all off, when they finally let her go, she had to be carried bodily from the place. What do you make of that?"

Holmes smiled thinly. "It's clear enough, Mrs. Hudson. What say you, Watson?"

❋ Solution on page 319 ❋

The Fifth Literal Oddity

Holmes' next little linguistic challenge came after dinner one restful evening. He had just solved a rather hair-raising case involving a murdered seaman, and we were making the most of a very welcome moment of peace and quiet.

"I have a pair of words for you, old friend," Holmes said.

"Pray, go ahead," I replied.

"They are 'facetiously' and 'abstemiously'. In addition, I'll also offer you the word 'subcontinental'. What do you make of them?"

✱ Solution on page 320 ✱

The Pleasant Lake

***The Peculiar Case of the Raven Child* dragged Holmes and myself up to the Gwynedd village of Abergynolwyn. A devilishly long way to go, but Holmes insisted we had to see some details for ourselves. So one grey morning, we found ourselves in a small chapel on the shores of a glacial lake, the Tal-y-Llyn, where the River Dysynni begins.**

Inside the chapel, a simple altar bore an exhortation regarding the ten commandments, along with the customary cloth and Bible. Above it, on the wall, a curious message was chiselled, clearly of some age:

P R S V R Y P R F C T M N

V R K P T H S P R C P T S T

Holmes glanced at it, and his eyes narrowed for a moment. Then he turned to me, with a certain light in his eye. "That last line is missing a final 'N'," he said.

"Clearly that's not all that's missing," I replied.

"I'll grant you that," he said. "There's precisely one other letter missing too – more than a dozen copies of it."

He would say no more, and we had to sit there until I'd decoded the message. It was not a comfortable time. Can you tell what the message is?

✻ Solution on page 321 ✻

Slick

Picking my way cautiously down Baker Street in the icy February morning was always a trying experience. It didn't help much that holmes often appeared to have the feet of a cat, and hardly ever slipped around. I, on the other hand, typically felt in serious danger of crashing to the ground with every step i took.

One morning, Holmes took note of my stumbling and suggested that I attempt to walk on the slickest, smoothest patches of ice I could find, rather than preferring those patches with a little texture to offer grip.

I, in turn, suggested that I was having enough trouble as it was.

"But, my dear chap, you'll find the smooth stuff easier to walk on than the rough. The smoother, the better."

He was right, as he inevitably is. Can you say why?

The Second Camouflage

I was sorting through my pocket change, which had become annoyingly weighty, when Holmes inflicted his third set of camouflage words on me. "Heartbreaker, journeyers, solipsistic and diagnoses," he declared. Having pulled my wits together and confirmed that I was supposed to locate the four small, thematically linked words hiding within each of the longer ones, I had him repeat them to me.

Can you find the answer?

✱ Solution on page 321 ✱

Forty-five

Holmes picked a slice of toast from the breakfast rack, but instead of buttering it, he thoughtfully tore it into four uneven pieces, and tossed them onto the tray.

"Mrs Hudson won't like that, old chap," I warned him. "You know how she is about food vandalism."

"Forty-five," he replied. I blinked.

"Curious number," he said. "Of course, they all are."

"Of course," I muttered, under my breath.

"You can split 45 into four chunks, four different natural numbers that added together produce it as their total. So far, so true of anything over 9. But these particular four numbers are somewhat special. Add 2 to the first, subtract 2 from the second, the third multiply by 2, and the fourth divide by 2. The result of each four operations is the same. Can you tell me the numbers?"

"I dare say," I replied. "May I finish my egg first?"

"If you must."

What are the four numbers in question?

✱ Solution on page 322 ✱

St Mary Axe

Holmes was reading a file that Inspector Lestrade had furnished him with some high-profile matter regarding purloined diaries belonging to a cabinet minister's younger daughter. Every so often, he'd snort or toss his head, rather like an ill-tempered stallion. Finally, he put the papers down, and turned to me. "Lestrade's documents say that Mr Lloyd takes precisely four hours to walk to and from his home in Stoke Newington to the City, not counting the 60 seconds he takes to hand an envelope to a small man in St Mary Axe. His outward journey is conducted at an average rate of five miles per hour, and the return journey three."

"Is that useful to know?" I asked innocently.

"Not in the least," Holmes replied. "Maybe you'd tell me how far it is from Lloyd's home to his small man in the city?"

Can you find the answer?

✷ Solution on page 322 ✷

Ronnie

Mrs Hudson was in high dudgeon over the supposedly high-handed way that one of her cousins, a gardener out in the home counties, had been treated by his latest employer.

"Ronnie agreed an annual salary of £500 plus a rather nice all-weather cape with the Terringtons. In the end, he had to leave them after seven months, because my uncle Hob had a nasty turn. The Terringtons gave him just £60, on top of the cape. Sixty quid! That's less than ten pounds a month. It's a disgrace."

"That's dreadful," I sympathized, but I'll admit that at the same time, I was wondering precisely how expensive the cape actually was.

Assuming the Terringtons are playing fair, what's the cape worth?

February

I was reading *The Times* of London when Holmes, having glanced at the date on the front of the paper, said, "Did you know that the last time we had a February with five Wednesdays in it was in 1888?"

Having given myself a moment to process this information, I confirmed that no, in fact I had not been consciously aware of that fact.

"It may interest you to calculate when the next occasion will be," Holmes continued.

Whilst I did not feel that the matter was especially fascinating, I went ahead and worked it out. Can you?

❋ Solution on page 323 ❋

Isaac

"Catch!" Holmes tossed an apple in my general direction.

I caught it shortly before it struck me in the chest.

He nodded. "You know, I trust, that everything falls at the same speed."

"Well, I seem to remember hearing something of the sort," I replied. "But drop a tumbler of scotch and a piece of paper, and tell me that again."

Holmes smiled. "Experimentation. Good. I should say then, that apart from the effects of air resistance, everything falls at the same speed. Gravity pulls on every atom of an object simultaneously, not just the ones on the outer surface."

"Hmm," I said. "Well, if you say so. It seems a little counter-intuitive, however."

"Indeed it does, Watson. Indeed it does. So, experimentation. Can you devise an experiment we can perform here and now?"

✻ Solution on page 323 ✻

The Code

We came across an encrypted sales ledger whilst investigating *The Adventure of the Frightened Carpenter*. It wasn't especially challenging to decode, but it was interesting, so I shall present a sample to you here for your amusement and possible edification:

```
GAUNT+
OILER=
------
RGUOEI
```

The trick to the code was reasonably straightforward. The fellow had selected a common ten-letter English word, one in which all the letters were different, and then assigned the digits from 1 up to 9 and then 0 to the letters. He then simply substituted the appropriate letter for each digit.

On that basis, can you find the key word?

❋ Solution on page 324 ❋

The Track

Our pursuit of the dubious Alan Grey, whom we encountered during *The Adventure of the Third Carriage*, led Holmes and myself to a circular running track where, as the sun fell, we witnessed a race using bicycles. There was some sort of substantial wager involved in the matter, as I recall, and the track had been closed off specially for the occasion. This was insufficient to prevent our ingress, obviously.

One of the competitors was wearing red, and the other blue. We never did discover their names. As the race started, red immediately pulled ahead. A few moments later, Holmes observed that if they maintained their pace, red would complete a lap in four minutes, whilst blue would complete one in seven.

Having made that pronouncement, he turned to me. “How long would it be before red passed blue if they kept those rates up, old chap?”

Whilst I wrestled with the answer, Holmes went back to watching the proceedings.

Can you find the solution?

✻ Solution on page 324 ✻

The Fence

Wiggins, the chief scamp of the Baker Street Irregulars, was reporting to us regarding movements afoot in Highgate cemetery. He looked unusually weary, but no less alert or mischievous for that.

"They're putting up some sort of statue, Mr Holmes," the boy said.

"I knew it," Holmes replied. "Are they fencing it off?"

"They are, sir. But they're having trouble."

Holmes perked up. "Oh? How so?"

"Well, they clearly want to use all the posts they have, and make an even fence. I heard one of 'em moaning that at a foot apart, they had 150 posts too few, whilst at a yard, they had 70 too many."

Our discussion went on for some time, but let me ask you this – how many posts did the would-be fencers have?

❋ Solution on page 325 ❋

A Chelsea Tale

"My Angie's fella, Trevor," said Mrs Hudson, "He's got a pal named Rick, and it was Rick's sister Sally who told me about the brother of her cousin's best friend, Roderick."

"Um, is that the cousin, the best friend, or the brother?" I asked, starting to sink.

Mrs Hudson gave me a very pitying look. "Roddie? He's Budgie's friend. Lovely lad, he is, specially considering."

I thought about asking what I was supposed to consider, but decided discretion in this instance was the better part of valour.

"Anyhow," she continued. "Roddie knows this guy who works out in Chelsea, if you can believe it."

That seemed entirely plausible, and I nodded accordingly.

"Well, Sally was telling me that Jez – that's the Chelsea chap, Doctor – got such a nasty fright at work the other day from a gigantic hornet the size of a robin that he leapt straight through the window he was standing at. It's eight floors up, Doctor."

"That's terrible," I said, genuinely shocked. "Poor man."

"Yes. He was sacked straight away, of course."

"Wait," I said, swinging back to total confusion. "What? Sacked? Wasn't he killed?"

"Killed? Not hardly. He a small cut on his ear from the glass, but no, otherwise he was totally fine."

"I don't understand," I had to confess. Do you?

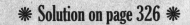

✻ Solution on page 326 ✻

120

The Fourth Wordknot

Holmes and I were in a comfortable tea-house with a clear line of sight to the front doors of St Paul's Cathedral. *The Adventure of the Impossible Gecko* had taken an unexpectedly clerical turn, and some extended observation was in order. When Holmes handed me a slip of paper, I at first mistakenly assumed it was something to do with the matter at hand. Not so. It was the fourth wordknot.

"You know the drill, Watson. Three loosely linked ten-letter words, first letters jumbled on the first row, you have to unpick them."

"Quite," I said, taking the paper. It read:

1. TUS
2. NUY
3. PDB
4. HEE
5. WER
6. SAR
7. CID
8. TOI
9. NER
10. REG

Can you find the solution?

✵ Solution on page 326 ✵

The Biscuits

Wiggins told us about an altercation amongst the Irregulars which had fallen to him to mediate. A small sack of biscuits had gone missing from their collective supplies, and it could have been any one of six suspects.

When he discussed the matter with the six, their stories boiled down to the following six statements:

Will: Stephen did it.

Max: Robin did it.

Mary: Will did it.

Stephen: I didn't do it.

Gwen: Max did it.

Robin: Yeah, Max did it.

His main annoyance with the affair was that only one of the six told him the truth. He immediately discerned the guilty party from that, of course. Can you?

✹ Solution on page 327 ✹

Dangerous Ladies

Holmes watched Mrs Hudson depart from our rooms with a somewhat rueful expression. "On the subject of redoubtable women, Watson, I have a little mental exercise for you. Two of the most formidable women in ancient history were undoubtedly Cleopatra, the last pharaoh of Egypt, and our very own Boadicea, who razed Colchester, London and St Albans to the ground."

"My word," I said. "There's a lesson there, Holmes – don't mess with a Norfolk lass."

He shot me a dark look before continuing. "Our best estimates say that the two ladies had a combined lifespan of 69 years. We know that Cleopatra died in 30 BC, and that Boadicea's death came 129 years after Cleopatra's birth. So when was Boadicea born?"

Can you find the answer?

✵ Solution on page 327 ✵

Square Sheep

"Intuition," Holmes told me, "is just a way of saying that your brain spotted an answer that your conscious mind did not. It can be a powerful aid to deduction for those in whom the awareness is less than perfectly honed, provided that you are ever-vigilant for the differences between a genuine intuition and simple imagination. Telling the two apart is a matter of practice."

So saying, he tossed me a box of matches. "Thanks," I said, somewhat doubtfully.

"Four of those, Watson, will make you a square. If you fancy a practical application, imagine that they are fences, and you are marking off a pen for a sheep or goat. Better yet, let us say that each match is the equivalent of a yard in length, in which case our square is one square yard in area."

"Square sheep, perhaps?" I offered.

"Say rather enormously fat sheep. Your challenge is to discover the minimum number of matches required to make a closed shape of at least ten square yards in area – a pen for ten of your obese sheep. You are not allowed to break the matches, by the by."

It took me a lot of trial and error before Holmes was satisfied with my efforts. Can you find a solution?

❋ Solution on page 328 ❋

Mr Andreas

During *The Adventure of the Maida Vale Baker*, we had to look into the financial affairs of Mr Andreas. They proved quite surprisingly regular, in the mathematical sense of the word. Some fifteen years before, the man had started an investment firm with his capital, of £1,600. His wealth then proceeded to grow by exactly 55 per cent every three years. It was quite uncanny how precise this was.

There was a reason for that, of course.

But for now, can you say to the nearest pound how much money Mr Andreas had after fifteen years?

❋ Solution on page 329 ❋

Davey

Wiggins had finished describing his latest discoveries to us, and rather than take off, he hung around to share an anecdote. "A funny thing happened to me on the south bank this morning, Mr Holmes."

"Is that so?"

"On my honour," Wiggins said, with an impish grin. "I was almost up to opposite the palace of Westminster when I happened to glance over my shoulder, and saw my old pal Davey heading in my direction, about 200 yards away. So I turned around, and headed towards him. Two hundred yards of facing each other later, him grinning at me every step we took, he was still 200 yards away. Can you credit it?"

"Very rum," Holmes said, allowing himself a small smile.

He had to explain it to me, but can you see what had happened?

Solution on page 329

The Watch

The Adventure of the Frightened Carpenter **led Holmes and myself to a warehouse, as I may have mentioned before. One of the more interesting things about that operation was the somewhat convoluted schedule that the four watchmen had devised for themselves. Their employers required that each man work two six-hour shifts a day with a break in between, starting precisely on the hour, so that there were always two men on duty, and both never changed shift at the same time.**

As we discovered later, each of the four men had their own personal requirements regarding their working hours. Jim wanted to start at midnight, and be entirely done by 4 p.m.; Dave wanted to be free between 10 a.m. and 4 p.m.; Peter wanted to relieve Dave after his second shift; Mike, finally, had to be on duty at 9 a.m..

What shift pattern did they finally settle on?

✻ Solution on page 329 ✻

The Fifth Wordknot

I received my fifth wordknot from Holmes over a rather nice luncheon at the Great Western Hotel at Paddington, a rather fine example of mid-century Second Empire architecture and design, with lavish ornamentation. The hotel, that is, rather than the luncheon, which was nevertheless quite outstanding.

I did my best to address Holmes's challenge adroitly, but I must confess that the goose was quite a distraction. The note he gave me is replicated below, and the task, as I'm sure you recall, is to unpick the three ten-letter words whose letters are scrambled in the ten rows below, first letters on the first row, second letters on the second row, and so on. The words are of course thematically related.

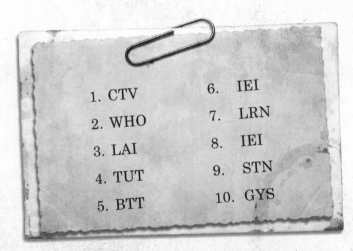

1. CTV
2. WHO
3. LAI
4. TUT
5. BTT
6. IEI
7. LRN
8. IEI
9. STN
10. GYS

❋ Solution on page 330 ❋

The Lease

Mrs Hudson was cleaning away our breakfast things. "That Archie, he does think he's a wit. Well, he's half-right."

"Archie?" I asked, in a moment of incaution.

"A cousin, on Mr Hudson's side," she said.

I breathed a sigh of relief. "How many cousins do you actually have, Mrs Hudson?" I couldn't help myself.

"Seventy-nine," she told me. "No, make that 78. That fool Neill died last month. Fell off a cliff. There's only 22 as I'd consider top shelf, though. Anyway, I was telling you about Archie."

"Indeed you were," I admitted.

"Well, Archie lives in a small place up Wembley way. He's on a 99-year lease, and I thought to ask him how much time there was left on it. So he only tells me, all smug like, that two-thirds of the time that's expired is equal to four-fifths of the time remaining. Of course, a gentleman like yourself wouldn't be fazed by that for an instant, would you?"

"Of course not," I managed. Holmes snickered from across the room.

How long is left on the lease?

✻ Solution on page 330 ✻

Tea

Holmes turned to look at me, fixing me with his gaze until I lowered my book. "Have you ever considered the plight of the humble grocer, Watson?"

I admitted that I had not, in general, spent a great deal of time attempting to evaluate the life of grocers, no.

"Scales can be a positively devilish business," he said.

"Is that so?"

"Most definitely. Imagine that you are such a grocer, in urgent need of dividing a twenty-pound bale of tea into two-pound packets. The only weights you have to use on your scale are one weighing nine pounds, and one weighing five pounds. What would be the least number of weighings you would need to divide up your bale correctly?"

What do you think?

✻ Solution on page 331 ✻

Loose Change

It occurs to me that an experience of my own may prove a worthy addition to this collection of problems. When I returned home to 221b from the trip to Hookland, I found myself rather short on ready money. I had kept receipts and other notes, so I had a solid idea of where it had all gone.

At the start of the journey, my ticket from Hookland back to London cost me precisely one half of the money I had available. Before boarding, I also bought a fortifying mug of tea for Holmes and myself, at a cost of sixpence. When we arrived back in London, it was lunchtime, so I treated the pair of us to a pub lunch at Waterloo, which cost me half of what I had remaining, plus ten further pence to boot. Half of what that left me went on getting back across town to Paddington. Then I gave sixpence to an old beggar outside the station, and paid nine pence for a quick shoe-shine. When I got home, I discovered that I had just one solitary sixpence left.

How much did I start out with? Feel free to calculate the sum in pennies.

❋ Solution on page 331 ❋

How Many Cows

During *The Adventure of the Wandering Bishops*, Holmes disguised himself as a Hookland farmer, and demonstrated an astonishing mastery of the frankly baffling local dialect. On those occasions where he had conversations with his supposed peers – as happened with alarming regularity – I was frequently left at a complete loss as to the topic of discussion. Still, our subterfuge proved a very useful necessity in coming to grips with the elusive self-professed major, C. L. Nolan, and his trail of intrigue and terror. But I must not permit myself to get distracted.

After one encounter with a fellow with the unlikely name of Podge, Holmes confessed that they'd been discussing theoretical cows.

"Mr Podge seemed most concerned regarding his black woodland cow," he told me. "He said that this beast had started producing one female calf a year, from the age of two, and to his apparent distress, each of these female calves had grown to follow the exact pattern of their mother, as had their own offspring, and so on. He was particularly worried about the time, 25 years from the birth of the black woodland cow, when apparently 'the time would be right', whatever that may denote."

"My word," I said. "Queer fellow. Wouldn't half of them have died of old age, or been eaten, or something?"

"He seemed to think that they would all – of some inevitability – still be alive. How many female cows would we be talking about at this point?"

Can you find the answer?

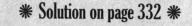

✻ Solution on page 332 ✻

Odd

Holmes was clutching some sort of disturbingly decorated thurible, and holding forth on the vital necessity of allowing one's mind to think outside of the rigidly inflexible train-tracks of conventional thought. The thurible, which had come from an abandoned church, was glittering in the sunlight as he waved it around the drawing-room. It kept drawing my eye, to my annoyance, as the peculiar script with which it was engraved made me feel more than a little uneasy.

"The superior mind must not be blinkered, Watson. Watson?"

"Ah, yes, Holmes. Not blinkered. Quite so."

"I'm glad you agree," he said, tossing the glittering censer from one hand to the other and back. "So. Write down five odd digits for me that will add up to fourteen."

I paused at that. "An odd number of odd numbers coming up even? That's impossible, surely?"

Holmes sighed. "What was I just saying?"

Can you find a solution?

❋ Solution on page 333 ❋

Draft

March was approaching slowly, and the weather outside was frightful. Snow, snow and more snow had been piling up for days, and despite the well-heaped fireplace, 221b was decidedly chilly. Holmes was standing by the window, gazing out onto the street, and making quiet deductions to himself about passing strangers, as was his occasional habit. Then he turned to face me.

"You'll have noticed that there's a cold draft coming from the window, my dear friend."

"I have indeed," I said.

"I can assure you that the window is perfectly sound, mechanically. There is no gap or chink in either glass or woodwork. So where's the draft coming from?"

That floored me for a bit. What do you think?

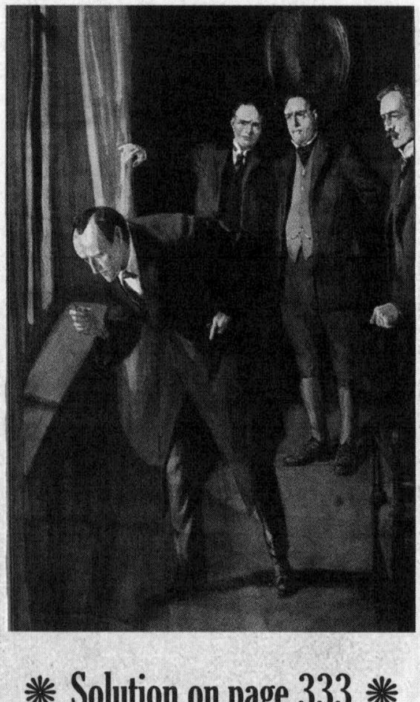

Solution on page 333

The Seamstress

During *The Adventure of the Impossible Gecko*, we interviewed a seamstress who'd seen a suspicious man loitering around outside her employers' manor house in rural Essex. The house was robbed a day later, and a priceless jewel-studded jade gecko – which really ought not to have existed, given all historical precedent – went missing. Naturally, the Turners recalled the information that the seamstress had passed to them the night before, so it was a clear necessity that we interview her.

When she arrived at 221b Baker Street, Miss Adams seemed polite and pleasant, if somewhat over-awed. Holmes looked her over, and spotted several sure signs of her profession, including needle-spotting on the second joint of her thumb, and a very specific callus on her index finger. Comfortable with her bona fides, he interviewed her.

We learnt from Miss Adams that it was a drizzly night when she saw the man out on the grounds, observing the house. She was working in a room on the ground floor, and caught sight of him near the tree-line, some 40 feet away. Although she was unable to see the man's face, she said that he was around six feet in height, and strongly built. He watched the house for several minutes, before turning around and slinking away. She immediately went to inform the Turners.

As soon as she left the building, Holmes leapt to his feet, grabbed a tattered coat from a closet, and dashed after her. All he'd spare me by way of explanation was that she was clearly lying. Can you say why?

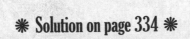

✱ Solution on page 334 ✱

Bees

"It's interesting," Holmes said, "the lengths to which people will go in order to obfuscate perfectly simple information."

"Imagine that," I said.

"Well, Watson, you of all people should be highly familiar with such manipulations." I must have looked slightly dismayed at that, for he followed up swiftly. "Having spent so much time exposed to academic research during your medical training."

"Ah. Yes, that. Damnable stuff, Holmes. Self-aggrandizement at its worst, often."

"Precisely." Holmes nodded. "Take this, which comes from a letter I received from an apiarist I have been corresponding with in Devon. He says, of a small hive, that one-fifth of the workers typically went to his azaleas, one-third to his roses, and a number equal to three times the difference between these two fractions to his geraniums, leaving the remaining worker to dart about uncertainly."

"Does he now?" I asked. "I suppose you'd like me to tell you how many worker bees there were in total?"

"Excellent, Watson. Indeed I would."

Any idea?

✻ Solution on page 334 ✻

Fruitful

Holmes had been downstairs to have a word with Mrs Hudson regarding cabbage, and returned carrying a large orange.

"Did you settle the cabbage matter to your satisfaction, old chap?" I asked him.

"Quite so," he replied. "That woman is a fountain of information."

"Indeed she is," I agreed, thinking of her frequent tales of her bewildering assortment of relatives and their in-laws.

"Did you know that she keeps a bowl of fruit downstairs?"

"Of course," I said.

"There's a number of pieces of fruit in there today. Given my depredations, all but two of them are oranges, all but two of them are pears, and all but two of them are apples. How many is that?"

Can you find the solution?

✻ Solution on page 335 ✻

The Third Camouflage

I was returning home from a shopping trip, carrying several quite sizeable bags, when Holmes accosted me on the street just outside the door to 221b. "Wait, Watson. Do not enter!"

I flinched slightly, surprised at his appearance, and stopped where I was.

"Tourbillion," barked Holmes. "Underfunded. Candyfloss. Tessellated."

After my initial panicked moment where I feared the poor fellow had suffered a major stroke, I realized that he was assigning me one of his camouflage puzzles. Four words, each containing a smaller word, such that the smaller words are thematically linked. I confess that my relief at his ongoing wellbeing quite drove the words from my mind, and it was quite a fight to retrieve them.

What was the uniting theme?

✻ Solution on page 336 ✻

Speed

Speed was something of an issue to the Baker Street Irregulars. When one lives as a street urchin, a swift pair of heels is an extremely important quality. So the Irregulars often engaged in competitive sprints – not so much for status, but to ascertain whose skills were more suited for which types of endeavour.

On one afternoon, Wiggins told us about some of that morning's races. The fastest member of the Irregulars was a twelve-year-old named Sid, who'd somehow found his way to London from Newcastle-upon-Tyne. He'd been putting a new recruit, named Raymond, to the test. In a series of 100-yard sprints, Sid had consistently beaten Ray by ten yards. Having seen Sid run, I was duly impressed by Ray's performance.

"At the end, after their rest break, Ray wanted one fair crack," Wiggins said. "So he asked Sid to start ten yards behind the line." He and Holmes both chuckled.

"I'm sure you can see what the outcome was, old chap," Holmes said to me. I snapped off an answer, and immediately regretted it. Can you find the solution?

❋ Solution on page 337 ❋

PART THREE

CUNNING

The Statuette

Holmes set aside his newspaper and looked up at me over breakfast one morning. "Do you suppose you have a head for business, Watson?"

"I dare say I'd be able to pick it up," I replied.

Holmes tapped the paper thoughtfully. "Let us suppose that you are a seller of antiquities. You have in your possession a rather pleasant statuette. A distinguished elderly gentleman comes in to your premises, and declares that the piece is familiar to him. He purchases it enthusiastically, not even blinking at your £100 price tag.

"Once the transaction is complete, the gentleman informs you that the piece is one of a pair; fairly valued by yourself as a singleton, but worth many times that amount if coupled with its mate. He offers to pay you a massive £1000 if you can obtain the other, and tells you his hotel. He leaves, and naturally you begin making enquiries about the statuette.

"Some days later, a fellow comes by with an identical companion to the statuette you sold. He says that he's heard you're looking for his piece, and is willing to part with it for £300. What say you? Does that sound like a good deal?"

What say you indeed?

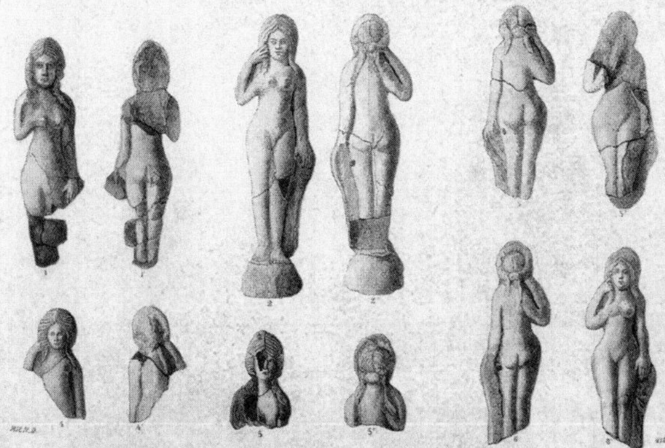

✻ Solution on page 339 ✻

Dedication

I took the opportunity, over a luncheon of Mrs. Hudson's fine ham and sliced tomatoes, to take my turn in throwing a little unexpected riddle at Holmes. He was amused, if hardly baffled, so I feel it may be of some entertainment to you.

There is a shop which is devoted to the sale of one particular staple of daily life. It sells many varieties of this particular device, all of which serve exactly the same broad purpose. Some of these varieties are made up of tens of thousands of individual, moving pieces, whilst others consist of less than twenty such parts. A few are completely solid, immobile throughout, and yet still function as well as the most complex. They may likewise range in size from taller and heavier than a man down to being less than the size of a fingernail, but the very tiniest can still have more separate moving parts than the largest.

Can you guess the identity of this device?

✻ Solution on page 340 ✻

The Green Stone

Holmes and I were pursuing an unfortunate incident connected to the theft of the Green Stone of Harvington. The owners, Rupert and Rebecca Coynes, had come into its possession some years before. On the evening of the theft, the couple had met for refreshments at a London hotel when Rupert had a seizure and collapsed dead. It was later found that he had been poisoned, and mere blind luck had helped Rebecca avoid the same fate.

After the Stone's return, Rebecca had difficulty understanding why she had lived whilst her husband had died. They had both been perfectly healthy and followed a very similar diet. Both their drinks had been laced with identical amounts of toxin, and Rebecca's resilience and constitution was no different to her husband's. To her credit, she refused to believe that it was some divine providence that spared her, but understandably, the matter plagued her with considerable guilt.

Sherlock Holmes bore Rebecca's anguished confusion placidly, and when her tears had subsided, said "Tell me, were you thirsty that evening?" Rebecca nodded, obviously perplexed. Holmes smiled, and said nothing, and it was left to me to explain.

❋ Solution on page 340 ❋

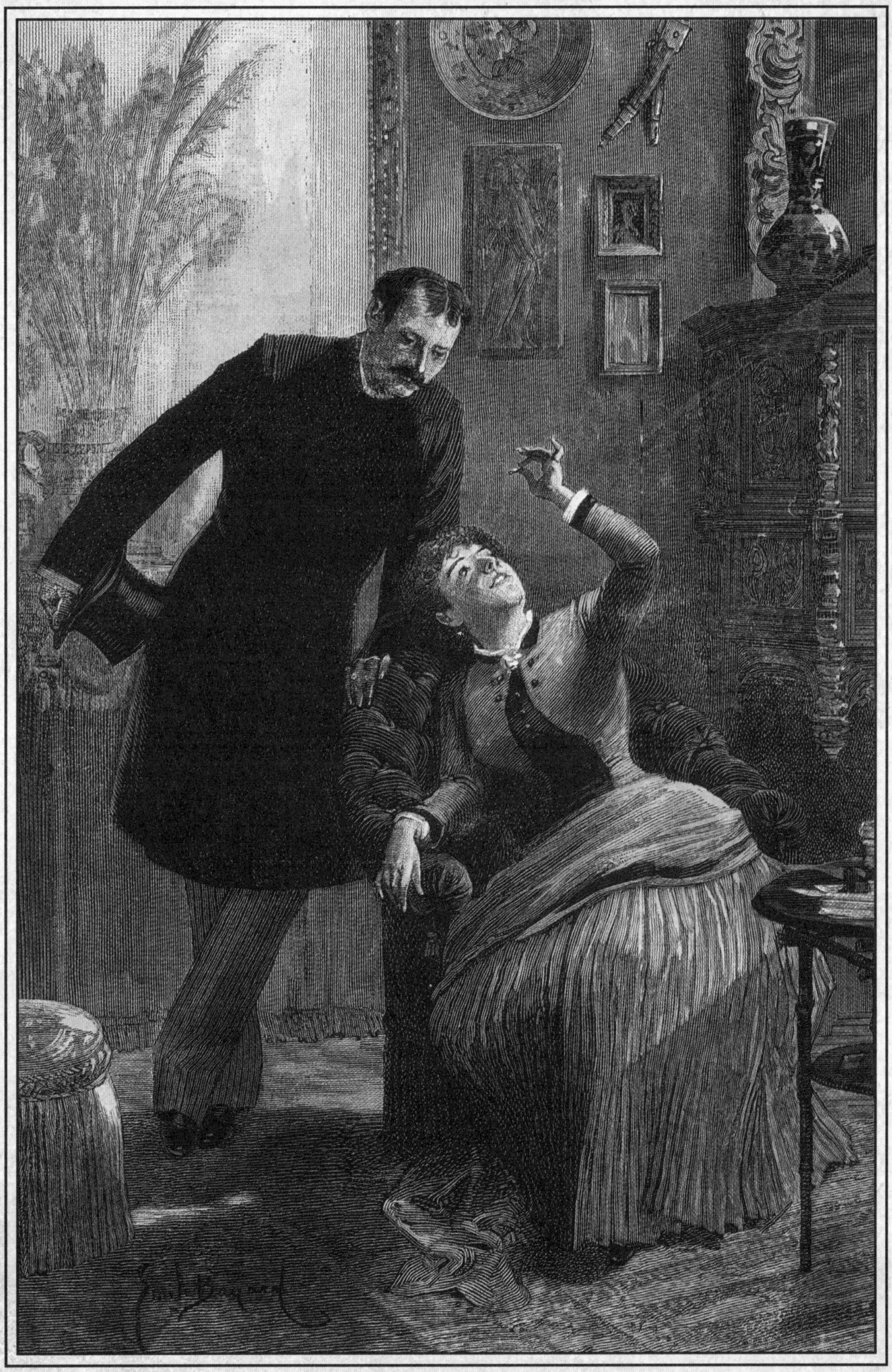

The Sixth Curiosity

"Mrs Hudson informs me that her greengrocer was unable to provide her with her usual 12" bundle of leeks at the market today, and instead gave her two 6" bundles."

"Ah well," I said, my mind not on leeks.

"He had her pay a little extra as well, for the effort involved in making the two bundles."

"Seems reasonable enough," I said. But was it?

Solution on page 341

The Cult of the Red Star

Holmes was reading one of his penny dreadfuls. After a short time, be put the pamphlet down and sighed. "It is obvious," said he, "that the murder was committed by the victim's father's brother-in-law. Or the victim's brother's father-in-law. Or, I suppose, the victim's father-in-law's brother. I hate it when the case is so transparent."

It didn't sound in the least bit transparent to me, and I said so. "You yourself cannot even decide between three possible murderers."

"Nonsense," Holmes said crisply. "There is only one possible candidate, and I have identified him precisely."

What did he mean?

✱ Solution on page 341 ✱

Afternoon

"Let's keep your mind on its toes," Holmes said to me as I was looking out of the window one afternoon.

I made no protest, so he continued.

"How many minutes are we now before 6pm,
if fifty minutes ago it was four times as many minutes past 3pm?"

Solution on page 342

The Sixth Literal Oddity

One afternoon, Holmes handed me a scrap of notepaper. It bore a short list of words, like so:

uncopyrightable

dermatoglyphics

misconjugatedly

hydropneumatics

"One of your word puzzles," I surmised.

"Indeed," said Holmes. "Taken together, these words are the longest English examples of what, exactly?"

❋ Solution on page 342 ❋

Suffocation

Lady Casterton was found suffocated to death in her bedroom shortly after 7pm, when the maid went to discover why her employer had not appeared for dinner. From an examination of the body, it was clear that she had been killed a little after six at the very earliest. Suspicion naturally fell onto her nephew, her inheritor, with whom relations had been strained in recent weeks. He would have looked like a prime suspect, were it not for the testimony of the maid.

"He left the house at 11 minutes to 6. I'm certain of it. I was in the drawing room, tidying. I heard him leave, clear as anything, and looked up to check the time. He doesn't usually depart before dinner, see? So I looked up at the clock, and thought to myself, 'Why, it's not even 10 to, yet.' So it can't be him. I won't see an innocent man swing."

With no other suspects or evidence of intruders, and the maid's physical weakness ruling her out, the police eventually turned to Baker Street for assistance. Holmes seemed interested briefly, but took a quick look inside the door, then called the maid over and asked her a single question.

Do you understand the situation?

❋ Solution on page 343 ❋

The Sixth Mental Trial

We were sitting at breakfast when Holmes said to me, "Let us return to my hypothetical friend for a moment, my dear Watson."

"The wily Alfie."

"Just so. Today, he is joined by several members of his family – Fred, George and Harry. The four were sitting down to tea together, when Alfie noted that George had the same familial relationship to Fred as he himself did to Harry. Furthermore, Alfie himself had the same familial relationship to Fred as George did to him."

"A knotty matter."

"Can you untangle it?"

Solution on page 343

Watch Out

"You know that I have no great love of the Alps," Holmes said. We had been talking idly about skiers. "One of the lesser known perils is that it can be difficult to keep the precise time."

"You mean you get distracted?"

"Not a bit of it," Holmes replied. "Both our pocket watches are scrupulously accurate. If I were to go and spend a period of time up in the Alps, making sure to keep my pocket watch at a healthy room temperature at all times, when I returned here our watches would show a noticeable difference. Despite the fact that the accuracy of my watch should not have suffered one iota from the experience. Can you account for it?"

❋ Solution on page 344 ❋

The Dinner Table

"My hypothetical friend Alfie is having a dinner party," Holmes informed me.

I prepared my brain as best I could for one of his typically baffling onslaughts.

"In addition to Bill and Charlie, he is also expecting Don, Eric, Fred and George."

"Quite a turn-out," I said.

"Alfie is setting places around a circular table, and wants to ensure everyone gets to sit next to everyone else, so he is having them change places between each of the three courses. He is however a little tired of George, and always fond of Bill. His intention is to arrange everyone around the table in alphabetical order for the starter. How should he arrange the men for the other two courses to ensure everyone sits beside everyone else, yet still keep Bill as close as that will allow, and George as distant?"

✵ Solution on page 344 ✵

The Bicycle

One afternoon, at my medical practice, I overheard a young patient attempting to extort a gift of a bicycle from her mother as a reward for the girl's good behaviour in complying with my ministrations. The mother was amused, as was I, but remained resolute.

"You can have a bicycle when you are exactly one third of my age, and not before. You are still too young, and I don't want you haring around on one of those things."

The little girl clearly deemed this acceptable, for she was perfectly sweet throughout her examination. I knew from my notes that she was 13, and her mother was 46. When I put the situation to Holmes, he was able to work out how long it would be before the girl got her bike in a flash.

Can you do so?

✱ Solution on page 344 ✱

Highland Fling

"Superstitious nonsense!" Sherlock Holmes slammed his newspaper down on the desk in irritation.

I enquired mildly regarding the nature of the story that had aroused my friend's ire.

"It is in the nature of the weak mind to ever seek supernatural intervention in even the simplest of matters," he replied, more calmly. "This article spins a tale of a supposedly Highland marriage, and the supposed curse that has been inflicted upon it. All utter nonsense."

"Of course," said I.

"A young couple chose this Candlemas just past for their nuptials. As the ceremony was progressing, a local girl burst in to the church and declared that as she had been passed over by the groom, she had ensured that the marriage would be a doomed one. As a sign, the church bell would not ring to celebrate their union. She then consumed some poisonous concoction, and staggered back out in a suitably theatrical manner. She was later found dead."

"I say!"

"The ceremony resumed, but the entire wedding party was afflicted with horror when, at the climax, the Church bell did indeed fail to sound. The bride fainted dead away, and several other ladies had to be attended to. When the groom and his man went with the vicar to investigate, they could find no sign of tampering, and indeed the bell worked again thereafter. So, being feeble-witted, they all declared it had to be the work of the devil in league with the spurned witch girl, and the bride has barely eaten nor slept since."

It was clear Holmes had a different explanation in mind. Can you imagine what?

❋ Solution on page 345 ❋

Big Squares

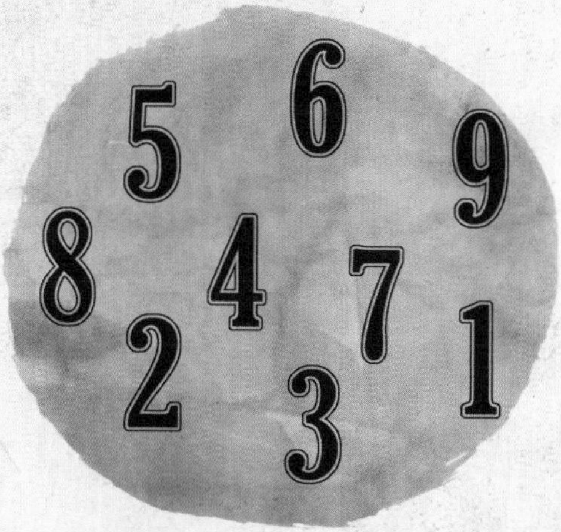

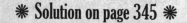

Holmes cornered me near the window, and expressed concern that his previous challenge to me involving the arrangement of each of the nine digits from 1 to 9 into a series of square numbers had not been stern enough.

I tried to persuade him that I felt most mathematically enlightened, but he was most insistent that I try again, this time to combine all of the digits into one single, massive square number. As if such a request were not enough, he casually added that it had to be the smallest possible such square.

I agreed as graciously as possible, and retired to my notepaper.

Can you find the answer?

✻ Solution on page 345 ✻

The Seventh Literal Oddity

"Tell me, Watson," Holmes said. "How many words in English use do you think there are that end with the letters -bt?"

"Well," I began, "there must be..."

"Careful man, give it a little thought."

I took his advice, and I'd suggest you do the same.

Solution on page 346

The Circus

It was a chilly November evening when Holmes informed me that he had obtained tickets to attend a circus on Clapham Common that very night. I expressed a certain amount of surprise, given that he had never shown enthusiasm for such diversions.

"Ah," said he. "I have had word that there may be some foul play afoot."

When we got there, we discovered a somewhat down-at-heel troupe, but none the less enthusiastic and committed for that. The performers included a small team of musicians and their conductor, a handful of clowns of various degrees of grotesqueness, a pair of aerial performers, a stage magician with assistant, two animal handlers, and the obligatory grandiose Ringmaster.

The performance was well-attended, and the audience seemed pleased enough as it unfolded along its predictable lines. During the trapeze act, something seemed to startle Holmes, and he snapped out of his inattentive reverie, leaning forward suddenly. Less than a minute later, tragedy struck. One of the trapeze artists mistimed his leap, and plummeted to the floor. The audience dissolved into a shrieking mass as the Beethoven screeched to a halt, and loud wails of anguish burst from the magician's assistant. I pushed my way into the ring, but it was hopeless.

"I'm afraid he's dead," I said to the horrified Ringmaster.

"Murdered," added Holmes, just behind me.

The Ringmaster and I spun round to look at him.

"Yes, murdered," Holmes said. "And we all watched the villain kill him, and did nothing."

What did he mean?

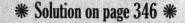

❋ Solution on page 346 ❋

Urchins

Wiggins was with us, receiving a briefing for a sensitive mission of observation. Holmes was most insistent that he go to extraordinary steps to avoid detection.

"I want you to use nine lads, Wiggins. Send them out in groups of three. You'll need to have them venture forth for six days. To help avoid detection though, I do not want any two boys next to each other twice. You may place them in the same group a second time, so long as they are not adjacent to someone they have been adjacent to before."

"No problem, Mr. Holmes," said the urchin, "just as you like." He sounded confident.

Could you have matched Holmes' instructions?

❋ Solution on page 346 ❋

The Third Portmanteau

I was taking my ease one evening in Baker Street, following a rather delightful dinner of stuffed quail that Mrs. Hudson had prepared for Sherlock Holmes and myself. I had thought that Holmes was conducting some abstruse chemical experiment or other, but was disabused of that notion when he appeared beside me and wordlessly handed me a rather eccentric illustration, which I have diligently copied below.

I recognised it for what it was, of course. "This is one of your devilish picture puzzles," said I.

"I see nothing escapes you," Holmes replied with a twinkle.

"So I am to consider each separate element of the image as a clue, and deduce the only possible location that fits all the evidence."

"You are," Holmes agreed. "If you are so able. Restrict your considerations to London however, Watson."

I gave it some thought, and was finally able to pronounce a solution which Holmes would accept. Where does the picture refer to?

❋ Solution on page 347 ❋

The Meadow of Death

"A couple were found dead in a quiet valley in the Highlands," Holmes said to me one morning, apropos of nothing.

"They were murdered, I assume?" It was rather rare for Holmes to take interest in cases where foul play was not involved.

"It seems not," was his surprising reply. "They were found lying next to each other, hand in hand, in a pleasant field carpeted with new spring flowers. There was no sign of whatever it was that killed them. They were less than a mile to the nearest village. There was no evidence of any sort of murderous assault, no broken limbs, nor any of the tell-tale signs that suicide might have left. Lightning would have left char marks, rocks would have caused clearly visible wounds, and the physicians found no evidence of poisons or disease. They did not appear to have been robbed, either. I have an idea, of course. But what do you make of it?"

The Egg

"Have you thought much about eggs, Watson?" Holmes asked me during breakfast.

"I prefer them poached, given a choice."

"I really referred to the shape of the shell."

I mused on that for a moment. "Not especially," I admitted.

"Are you not curious as to why they are that particular drop-like shape, rather than being spherical, which would make them stronger?"

"I suppose it is an interesting question, yes."

"And what answer would you come up with?"

❋ Solution on page 348 ❋

The Eighth Literal Oddity

Finding myself at an idle moment on a quiet September afternoon, I asked Holmes if he happened to have any little word trial prepared which he had been saving up to vex me with. That may strike you as a little masochistic, but I was looking for a diversion.

He searched his memory for a moment, and nodded. "I'll offer you 'regimentations' and the mineral 'nitromagnesite'. What distinguishes them?"

✱ Solution on page 349 ✱

Gold

Holmes and I apprehended a vicious gold-smuggler in Epping one nasty September evening. He was a particularly unpleasant sort, and it was a genuine pleasure to hand him over to Scotland Yard.

He had been in the middle of preparing a consignment of gold slabs for shipment to France – 800 of them, each one 11" wide, 12½" long, and 1" deep. A king's ransom indeed.

Holmes pointed out to my attention that the box he had packed them in was square, and sufficiently high that it exactly contained all of the slabs with no wasted space left over. Further more, less than a dozen of the slabs had been stood on an edge.

Can you discern the dimensions of the box?

✻ Solution on page 350 ✻

Stones

One pleasant Sunday afternoon, Holmes had the Irregulars gather him up a basket of precisely fifty stones. Then starting from the step of 221b Baker Street, towards St. John's Wood, Holmes started laying the stones out with an ever increasing gap between them. He placed the second stone one yard from the first, the third three yards from the second, the fourth five yards from the third, and the fifth seven yards from the fourth.

At this point, he returned to where the rest of us were standing, watching him curiously.

"Young Wiggins, what would you say if I told you that I would place all fifty stones according to this pattern, and then pay you a farthing to pick them back up – but strictly one at a time, bringing each back to the basket here at the start before going to fetch the next?"

"I'd tell you to bugger off, Mr. Holmes, Sir."

Holmes laughed. "Quite right too."

But why?

Solution on page 350

The Seventh Curiosity

Shortly after Christmas one year, I was relaxing and enjoying the season when Holmes' thoughts turned to the tragic Massacre of the Innocents, King Herod's vile infanticide which we remember on December 28th.

"It is said," Holmes mused, "that after the deed, a number of the unfortunate mites were buried in sand, with only their feet sticking up to indicate their presence. How do you imagine that they told the boys apart from the girls, on such scant evidence?"

❋ Solution on page 351 ❋

Fencing

"A good detective must be a man of science, Watson."

I of course agree with this sentiment, and said so. Among the many things that my time with Sherlock Holmes has taught me is the paramount importance of even the most seemingly irrelevant physical clue.

"What do you know of the science of acoustics?"

"As much as any common lay-man," I allowed. "I'm confident in saying that the old folk myth about a duck's quack having no echo is utter bunk, and physically impossible besides."

"Imagine you are putting up wooden fence posts in a large field, perhaps to prepare an enclosure for sheep."

"Very well." I duly complied, painting the scene with a little light drizzle, and a hilly backdrop.

"When you start, near a stone building, you can hear a clear echo coming back to you. Later, near the middle of the field, the hammering noise you make is dull and flat. But later still, in another part of the field, you can hear a clear ringing noise. Do you know what could cause such an effect?"

✱ Solution on page 351 ✱

The Soho Pit

We were walking through the Soho area of London one morning, in search of one of Holmes' less reputable contacts. As we strolled down Dean Street, we passed a workman engaged in digging a hole for some purpose or other.

"You, sir, are five feet and ten inches in height," Holmes declared to him.

The man nodded. "And when I've gone twice as deep as I am now, then my head will be twice as far below the level of the pavement as it is above it this instant."

Holmes told the fellow how deep his hole was going to be, and got a respectful nod in return. Could you have done so?

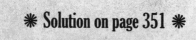

✱ Solution on page 351 ✱

The Seventh Mental Trial

"I have decided that today I know two hypothetical men, my dear Watson. Alfie and Bill."

"As you wish, Holmes," I said. "What do they look like?"

"Fishmongers," said he.

"So. Alright, I'm picturing a pair of hypothetical fish-mongers."

"It matters little, in truth. The case is that Alfie has twice as many sisters as he has brothers, whilst his sister Mary has the same number of sisters and brothers. Bill, by comparison, has three times as many sisters as brothers, but his sister Nancy has the same ratio of brothers to sisters as Mary does. Assuming both have just the bare amount of siblings required to fulfil their conditions, who has the more brothers, Alfie or Bill?"

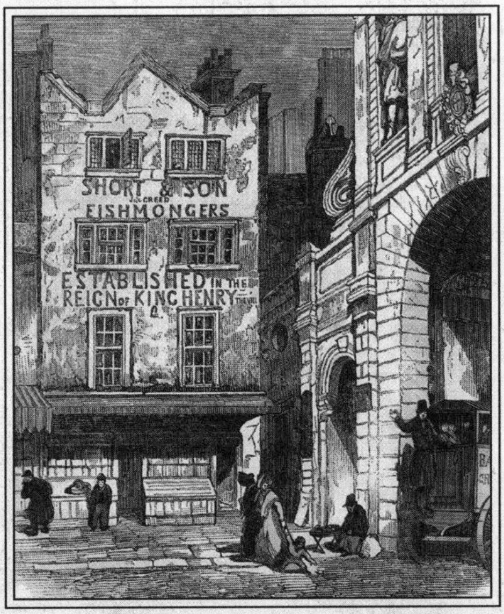

Solution on page 352

The Hanged Man

A rather perplexing crime had prompted Scotland Yard to summon Mr. Sherlock Holmes and myself to Draper Street. A temperamental young artist of some promise had been found hanged, and the police were at a loss to explain the murder.

His absence around town having been noted, the young man had been discovered in his rooms, behind doors so firmly locked and bolted that it took three stout constables to batter them open. The window was similarly secure, and anyway, it looked straight down onto the road some four stories below. The body itself was hanging by a short cord from a light fitting in the ceiling, nothing but air and dark carpet beneath its booted feet. In fact, there was no object whatsoever in evidence that the young man could possibly have stood upon with which to take his own life. The room was perfectly tidy, and the maid assured us that everything looked to be in its usual order, with nothing missing, and no additions. The police were certain that the killer had tidied up after the murder, but didn't know how he had exited the room.

Sherlock Holmes walked through the door, glanced around once, and snorted in derision. He knelt by the corpse, touched the carpet, and then rose again. "Really, Lestrade," he said, drying his fingers on his handkerchief. "You've excelled yourself this time. The situation is perfectly clear."

Would you consider it so?

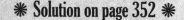

❋ Solution on page 352 ❋

A Hearty Drop

"My hypothetical friend Alfie," Holmes said, "wishes to divide a keg of ale equitably between Bill, Charlie and himself."

"I dare say he does," I retorted. "That undoubtedly explains his hat problem."

Holmes was unruffled. "The keg contains a whole six quarts, but the men find themselves with just a 2½ quart pail and a three-pint pickling jar, fortunately both perfectly clean."

"Can you not imagine them a hypothetical pint glass?"

"I cannot," Holmes replied. "That being so, can you tell me how they might most efficiently divide and consume the ale so that each gets his four pints?"

✻ Solution on page 353 ✻

The Barn

Norfolk was the setting for this particular problem. Inspector Lestrade brought word to Baker Street one chilly February morning that a colleague of his up in King's Lynn was having persistent trouble with a raider who specialised in robbing the warehouses of the shipping companies out there. The investigation had been proceeding well, until a sinister incident unnerved the superstitious local constabulary enough that help had to be sought. Perhaps inevitably, the problem found its way to Mr. Sherlock Holmes.

The villain had struck on a snowy Friday night, and made off unseen with a substantial quantity of goods. Witness statements suggested the villain had headed west out of the town, and once the storm had abated, and dawn had broken, the police found a crisp, deep hoof-print trail clearly leading over the fields. They followed the prints to a disused barn, steeled themselves, and threw open the door, ready to apprehend the thief.

The barn, however, was empty, save for a few small discarded bits of farming equipment. The snow was deep enough that even a sparrow's passing would be clearly noted. There were no drag-marks where prints could have been eliminated. There were no other ways out of the barn. The raider had ridden into the barn and vanished into thin air, according to the disturbed constables, "like the very Devil himself."

Holmes listened to Lestrade's tale, and just arched an eyebrow, clearly amused. The inspector's wounded expression simply made Holmes's eyes twinkle all the more. Can you explain?

✵ Solution on page 354 ✵

Solaris

Holmes has never been especially interested in matters astronomical. He maintains – and not without a certain justification, I suppose – that the revolutions of the heavenly bodies have very little impact on the solving of crimes. He knows the moon's phases, and is aware of upcoming eclipses, but otherwise maintains that he cares little for which astronomical body moves around which, or how swiftly.

Whilst I empathize with his focus, I feel a little differently. We live in a magnificent universe, and it seems a shame to me to not pay at least a little attention to its wonders. There is little so awe-inspiring, to my mind, as gazing up at a sky full of uncountable stars, knowing that any of them might be home to a planet with an intelligent being looking in my direction.

You know, I trust, that the Earth revolves upon its axis once per day – that being how the day is formed – as well as rotating entirely around the Sun once a year, in a counterclockwise direction. So my question is this: Does your speed of rotation (in relation to the Sun) change during the day, and if so, at what time are you moving the fastest?

✻ Solution on page 354 ✻

A Worship of Writers

During *The Adventure of the Third Carriage*, we found ourselves attempting to unravel the specific details of a collection of writers who came by train into London. The six of them entirely filled one compartment of the carriage, seated as there were in two rows of three, facing each other.

The facts that we managed to glean from the ticket inspector and other passers by are these. The six men were called Tomkins, Archer, Squires, Whitely, Appleby and Gardner. Between them, their specialities covered short stories, histories, humour, novels, plays and poetry, and each was reading the latest work of one of the others in the carriage.

Squires was reading a work by the person sitting opposite him. Tomkins, who is not the historian, was reading a volume of short stories. Archer, the novelist's brother-in-law, was sitting between the humorist and the short-story writer, who, in turn, was opposite the historian. Whitely was reading a play and sitting opposite the novelist. Appleby, reading the humorous book, was next to the playwright. Tomkins was sitting in a corner. Gardner, finally, hated poetry.

Who was the novelist?

Solution on page 355

Loggers

In Sussex, Holmes and I ran into a pair of woodcutters named Doug and Dave. There was an air of the unreliable about them – not helped by a clearly discernable aroma of scrumpy – but they nevertheless proved extremely helpful in guiding us to a particular hilltop clearing some distance outside of the town of Arundel. A shadowy group had been counterfeiting sorceries of a positively medieval kind, and all sorts of nastiness had ensued.

The Adventure of the Black Alchemist is not one that I would feel comfortable recounting, and if my life never drags me back to Chanctonbury Ring I shall be a happy man. But there is still some instructive material here. Whilst we were ascending our hill, Doug and Dave made conversation by telling us about their trade. According to these worthies, working together they were able to saw 600 cubic feet of wood into large logs over the course of a day, or split as much as 900 cubic feet of logs into chunks of firewood.

Holmes immediately suggested that they saw as much wood in the first part of the day as they would need in order to finish splitting it at the end of the day. It naturally fell to me to calculate precisely how much wood that would be.

Can you find the answer?

✻ Solution on page 355 ✻

The Sixth Wordknot

I was in a tailor's shop on Jermyn Street when Holmes sprang his sixth wordknot upon me. In fact, I was being fitted for a jacket, and the tailor was most strict that I withhold from moving. It certainly made it harder to concentrate, and not having access to a pencil didn't help one bit, I can assure you. I wasn't even able to take the slip of paper, which Holmes cheerfully held out in front of me for reference.

I impose no such unreasonable strictures upon you.

As before, the slip of paper bore ten rows of three letters, each one containing one letter, in normal sequence, of a ten-letter word. The letters in each row were in no particular order, however, making the task of unscrambling the three loosely themed words quite challenging.

The rows were as follows:

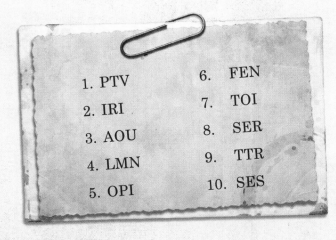

1. PTV
2. IRI
3. AOU
4. LMN
5. OPI
6. FEN
7. TOI
8. SER
9. TTR
10. SES

✵ Solution on page 356 ✵

Duck Duck Goose

The Peculiar Case of the Raven Child **took Holmes and I to the Dysynni Valley. Whilst much of what we encountered there was odd to say the least, there was at least a horrible logic to it, at least when examined after the fact.**

The same could not be said of a sign we saw outside one farmer's cottage. "Two chickens for a duck; three chickens and a duck for two geese," it declared, in wild handwriting. In smaller, neater lettering beneath, there was a further offer: "Three geese, one chicken and two ducks for 25 shillings. NO CHANGE."

"Eccentric fellow," I observed to Holmes.

"Probably spent the night alone on the top of Cader Idris," he replied. "Still, there's enough information there to work out the price of a duck, if you assume his 'no change' means that each bird costs a whole number of shillings."

Can you work out the value of a duck?

✱ Solution on page 356 ✱

The Jeweller

During *The Adventure of the Impossible Gecko*, we had reason to examine the movements of a certain jeweller of Hatton Gardens, a fellow named Stewartson. The Baker Street Irregulars were despatched to keep an eye on his movements, particularly with regards to the timing of his journey to and from work.

When Wiggins reported back to us, he informed us that Stewartson often took a handsome cab to and from work, and on those occasions, his total journey time to and from his shop was 30 minutes. On some mornings, however, he walked into work, and then caught a cab home when he finished. On those occasions, his total journey time was one and a half hours.

I made some comment to the effect that Wiggins could just have told us how long it took the fellow to walk to work, and Holmes archly replied that he'd done just that.

How long was Stewartson's walk to work?

❋ Solution on page 356 ❋

The Note

Holmes had been tinkering away in his study for the best part of a couple of hours, testing a range of pungent chemical experiments, when he came out bearing a purple-speckled notebook.

"Take a look at this, old chap," he said, and passed it over.

I took the notebook, and was about to examine it when Holmes turned on his heel and returned to the study. "Let me know when you've cracked it," he said, before closing the door.

Mystified, I opened the book, trying to avoid the purple splotches. The front page was the only one to bear any writing, and its contents were these:

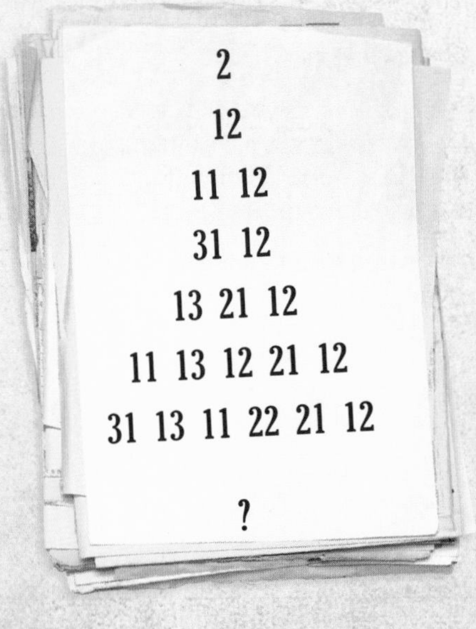

What should the next line be?

✻ Solution on page 357 ✻

The Legacy

I remember reading in the *Evening Standard* of an instance where an old soldier died childless, and left his modest bequest to his nephews, Ronald and Frederick. It was just below a silly story about a Canadian poltergeist. The piece was of interest only because of the somewhat tangled way in which the deceased had specified the money be divided. The newspaper took a humorous slant on the story, playing up the perplexity of the lawyer involved, and painting the dead man as an enthusiastic prankster. The truth of these claims is left to your personal judgement regarding the veracity of newspaper reporters.

However editorialized the story might have been, the base facts were that the fellow left £100 precisely, and determined the allotment of inheritance by saying that subtracting a third of Ronald's legacy from a quarter of Frederick's would give a difference of £11.

How much did Ronald get?

✱ Solution on page 357 ✱

Children

Having brought up some breakfast for Holmes and myself, Mrs Hudson rather spoiled my appetite by informing us that her cousin Davey and his wife were trying vigorously for a family. Whilst I was still attempting to get rid of the mental images thus conjured, she continued by saying, "They've decided they'd like to have four children, nice and quickly."

As a doctor, I naturally found the idea of both "nice" and "quickly" being applied to four pregnancies to be somewhat implausible, but I held my peace.

Mrs Hudson continued blithely on. "They're hoping not to get all four children the same sex. The real question, of course, is whether they're more likely to have two of each, or three of one."

"I'm sure the good Doctor could answer that for you," Holmes said, arching an eyebrow in my direction. "Assuming that they're equally likely to have a boy or a girl each time."

"Oh, yes," said Mrs Hudson. "Thank you, Doctor." I'm sure I saw her suppressing a mischievous grin.

Can you work out the answer?

Solution on page 358

The Trunk

Holmes and I were walking along a sleepy lane in Hookland, making our way back to the inn at which we had secured lodgings after scouting out the estates of the supposed major, C. L. Nolan. Up ahead, a tractor was slowly pulling a chained tree trunk along the lane. Fortunately it had been trimmed of its branches, but it was still an imposing sight.

When we'd overtaken the thing, Holmes surprised me by turning sharply on his heel and walking back along the trunk. I stopped where I was to watch him. He continued at a steady pace until he'd passed the last of it, then reversed himself once more, and walked back to me.

"Come along, old chap," he said as he walked past.

Shaking my head, I duly followed.

"It took me 140 paces to walk from the back of the tree to the front, and just twenty to walk from the front to the back," he declared.

"Well of course," I said. "The tree was moving, after all."

"Precisely," he said. "My pace is one yard in length, so how long is that tree-trunk?"

Can you find the answer?

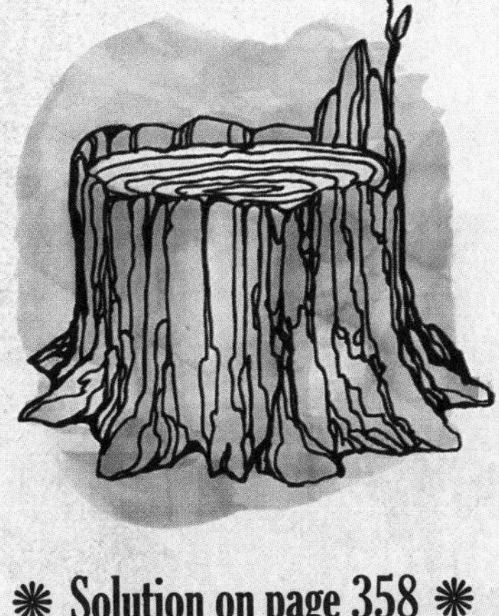

❋ Solution on page 358 ❋

The Revenge

Edward Blaydon was the captain of the *Revenge*, an ill-aspected sloop that claimed Cape Town as its home berth. This was during *The Adventure of the Sapphire Gin*, and a very strange affair it was too. Holmes had lured Blaydon to a luncheon in St. James', where we met him in the guise of shady exporters to ostensibly discuss the transport of a cargo from Whitby to Varna, on the Bulgarian coast.

"I know the Black Sea like the back of my hand," Blaydon said confidently. "I can get your merchandise into Varna, no questions asked, and that's a guarantee. I'll do it in under a week, too."

"That sounds very promising," Holmes replied. "Are you certain that your ship is up to the task?"

"The *Revenge*? Ha. Of course. I admit that it's not much to look at, but that's one of the fastest packet-runners you'll find in any of London's docks."

Holmes nodded thoughfully. "I noticed that you're registered in Cape Town. Is that where you're from?"

"Where's any seaman from, Mr Gordon?" Gordon was Holmes. I was going by Hendricks. "I belong to the oceans. Ports are just places where you buy booze, food, and other little niceties. I'm a Portsmouth lad, originally. But I've spent my time in the shadow of Table Mountain, if that's what's worrying you."

A little while later, we took our leave with some vague promises and assurances. As soon as we were out of the restaurant, Holmes shook his head disapprovingly. "I assume that you realized our friend was no sailor, Watson? Anyone hearing him would have."

What did he mean?

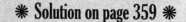

✱ Solution on page 359 ✱

The Field

One of the side effects of our trip to Hookland was that for several days thereafter, Holmes was given to couching his little mental exercises for me in agricultural terms. I suppose it did make something of a change to be considering matters pastoral rather than, say, fiscal or horological. There was something a little odd about it, however. Either way, it came to an end when *The Adventure of the Wandering Bishops* did.

As a practical example, consider this problem that Holmes set me during that period. There is a particular field which three of a farmer's animals – a cow, a goat, and a lamb – are set to graze. If it were just the cow and the goat, they would graze it bare in 45 days. Without the cow, the goat and the lamb will consume all the grass in 90 days. Absent the goat, the cow and lamb will eat all the pasture in 60 days. The farmer, however, has turned all three loose in the field. How long will it take the three combined to graze out the field?

You may assume for the sake of simplicity that the growth of the grass is irrelevant.

✻ Solution on page 359 ✻

The Type

During *The Adventure of the Third Carriage*, we spent some time talking to a printer. Holmes was after some nugget of information, but felt that the matter needed to be addressed obliquely, so we spent more than an hour with the fellow.

He was nice enough, as printers go, but he was somewhat fixated on a batch of calendars that had been commissioned from him. They were of the style of one month to a page, and had to be printed in a very specific – and expensively ornate – typeface. Because of this, the man was keen to minimize the number of movable type letters that he had to purchase.

He was quite proud of himself for having found the thriftiest solution that would allow him to print the names of the months in full. Using all capital letters was part of it, of course, but the main portion involved ensuring that he had just enough individual letters to assemble any given month.

Can you work out how many letters he had to purchase?

❋ Solution on page 360 ❋

Stabbing

"It was the butler who found my father on the floor of the study, Mr Holmes." Emma Porter was a pleasant-seeming woman in her late twenties, her face heavily scored with grief. "He actually stumbled over the body in the darkness. The fire had gone out, you see. His shrieks woke the maid and myself up."

"Did you have any reason to suspect your father was in danger?" Holmes kept his voice politely neutral in tone.

"No, of course not. I mean, he had to lay a fellow off yesterday, and he had a rival or two, but who would stoop to brutal murder over chauffeuring?" Her eyes welled with tears.

"Why did he sack that chap?"

"Drinking," she said. "At least, that's what I understood."

Holmes frowned slightly. "Did he ever drive clients around himself?"

"Almost never, but perhaps if he was desperately short-staffed he might have. He generally kept himself distant from the drivers."

"I see," Holmes said. "And he was found dead shortly after midnight."

"That's right," she said. "The butler was on his way to bed, but noticed that father was on the floor as he passed the study. I had been asleep for some hours by that point. The maid would have been in bed by eleven, too. All the windows were closed, of course. The police said that he'd been stabbed repeatedly. It just doesn't make sense." She folded inward on herself gently.

"I'm confident we'll find the answers very soon," Holmes said. "We already have our primary suspect."

Who does Holmes suspect, and why?

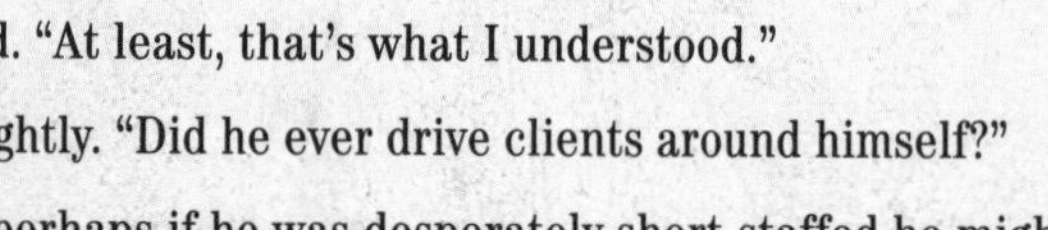

✻ Solution on page 360 ✻

The Manager

Once the safety of the frightened carpenter was assured, and the tome located to a reasonable degree of safety (if not actually recovered), Holmes and I had occasion to speak to a rather evasive little warehouse manager and his somewhat apologetic deputy. The deputy was clearly of better character, so whilst I distracted the manager with some discussion of high-grade medical steel, Holmes chatted to the younger man.

Later, as we departed, Holmes told me a curious thing. The deputy, he said, confessed to Holmes that he had actually enquired about his boss's age a few days beforehand. He was told that the manager was twice as old as the deputy had been, back when the manager had been the same age as the deputy now was.

We already knew from our researches that the manager was 48. How old did that make the deputy?

✻ Solution on page 360 ✻

Getting Ahead

Flicking through a book of European history, I came across a rather odd account, which I shared with Holmes.

"According to this text, which I admit is somewhat sensationalized, during the French revolution, the locals of Nîmes used to wager on the sizes of the severed heads of nobles and other supposed enemies of the revolution. The task was to estimate how large the head would be once it had been dipped in wax, but before it had been set out for display. People would bring along vegetables, sometimes carefully trimmed, which they felt would best match the head of a particular condemned person. The closest guess won the pot."

"Ingenious and enterprising," Holmes replied. "Thoroughly French."

"It seems like the very devil of a thing to judge," I said.

"Really?" Holmes sounded amused. "Can you not think of a simple way to get a precise verdict?"

Solution on page 361

Bicycle

I noticed Holmes looking distracted one morning over breakfast, tossing a piece of toast into the air before catching it again, over and over like a cat with a toy.

"Something on your mind, old man?" I asked him.

"The valencies of sulphur," he replied. "Particularly in the way that they relate to its propensity to form astringents with zinc."

"Ah," I replied.

"Here's something mostly unrelated for you to chew over, my dear Watson. Say you and I have a single bicycle between us, and no other transport options save walking. We want to get the both of us to a location eighteen miles distant as swiftly as possible. If my walking speed is five miles per hour compared to your four, but for some reason – perhaps a bad ligament – my cycling speed is eight miles per hour compared to your ten. How would you get us simultaneously to our destination with maximum rapidity?"

"A cab," I suggested.

"Without cheating," Holmes replied, and went back to tossing his toast in the air.

Solution on page 362

The Canvas

"Let us say that I needed to paint a very particular picture," Holmes said to me one afternoon.

"I would find such a proposition alarming, given your utter absence of any previously displayed artistic talent."

"You do me a disservice," Holmes replied. "But that is not important. This painting needs to occupy precisely 72 square inches, and measure a whole number of inches on each side. Furthermore, it needs to have a clear border of exactly four inches above and below, and two inches to either side."

"That is quite specific," I observed.

"Very much so," he said. "What is the smallest canvas I could fit such a painting on?"

✻ Solution on page 362 ✻

Pig

In Hookland, Holmes and I discovered that the elusive C. L. Nolan had made a suspiciously large purchase of livestock. Converting all the assorted value to shillings for simplicity, he bought pigs at 95s each, and sheep at 97s each, for a grand total of 4,238s – well over two hundred pounds sterling. The dealer who furnished us with this information was still somewhat dazed by the entire transaction. About the only other pieces of information that we got out of the fellow were that Nolan paid entirely in crown coins of all things, and that he would somehow arrange for the livestock to be transported to a number of destinations over the next few weeks.

It was very peculiar, which honestly rather matches my overall opinion of Hookland as a county.

As we left the dealer, Holmes said to me, "So how many pigs did he purchase?"

It was late that night before I could furnish him with an answer. Can you find one?

✵ Solution on page 363 ✵

The Seventh Wordknot

I received my seventh slip of wordknot paper from Holmes as we were bouncing down the horribly uneven streets of Bethnal Green in a cab. At the time, it seemed all too plausible that the driver's mind had been seized by fiends or, at the very least, some esoteric specimen of mental disturbance. Holmes had clearly been waiting for precisely such an occasion, for he whipped out the note with a delighted flourish, and presented it to me.

I received it with lamentable ill grace. On it were the usual ten lines of three jumbled letters, each row being formed by taking one letter from each of three ten-letter words, starting with the three initial letters on the first row, and proceeding regularly to the ten final letters on the tenth row. The task of unpicking the three loosely themed ten-letter words was not helped by my ongoing fear of imminent disaster, nor by my fight to prevent my breakfast from attempting escape.

The rows of letters were as follows:

1. DPM
2. IOI
3. CUS
4. HAN
5. TOR
6. NEE
7. EBS
8. SAQ
9. TUN
10. KEY

Can you find the words?

✱ Solution on page 364 ✱

Match Two

As Holmes put it when setting me this challenge, "You may find that a bit of mechanical aid proves of assistance with this one, my dear Watson." In other words, get some tooth-picks or matches.

The task is, using matches, to remove seven-tenths of five and in so doing, leave exactly four remaining.

It is quite obvious when you know how it is done, but to be frank, I did struggle for a while with this one. Holmes was quite steadfast in refusing me any sort of hint, and merely sat there, poring through a rather sensationalist volume of criminal activity that had taken place in Leeds over the past few years. From what little I saw of it, it must have been depressing reading. Not, of course, that I should wish to give the impression I that I am singling Leeds out as especially criminal; merely that Holmes' interest in crime was entirely catholic.

Anyhow, Leeds is by the by. Can you find the solution?

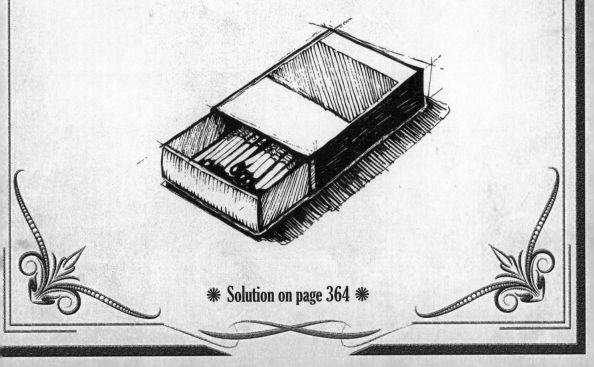

✻ Solution on page 364 ✻

Curio

"I have a little mathematical curio for you," Holmes told me one afternoon.

I eyed him warily. "Oh?"

"There are two separate pairs of numbers between one and nine which, when each is squared, and these squares are added to the product of multiplying the numbers together, give you a total which is also a square. Can you identify one of the pairs?"

"Let me just straighten that out," I told him. "Two different single-digit numbers, no zeroes. Multiply them by each other, and by themselves. Add the three totals together, and get a square number. Find one of two solutions."

"Precisely so," Holmes said. "There are only 81 pairs, if you don't fancy tackling the algebra."

Can you solve the problem?

✻ Solution on page 364 ✻

Engine Trouble

It is a long haul from Bangor to London by train, particularly when your route requires several changes. The Dysynni Valley is beautiful, in a stark sense, but it's a devil of a haul from Baker Street. Our journey back was not helped by an engine problem that one of the trains on our route developed.

We'd been on this particular leg of the journey for an hour when our speed was suddenly cut to three-fifths of its former magnitude. Consequently, we were two hours late arriving at our destination, and missed our connection.

The guard did apologise on behalf of the driver, and informed us that if the problem had developed 50 miles later, we would have arrived 40 minutes sooner, and made our connection. This was not any great comfort.

Can you calculate how long this particular leg of the journey was?

❋ Solution on page 365 ❋

Recall

Memory is a curious thing. I recall a conversation with Holmes on the matter, where he proposed that there were in fact many different forms of memory – immediate, autobiographical, muscular, visual, audial, linguistic, and more – and that different people would often have varied facilities in these areas. Certainly, I knew a fellow with a very sharp memory, who could recall a snatch of song or read passage from a decade ago with perfect alacrity, but had genuine trouble recalling what he'd done the day before, and had to work his birthday out by starting with the current date.

At the conclusion of the discussion, Holmes proceeded to test my immediate memory with a rather confusing little mental calculation.

"Tell me," he said, "what is the number which when tripled, and this product increased by seventy five percent, the result divided by seven, the quotient reduced by a third, the result multiplied by itself, this square reduced by fifty-two, the square root found of this remaining difference, this root added to eight, and the sum divided by ten, results in the number two?"

Luckily, I have good short-term recall. You have the advantage of being able to refer back to the problem.

✻ Solution on page 365 ✻

Moran

As you may be aware, Holmes and I on occasion tangled with an extremely lethal fellow by the name of Colonel Moran. Holmes believed him to be the second most dangerous man in London at one time, and was almost certainly correct.

One of the incidents which led Moran to leave the army was a disagreement over a brutal firearm that he had personally invented. There was a call at the time for improved weapons, with a substantial purse waiting for people who could match the stringent requirements. Moran put forth a repeating rifle which, he said, would fire 60 shots at the rate of one every five seconds.

It is true that the assessing panel, who were men of good character, were ill-disposed to accept Moran's petition. Even then, he had the reputation of a brutal, nigh-uncontrollable monster. Still, they had technicians test the device. The panel accepted that Moran's gun took five minutes to fire 60 shots, and then rejected the rifle on the grounds that it did not live up to his claims. Moran was incandescent, and within six months, had become a career criminal specializing in assassination and card-sharping.

Was the panel's assessment of failure accurate?

❋ Solution on page 366 ❋

The Eighth Wordknot

You are probably familiar with Mr Joseph Paxton's glittering masterpiece, the Crystal Palace. Holmes and I were within its glass confines one afternoon. A fellow by the name of Andrew Hodder was going to be within the Alhambran Court, and for several reasons, Holmes felt it wise to observe him.

Mr Hodder duly arrived, and swiftly took a seat, then started sketching. After a minute or so, Holmes decided that Hodder was clearly going to be some time, and handed me the paper on which was recorded the eighth wordknot. As on previous occasions, this took the form of ten rows of three letters, thus:

1. HRH
2. EAO
3. SON
4. DDT
5. CWR
6. AIU
7. FIN
8. KNF
9. EEE
10. DDD

Three loosely related ten-letter words were obscured within, their first letters on the first row, their second letters on the second row, and so on. My task, which I hand down to you, was to unravel the three words.

Can you find the solution?

✻ Solution on page 366 ✻

Barnabas

We met up with Wiggins one fine spring morning to find him in particularly high spirits. When we enquired, he explained that he'd helped an ageing gardener of his acquaintance to dig a client's ditch the afternoon before, for which he had been handsomely paid.

"He tried to give me three half-crowns," Wiggins said, sounding slightly awed. "Said it was what he'd be paid for the ditch, and as I'd done most of the work, and helped him out of a spot besides, I could take it all. I only took what was fair, though. Greed is bad for business, and this way maybe he'll have me help out some other time."

"Very admirable," I told him. "What was your fair share?"

Wiggins grinned, and winked at Holmes. "Thought you'd ask me that, Doctor. Look at it this way. Old Barnabas was able to dig as rapidly as I could shovel the loose dirt out of the trench, but I could dig four times as fast as he could shovel out dirt. It's not that either of us was worse at shovelling than at digging, you understand. It's just slower. The effort rate is the same. So you tell me, what do you think is fair?"

It took me a while to find an answer. Can you do so?

❋ Solution on page 366 ❋

The Forty-four

Mrs Hudson seemed out of sorts. It was nothing that I could immediately put my finger on, but something was amiss.

I offered her a smile. "Are you feeling quite alright, Mrs Hudson?"

She sighed. "I'm fine, Doctor. Thank you. I'm concerned about my uncle Michael. I saw him on Sunday for the first time in several years. He lives down on the Lizard now, you know, in Cornwall. At one point the conversation turned to age, and I asked him how old my cousin Minnie was now. He fell silent for a moment, and then told me that she was 1,280 years old! Then he corrected himself, and said that she was 44. But her older brother Douglas was 40 last year. I got to the root of it in the end – he first multiplied her age with his own, and then subtracted hers from it. I'm afraid his mind is going."

"I'm dreadfully sorry to hear that," I told her. "It's a terrible business."

She thanked me, and carried on. After she'd left, I found myself pondering the ages of Minnie and her father. Can you work them out?

❋ Solution on page 367 ❋

The Murder of Molly Glass

The death of Molly Glass seemed like a tragic suicide. The woman in question, who was married and in her thirties, but childless, was found dead inside her bedroom. The room contained a gas fire, connected to the mains, as is so common nowadays. The gas was switched on, but unlit, and this was most definitely the cause of death. Post-mortem indicators made this perfectly plain. The windows of the bedroom were firmly closed, and latched from the inside. They were unbroken and undisturbed. The bedroom door was also locked from the inside, and there were no other means of egress.

Mrs Glass's mother was most insistent that her daughter would never have taken her own life, and refused to believe the police's complacent insistence on suicide. The lack of any sort of note did certainly encourage the possibility of such speculation. And so the case duly came before Holmes. He glanced at the details, and then tossed them aside declaring that it was clearly murder, that her husband was mostly likely the culprit, and that his expertise was needed no further in the matter.

He was, of course, correct in all points. But how was it done?

❋ Solution on page 367 ❋

PART FOUR

FIENDISH

The Eighth Mental Trial

"My hypothetical friends, Alfie and Bill, have an acquaintance," Holmes said to me one afternoon. I understood this to mean that he had another mental challenge for me.

"Soon you will have an entirely hypothetical village," I said.

"That may happen, my dear Watson. But today, we are concerned just with the addition of Charlie. Poor Charlie has run out of lamp oil at an inopportune moment. Alfie and Bill both have reasonable stocks – Alfie has eight pints, and Bill has five. The two decide that the comradely thing to do would be to pool their oil, and divide it up into thirds. This they do, and to repay their kindness, Charlie hands over thirteen farthings."

"Who will be their next friend?" I asked. "David?"

"Unlikely," said Holmes. "But for now, in the interests of equity, tell me, how should the money be divided?

❋ Solution on page 369 ❋

In Paris

"You may recall that the World's Fair was held in Paris a few years back," Holmes said.

I nodded. "Quite the show."

"Quite. Did you hear about the missing brother?"

"No?" I leaned forward, curiosity engaged.

"A funny business. An American lady and her brother arrived at the Ritz the afternoon before the fair, and checked in to their rooms. They had dinner together, but the lady was tired, and her brother flat-out exhausted, so they called it an early night.

"The next morning, the lady was surprised that her brother did not appear at their agreed-upon time for breakfast. She asked the waiter if he had already eaten, and received just a puzzled stare. When she went looking for his room, number 13, she was unable to find it, and had to seek help from the staff. The concierge superciliously informed her that there was no Room 13. The manager, when he appeared, said the same. All the staff insisted she had arrived alone and eaten alone the night before. The registry book showed just her name. The rooms on the first floor went straight from 12 to 14. Despite her very great distress, she could find no evidence her brother had ever existed."

"My word," I said, perplexed.

"What do you suppose was going on?"

❋ Solution on page 370 ❋

Six-sided Dice

"A simple little question for you, Watson."

Holmes tossed me a standard die, which I caught.

"The humble die conceals many mysteries and is at the heart of many adventures. Given that each pair of opposite faces on the die must always add up to seven, how many different ways are there to set out the numbers on three separate dice?

✻ Solution on page 370 ✻

The Ninth Literal Oddity

"Are you ready to give your mind a stern lexical test, Watson?"

I confessed that 'stern' sounded a little daunting, but so long as there was no dire penalty for failure, I was prepared to do my best.

"That's the spirit, old chap. The nine-letter word 'checkbook', an American coinage from our own 'chequebook', possesses an unusual quality. This is shared with a small number of other words, all shorter, including our very own 'exceeded'. What do you imagine that it is?"

Solution on page 371

The Eighth Curiosity

"Girdle the Earth!"
"What?" I snapped to attention, reasonably startled.

"In your mind, man. Girdle the Earth. With steel, I dare say, for structure. Now assuming – fallaciously, of course – that the Earth were perfectly flat and round around the equator so such a girdle could be circular, place it so that it is exactly flush with the Earth."

I complied.

"Now, if you added six yards to the length of that girdle, how far do you suppose that would raise it off the surface?"

❋ Solution on page 372 ❋

The Fish Murder

A regular police patrol found Mister Frank Hale gasping his very last breath in the streets surrounding Billingsgate Fish Market in the early hours. He had been stabbed through the neck, and clearly it had happened very recently. On the basis that his killer had to still be nearby, the constables chased down and apprehended the only other fellow on the street.

Like Hale, Rick Weir was a fish merchant, and the police were able to show that the pair were at least rivals professionally. Under questioning, Weir maintained total ignorance of the event, and claimed that he had fled the police simply out of an instinct born from confusion. As evidence of his innocence, he pointed out that he had nothing on his person that could remotely be used as a murder weapon, nor had he discarded any such item. The police searched the area thoroughly, but could find nothing that might have plausibly caused Hale's rather irregularly-shaped wound.

With nothing more to go on than the victim's damp shirt collar and ragged stab-wound, Scotland Yard was on the verge of allowing Weir his freedom. It was at that point that Holmes heard of the case, and scribbled a quick note to Inspector Lestrade. Weir was formally charged with the murder in less than an hour.

Can you imagine what thought had occurred to my companion?

❋ Solution on page 372 ❋

Sheep

"Sometimes, my dear Watson, you have to think outside the boundaries of the sheep pen."

"A curious turn of phrase, old friend."

"But deliberate," Holmes said. "You have four sheep pens of equal size. How would you place fifteen sheep to ensure that each pen contained the same number of sheep?"

I thought about it for a little while. "It seems impossible, without butchering a sheep."

"Such exertions are unnecessary," said Holmes, "but do not forget my earlier admonition."

✱ Solution on page 373 ✱

Get a Hat

"My hypothetical friend Alfie's dinner party had six guests," Holmes said. "That meant that there were seven hats. By the time it came to depart, the men were too wearied by their exertions at the table to take notice of which hat they obtained."

"No doubt," I replied. "I suspect any normal man would be fatigued by an evening in your prodigious mind, my dear Holmes."

"Perhaps," he replied. "But either way, the truth is that after all had left, no man had the correct hat, not even Alfie. How many possible variations are there of this mishap?"

❋ Solution on page 373 ❋

The Fourth Portmanteau

"I have another picture for you to puzzle over, Watson."

Sherlock Holmes passed me the extraordinary illustration which I have reproduced here.

"It contains all the visual clues you could possibly require to positively identify one particular spot in London. When you can place the relevance of each element of the picture, you will be able to allow no possible doubt regarding the location to which it refers. Be stout; the solution is not quite as obvious as some of the other images I have passed you."

I turned my attention from my friend to the drawing he had given me. To where does it refer?

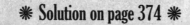

✻ Solution on page 374 ✻

Nephews

We were in the area near King's Cross railway station one morning, pursuing a matter involving a larcenous baker's nephew. I should make it clear that the larceny was on the baker's part; the nephew was quite innocent. As that may be, I was deep in thought when Holmes said to me, "Watson old chap, do you know that it is possible to be both the nephew and uncle of a fellow at the same time?"

That brought me up short. "Surely not," I protested.

"Oh yes," Holmes said. "All perfectly within the law, too."

"How can that be?"

"Why don't you tell me," he replied.

Solution on page 374

The Ninth Mental Trial

"I have another mental exercise for you, my friend."

I looked up from my book. "Very well, my dear Holmes. I'm sure it is to my benefit."

"Immeasurably," came the reply. "Consider for a moment that you have been given a counterfeit shilling in amongst your money. It is ever so slightly lighter than it ought to be, but it is otherwise indistinguishable from the real thing. You cannot tell by hand, but you have a balance scale. What is the least number of weighings that you can perform upon the scale to discover the precise identity of the counterfeit?"

❋ Solution on page 375 ❋

Twenty Thousand Leagues

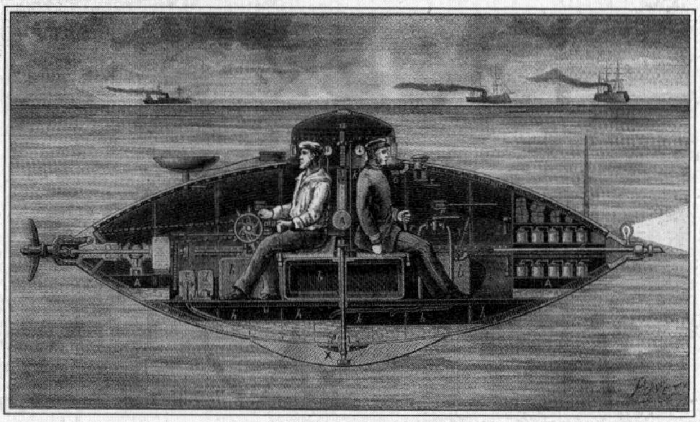

"As I recall Watson, you've read Mr. Verne's tale about Captain Nemo and his miraculous underwater submersible, the Nautilus."

I nodded. "I have. I enjoyed it, but I fear that it would offer you little. The villainies it contains have little mystery to them."

"So I gather," said Holmes. "Although I believe the French are currently testing a similar – if much less fanciful – device with a marked degree of success. I cannot help feeling that the captain of any such device would spend his entire time living in mortal terror of accidentally touching the bottom of the ocean."

"The risk of damage to the structure, you mean?"

"Well yes, there is that, but no, I was thinking of a danger that would apply to the mildest sandy bottom as much as to a jagged shelf. More so, even."

What did he mean?

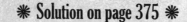

✱ Solution on page 375 ✱

The Shoreditch Bank

Sherlock Holmes and myself encountered a cunning method of bank robbery in Shoreditch on one memorable occasion. The manager was diligent in his security arrangements. The bank's safe was a massive thing, complex enough that even a skilled thief would take an hour or more to get into it, and this with cutting tools that would leave very obvious scarring. This in turn was locked in the manager's office. The office door had a small viewing port set into in. The guards' rounds of the bank brought them past the manager's office every six minutes, and they always paused for a moment to peer through the port and inspect the safe.

Despite these precautions, when the cleaning lady went into the manager's office early on Monday morning, to start tidying up before the week began, she immediately realised that the bank had been burgled. The security men were utterly confounded, they and their colleagues having faithfully checked the safe every few minutes, all through the weekend. Given the length of time that it would have taken for the safe to be opened, and the regularity of the guards' observations, can you imagine how the criminals had found the time to get it open?

❋ Solution on page 376 ❋

Markham

"A very simple matter this one, Watson." Holmes indicated an illustration on his desk, which outlined the details from the scene of the recent Markham murder. "I feel confident that even you should be able to see through to the heart of the crime."

I reminded him that I was not familiar with the particulars of the case.

"Markham was in his study, working. His wife was in the drawing room, and has said that although her husband had been a little preoccupied recently, she had no idea that he was in danger. She realised that she could hear conversation through the wall: her husband sounding agitated, and a rougher man's voice which she could not clearly make out. Then there was a blood-curdling scream, a heavy thump, and silence. She rushed to the study door in a panic, but finding it locked on the inside, dashed out and around the side of the house to the study window. It too was locked tight, and the curtains drawn. Her statement is corroborated by the maid.

"Her cries for help brought the assistance of the police, who battered down the door and found the room as shown, and the window still firmly locked and barred from the inside. Markham was dead of course, with a hunting knife through his heart. Both the widow and the maid insist that no intruder could have escaped without their notice, and the police admit that they can find no signs of egress.

"So tell me. Who killed Markham?"

✻ Solution on page 377 ✻

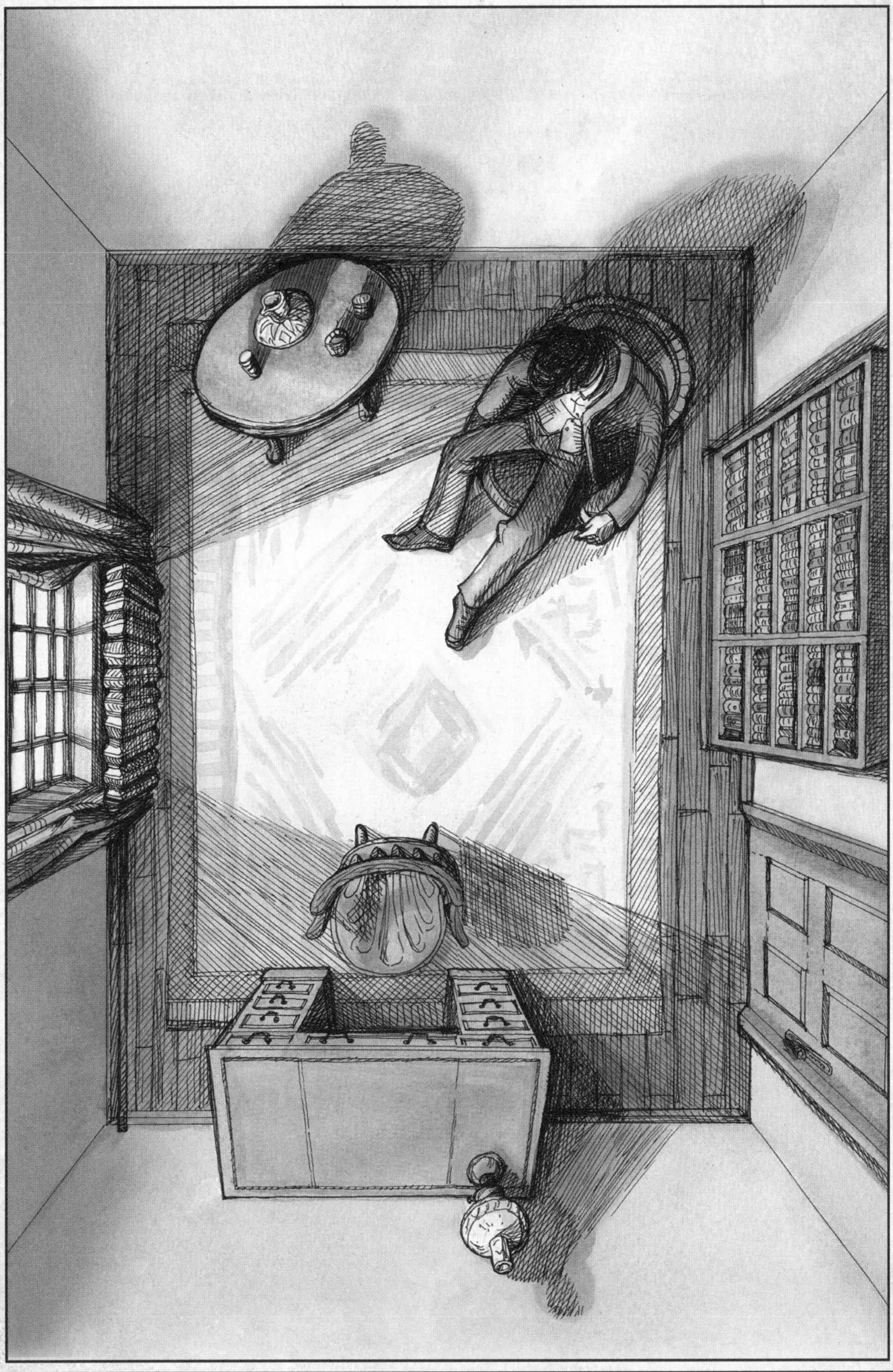

Montenegro

Holmes made the acquaintance of a pair of charming rogues from Montenegro at one point, and, I gather, obtained all sorts of useful tid-bits from them. One of the items that he obtained was a curious little dice game.

The game is played with three regular six-sided dice. Each player selects two separate odd numbers that the three dice sum to. The four numbers must all be different, so in fairness, they take turns to select their numbers. They then throw the dice alternately; whoever throws one of their numbers first wins, although the opponent has one last chance to throw their own number and make for a draw.

The question is whether it is possible for the two players to have exactly identical odds of winning the game.

✻ Solution on page 378 ✻

Wimbledon Common

Holmes turned to me with a wry smile and tapped his *Morning Post*. "In here, Watson, we have the story of a cabbie who picked up a fare in Putney yesterday morning, took the fellow out into Wimbledon Common, and then bludgeoned him to death with a cudgel he kept under his seat. Why do you suppose he did so?"

"A vicious mugging?"

"Not so; the corpse was found with wallet and all effects."

"Some bad blood, then?"

"The two men had never even heard of each other before, let alone laid eyes on each other."

I thought for a moment. "Well, is the driver just demented?"

"Not a bit of it," said Holmes. "He is entirely rational, and has an explanation that he clearly feels justified his action. He will undoubtedly swing for it, although they might be more lenient if he were tried in Paris."

Can you guess what the reason was?

Solution on page 378

The Tenth Mental Trial

"Let us return one more time to my hypothetical friends, Alfie and Bill. Imagine that you are with the pair of them in the office of a curious prison warder. Charlie's presence is not required."

"I am in prison with a pair of fishmongers," I noted.

"You are all innocent, of course," Holmes replied. "Sad victims of a miscarriage of justice, fear not."

"My mind is at ease."

"Capital. The warder shows you all five coloured signs, two black and three white. He then has you turn around in a line, and affixes a sign to the back of each of your prison uniforms. The warder informs you that the first man to correctly identify the colour of his sign will walk free; but identify wrongly, or collude, and your sentence will be extended. Then he allows you to turn around and inspect each other. You see that both Alfie and Bill are wearing white signs. The other two look at you, and at each other. What colour is your sign?"

✻ Solution on page 379 ✻

Carl Black

"Did you see the item about the death of Carl Black, Watson?"

"Who?"

"A former steel baron from New York. He was kidnapped last year by Serbian radicals during an exploratory business trip to the area, and ransomed for a very princely sum. He was lucky. Many such victims are never returned. Black resigned from the company immediately afterwards, although of course the firm's travel insurance covered the actual cost, and he moved to the south of France."

"Was he murdered?"

"No. Boating accident. A bit of foolishness, with serious consequences, but nothing in the least bit sinister about it."

"Oh," I said, increasingly mystified.

"Note that Black's former company was in good financial shape for the first time in five years, and that although relations were cordial, he had possessed no formal ties to them for almost twelve months. The interesting question then becomes, why was his former business partner caught trying to burn down Black's chateau three nights later?"

A good question.

✵ Solution on page 379 ✵

A Matter of Time

"Come, Watson," said Holmes to me one afternoon. "Indulge me in a little matter of creative thought."

"Of course," I replied, with just a hint of trepidation.

"Suppose you need to exactly measure the passage of 45 minutes before making a timely entrance. You are required to wait in some dreary room, without a pocket-watch or convenient clock. You do, however, have two lengths of tallow-dipped stick, and a box of matches. The sticks are certain to burn for an hour precisely, but they will not do so at a constant rate.

"Variations in thickness and other defects of construction mean that after 30 minutes, just a small length of stick may be consumed, or alternately a great length. There is no guarantee that the pattern will be the same from one stick to the other. Yet these inadequate sticks are all you have at your disposal. How then would you use them to measure the time correctly?"

How indeed?

✻ Solution on page 380 ✻

The Ladies of Morden

The Ladies of the Morden Whist Circle came to our attention in regard to a daring little robbery that had occurred in Balham. The case was solved easily, but Holmes was more interested in their playing regimen.

There were twelve ladies, and they so arranged themselves that over eleven evenings, each of them played no more than once with the same lady as a partner, nor more than twice with the same lady as an opponent. By this, they managed to ensure that every member played every other member in all possible quadrants.

Can you work out how such a thing might be achieved?

❋ Solution on page 380 ❋

The Final Portmanteau

"Another of your damnable images, Holmes?" My eager expression removed any sting the words might have seemed to carry. The truth was, I rather enjoyed poring over the things.

"Yes indeed, old friend. This one should provide you with a genuine challenge, too. Each aspect of the picture is a carefully-crafted clue. Taken together, all the clues point to just one place in London. This is the last of them for now, so I have naturally saved the best for the occasion."

He handed me the drawing, which I have replicated for you to examine. "Thank you, Holmes."

"You are of course welcome, but I'd not be too hasty. You may be cursing me before you solve this one."

It took a while, but I did indeed crack the mystery. Can you?

✻ Solution on page 381 ✻

The Final Curiosity

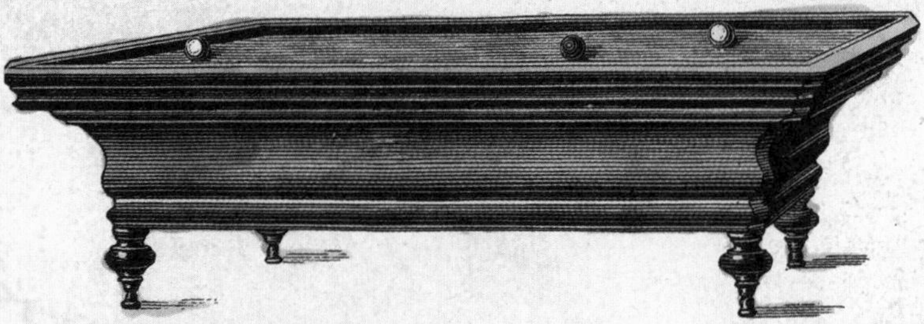

"Tell me, Watson. Do you imagine that a perfect billiard table is absolutely level?"

"Of course," I replied.

"Oh? How curious. Would you like to guess why you are wrong?"

Solution on page 382

The Eggtimer's Companion

In the course of the rather odd affair of the Eggtimer's Companion, Holmes and I came across a pair of feuding families in Highgate, the Adamses and the Southwells. Both families consisted of a mother, father and two children, and it was interesting to note that the sum totals of the ages of each family was 100 years.

The coincidence was increased by the fact that in both families, the daughter of the house was older than her brother, and if you added the squares of the ages of the mother, daughter and son together, you would get a total which exactly matched the square of the age of the father.

Miss Southwell was one year older than her brother however, whilst Miss Adams was two years older than hers. Armed with that knowledge, Holmes maintained, it was perfectly possible to discern the age of each of the eight individuals.

Can you deduce the ages?

❋ Solution on page 382 ❋

The Final Mental Trial

"I'd like you to consider the following sequence of numbers, Watson. They are: 2, 5, 8, 11, 16, 14. What number less than 20 is the next in the line? I assure you that you do not need any mathematical aptitude to arrive at the correct answer."

2, 5, 8, 11, 16, 14...

❋ Solution on page 383 ❋

Down on the Farm

I remember one particular occasion that pulled Holmes and myself out to an uninspiring pasture in West Sussex. A local farmer had noticed his sheep behaving oddly, and on investigation discovered a body in the middle of his field, in seemingly undisturbed grass. The body had been moved, but of course we had to slog out through the summer sun to examine the site. While we were looking around, Holmes discovered the top half of an unlit match, which he declared to have come from the corpse by dint of position and freshness.

A short while later, we got to examine the body itself, which had been moved to a more suitable location. He had been a middle-aged fellow, clearly of some means. Cause of death appeared to be general physical trauma, which included crushed ribs, smashed jaw and broken legs as well as the skull damage which had most probably finished him. He was dressed in soft shoes, stout woollen trousers and a sturdy leather jacket trimmed with fur. He had no personal possessions however, not even a watch.

Holmes took one look at his bootlaces and declared the man to be a Prussian, and then remarked that the style of his hair indicated he had been passing himself off as British, so he was probably a spy.

So declaring, he then asserted that the reason – and method – of his death were painfully obvious. Can you work out what he meant?

❋ Solution on page 383 ❋

Board

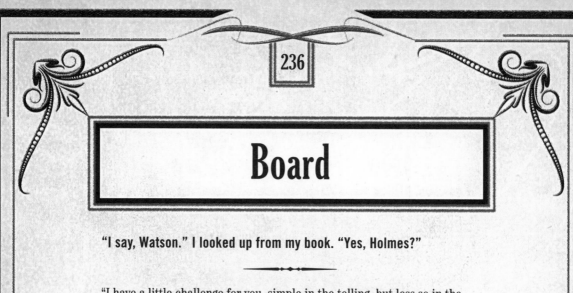

"I say, Watson." I looked up from my book. "Yes, Holmes?"

"I have a little challenge for you, simple in the telling, but less so in the execution. There are 64 squares on a chessboard, but how many different squares and rectangles can one or more of those squares be formed into?"

❋ Solution on page 384 ❋

The Night Watchman

We were called to the scene of a violent robbery down by the Thames, where a hapless night watchman had been murdered, and a consignment of shipped goods stolen. The poor watchman was dumped in the river after being killed, and the water immediately caused his pocket watch to stop working.

That would have given the time of the robbery, had one foolish policeman not tried to get the watch working again, and scrambled the time. Holmes was furious of course, but all the unfortunately constable could recall was that the second-hand had just passed 49, and that the hour and minute hand were perfectly aligned together.

Holmes recognized that the hands on the watch were of the constantly sweeping variety, rather than the type which clicks from division to division, and declared that this made the time of the robbery perfectly obvious.

What was the time on the watch when it stopped?

✱ Solution on page 384 ✱

The Final Literal Oddity

"I have saved the best for the end," Holmes declared.

I felt my eyebrows raise. "What's that?"

"One final trial of your authorial muscle, Watson."

"Ah. If it is anything like the last..."

Holmes shook his head. "Not a bit of it. This one will genuinely tax your ingenuity."

"Very well," I replied, with a little trepidation.

"I want you to find me an English word which has each of its letters repeated exactly three times. I'll warn you now that I know of only one, and its etymology suggests an Italian derivation. I would discount any contrived word which was simply the same syllable repeated three times as being an unworthy answer."

Solution on page 385

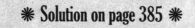

Intersection

Walking through Charing Cross, Holmes drew my attention to a pair of wires. Each was fastened to the top of one pole, and ran straight down to the foot of the other.

"Those poles look to me to be five and seven feet high," Holmes declared.

"I dare say you're correct," I replied.

"Can you tell me how high off the ground the wires are when they intersect?"

"Possibly. How far apart do you think the poles are?"

"My dear Watson," Holmes said, "I assure you that is completely irrelevant."

What do you think the answer is?

✻ Solution on page 385 ✻

Pipe Dreams

Whilst I was serving in the army, I spent some time in Afghanistan, and there I came across a curious treatise that had been translated into English. The document, entitled *The Red Tower,* claimed to be the work of one Ghirgiz al-Uqbar, a name that suggested a non-local origin. It was a highly whimsical piece, but one section in particular is worth recalling for my current purposes.

In this section, the author decries the even population balance between men and women, suggesting that there ought to be more women, so that harems could be larger. From this highly dubious suggestion, he goes on to state that if he were ruler, he would pass an edict that required a woman to stop having children if and only if she had a son. Thus, he reasoned, families would have many daughters but just one son, and in a score of years, there would be a surfeit of unmarried young women.

His plan was clearly insane, but do you think it would have worked, if somehow implemented rigorously?

✻ Solution on page 386 ✻

The Old Ones

A curious incident in Bethnal Green came to my attention one Tuesday morning, in the *Evening Standard*. A fellow walked into a pub on the Cambridge Heath road, and asked the man behind the bar for a glass of water. The response was immediate – the man pulled out a gun, and immediately shot the would-be customer dead.

Unfortunately for the murderer, there was a witness he was unaware of, one of the regular serving girls. She escaped detection, and was able to describe the day's horror to the police. She was also able to confirm that the murderer did not appear to have known the victim or harbour any sort of grudge against him, but also did not seem to be killing simply for the dark joy of it. According to the newspaper, the police even mentioned that the victim had not had hiccups.

Can you find the reason why this murder happened?

✻ Solution on page 386 ✻

The Pleasant Way

During *The Peculiar Case of the Raven Child*, Holmes and I had cause to examine the movements of a suspicious fellow named Rowlands. I won't bore you with the specifics of the intrigue here, but one morning, Rowlands set out to walk over the hills from Tywyn to another town a modest distance away. At precisely the same time, his acquaintance Jones left Rowlands's destination, heading for Tywyn.

Their movements were notably suspicious. The pair met briefly at the point ten miles from Tywyn. Spending identical amounts of time in their destinations, they set off on their return journeys in such a manner that they met again, this time twelve miles from Jones' original starting point. Their walking speeds, of course, were consistent throughout.

How far apart are the two towns?

Solution on page 387

Fashion

On one occasion, Holmes and I were asked to solve the robbery of a number of dresses from the workshop of a recently deceased ladies' tailor to the upper echelons of society. Holmes took a short look at the particulars of the case, and sent them all back to the gown-maker's son with a scribbled note to the effect that it could only be one particular seamstress, with the help of her husband.

However, glancing through my observations some period later, I observed certain facts about the robbery which led me to an interesting little exercise. The stock at the workshop had been very recently valued at the princely sum of £1,800, and when examined after the theft, comprised of precisely 100 completed dresses in a range of styles, but of equal valuation. However, there was no remaining record of how many dresses had been there beforehand. The son did recall his father stating, of the valuation, that if he'd had thirty dresses more, then a valuation of £1,800 would have meant £3 less per dress.

Are you able to calculate how many dresses were stolen?

✱ Solution on page 387 ✱

The Fourth Camouflage

I'd just scalded the roof of my mouth on a surprisingly hot spoonful of Scots porridge one morning when Holmes decided to seize the moment and throw one of his camouflaged word puzzles at me. The words he called out to me were stonecutter, tardigrades, cassowaries and matrimonial.

I knew from bitter experience that Holmes would not repeat the words, so made an effort to memorize them whilst simultaneously attempting to resist the urge to yell aloud at the pain in my mouth.

The task, as ever, was to discover the four smaller words, one within each of the longer, that were united by a common theme.

Can you do it? I recommend not burning yourself in the mouth before beginning. It is not helpful.

✱ Solution on page 388 ✱

The Apple Market

We stumbled across a practical instance of this odd little puzzler whilst in Hookland. Rather than try to replicate our experience exactly, however, I shall endeavour to abstract it slightly, so that it is easier to see to the heart of the matter. Hookland, as I have mentioned earlier, is a strange county.

The market held a group of three apple-sellers, friends with different species of apples to sell, and thus different prices. One of the ladies sold her apples at two for a penny, the second at three for a penny, and the third at five for tuppence. Around 11 a.m., however, both of the first two ladies had to suddenly depart. Each had 30 apples remaining. These 60 were handed to the remaining friend, who proceeded to sell them at her usual price of five for two pence.

If the two missing ladies had stayed to sell their stock, they would have brought in 25 pence between them. Now three apples at one penny and two apples at one penny together clearly equals five apples for tuppence. However, when the third lady sold her friends' stock, she brought in only 24 pence, as 60 divided by five is twelve, and split that evenly between her friends.

So where did the odd penny get to?

✻ Solution on page 388 ✻

A Pair of Fours

Holmes took a puff on his pipe. "You are familiar, I trust, my dear Watson, with the principle of expressing a whole number in terms of a different number plus some mathematical operators."

I nodded. "Such as four being two times two, you mean."

"Precisely. And 63 being two to the power of two times two plus two, with two divided by two subtracted from it."

I jotted (2^(2*2+2))-2/2 down on a notepad, resolved it to (2^6)-1 = 64-1 = 63, and nodded again.

"Capital," Holmes said. "So can you likewise find a way of expressing 64 using as many mathematical operators as you like, but only two instances of the digit 4, and no other digits? It may take you a little time."

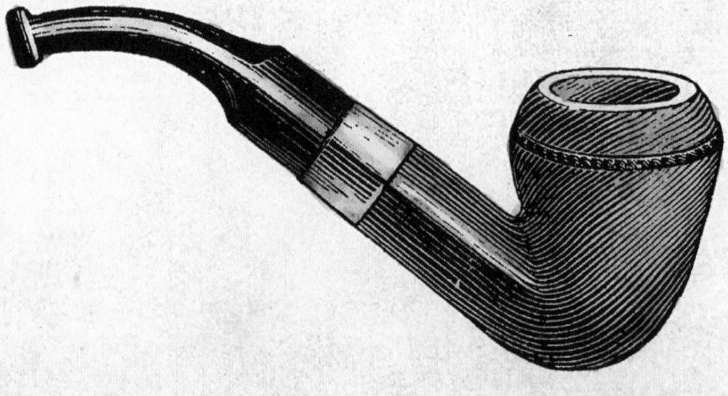

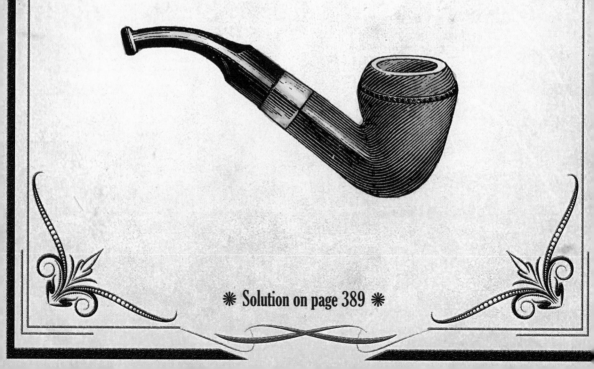

✻ Solution on page 389 ✻

Andrew

Holmes and I have encountered many highly peculiar individuals over the years. One of the most singular, however, was a fellow by the name of Andrew who was caught up in *The Adventure of the Black Alchemist*. Despite a certain preoccupation with fried-egg sandwiches, he was a quick-witted and resourceful fellow, and his heart was in the right place, both metaphorically and medically.

I vividly remember him explaining to Holmes and myself that he had lost his pocket watch in a scuffle with a cloaked and hooded figure whom he suspected of being an occultist. He went on to explain that on occasions when he forgot to wind his carriage clock at home, he would rectify the problem by visiting his friend David, who somehow always anticipated his arrival. Then he'd spend the evening there, and return home, correctly setting his clock when he arrived back.

It occurred to me that this must be rather haphazard, as he had no way of precisely telling the duration of the return trip, but he countered that as long as he took as long going there as he did getting back, it didn't matter.

What was his method?

✻ Solution on page 389 ✻

Rock Paper Scissors

Wiggins grinned at me. "You've not played Rock Paper Scissors before, Doctor?"

"Doesn't ring a bell," I told him.

"Two of you randomly pick one of the three, and shout your choice simultaneously. There are hand gestures, too. If you both get the same, it's a draw. Otherwise, scissors beats paper, paper beats rock, and rock beats scissors."

"So it's a way of settling an argument," I suggested.

"You were brought up wrong, Doctor," Wiggins said gravely. "Look, try it this way. I played a series of ten games with Alice earlier. I picked scissors six times, rock three times, and paper once. She picked scissors four time, rock twice, and paper four times. None of our games were drawn." He glanced at Holmes, who nodded. "So then, Doctor. What was the overall score for the series?"

✻ Solution on page 389 ✻

Old Hook

An event that occurred during *The Adventure of the Wandering Bishops* inspired Holmes to devise a particularly tricky little mental exercise for my ongoing improvement. There were times when I thoroughly appreciated and enjoyed his efforts, and times when I found them somewhat unwelcome. I'm afraid that this was one of the latter occasions. It had been a bad week.

"Picture three farmers," Holmes told me. "Hooklanders. We'll call them Ern, Ted, and Hob."

"If I must," I muttered.

"It will help," Holmes replied. "Ern has a horse and cart, with an average speed of eight mph. Ted can walk just one mph, given his bad knee, and Hob is a little better at two mph, thanks to his back."

"A fine shower," I said. "Can't I imagine them somewhat fitter?"

"Together, these worthies want to go from Old Hook to Coreham, a journey of 40 miles. So Ern got Ted in his cart, drove him most of the way, and dropped him off to walk the rest. Then he went back to get Hob, and took him into Coreham, arriving exactly as Ted did. How long did the journey take?"

Can you find a solution?

Solution on page 390

Art

One of my medical patients came to see me with a sore arm, but he seemed far more interested in his financial situation than his medical one. It can be that way for some people, particularly men in my experience – aversion to considering unpleasant medical possibilities leads them to emphatic fixation on something utterly unrelated. The fellow just had a light sprain, but that didn't stop him rabbiting on about some art dealing he'd been attempting.

Despite my best attempts otherwise, he resolutely insisted on informing me that he'd sold two paintings the day before, each for £75. One of these produced a 25 per cent profit, but the other yielded a 25 per cent loss.

I informed him absent-mindedly that it could have been worse.

"Not at all," he replied. "It was a very bad day."

I back-pedalled a little to avoid offence, and told him I was referring to his arm. But do you know what he was talking about?

❋ Solution on page 390 ❋

The Ninth Wordknot

I'd barely blurted the answer to Holmes's devilish two-fours puzzle when he produced a slip of paper with a flourish and a quite evil smirk, and handed that over too. Sure enough, it proved to be one of his wordknots, and a stern one to boot. I looked wistfully out of the window, at the rather fine afternoon I was missing, and set myself back to work.

The paper bore the letters:

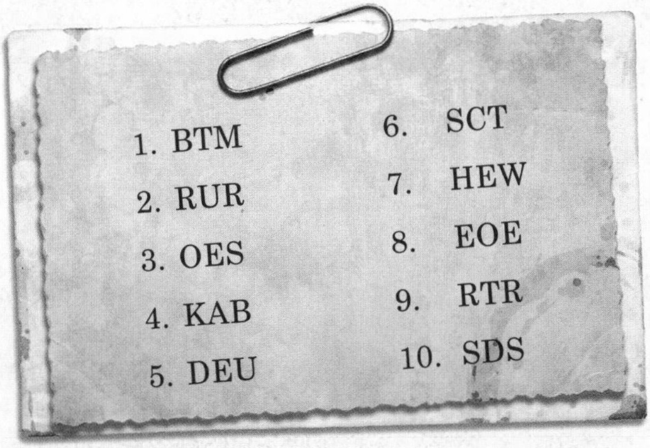

Each row held one letter from each of three words, jumbled into no particular order. These letters were all from the same position in each word, and presented in correct sequence, so that the first row held the first letters, the second row held the second letters, and so on and so forth. My task, of course, was to discover what the three ten-letter words were. I knew only that they would be loosely related.

❋ Solution on page 391 ❋

The Seven

Mrs Hudson eyed me grudgingly from over her stack of retrieved teacups. "My cousin Daisy took her two and her sister Allie's five to see a Punch and Judy show last week," she said.

"Oh, yes, the Neapolitan puppet thing," I replied. Visions of devils, mistresses, and wanton violence floated before my mind's eye. "Is that entirely suitable for children?"

"It is nowadays," she said. "More or less. They apparently enjoyed it anyway, the scamps. But that's not the point. The point is that there are three girls amongst the seven, and four boys, and they sat themselves utterly haphazardly in a row. What do you think that the chance was that the end-spots were both occupied by girls?"

That stopped me in my tracks. Can you work it out?

Bridge

The game of bridge is an interesting new Russian spin on that perennial pub favourite, whist. One of the things about it which I find the most curious is its seemingly boundless propensity to end up in the newspaper. It seems nowadays that hardly a week goes by without some mention of it in either the *The Times* or the *Evening Standard*.

The other day, I came across a story about a quartet of bridge players whom had each been dealt all thirteen cards of one suit – a phenomenon known as the "perfect deal".

Dismissing those perfect deals that arise from deliberate tampering or ineffective shuffling, how many such events would you expect to occur nationally over the course of one year?

✻ Solution on page 391 ✻

The Fifth Camouflage

After an unpleasantly long chase through the eastern portion of the City of London, Holmes and I had successfully apprehended a fellow by the name of Raphael Stevens. He was up to his neck in *The Adventure of the Sapphire Gin*, and there were certain pieces of information which we needed from him. Clearly, he had not been willing to speak to us. I was forced to restrain him while Holmes put his questions.

Eventually, we had the knowledge we needed. I let Stevens go, and slumped against a wall, exhausted – which, naturally, was the exact moment when Holmes decided to challenge me with one of his word camouflages.

"Displayable," he said. "Hideosities. Totipotent. Browbeaten."

A groan escaped me. "Really, Holmes?" I asked.

"Crime never waits for your convenience," he said, severely.

So I had to find the answer. Four shorter words, one per longer word, that formed a thematically linked set.

Can you find the theme?

❋ Solution on page 392 ❋

The Enthusiast

Colin White's murder came as a nasty shock to the London chess-playing community, particularly when police let it be known that they suspected that a fellow player. Brian Campbell was one of three men who'd visited White that last day, according to a diary entry from that morning. A fellow player of some repute, he'd often been quite critical of White's eccentricities. In addition to Campbell, another chess-player had paid White a visit, a younger man named Tom Wilton, who was said to rather look up to the deceased. Finally, he'd also had a visit from his cousin, Alan Lloyd, a genial chap with a devout love of fishing. Unfortunately, White had listed the men in alphabetical order, rather than time.

Inspector Lestrade was somewhat beside himself, because, following legal advice, none of the men were prepared to make any sort of statement whatsoever. Holmes agreed to help, and a few hours later, he and I were in the dead man's flat.

"We've kept it as it was," Lestrade told us. "We found him in the sitting room, stabbed."

The room was large and restrained. The big central table held four chess boards, one of them set up with a match in the mid-game. I am no chess expert, but I could tell white was winning handily, dominating the board with a line of major pieces, its bishops immediately either side of a rook. Aside from that, there were some small pieces of Greek statuary, a long shelf of books – on chess, inevitably – and a plain ashtray. I considered that perhaps a game had gone badly astray.

Holmes poked around, examined a couple of books, and then turned to Lestrade. "The identity of the murderer blindingly obvious," he said.

I didn't know what he meant at the time. Do you?

❋ Solution on page 392 ❋

The Ribbons

This particular puzzle was another of Holmes's abstract contrivances, inspired, so far as I was ever aware, by a conversation that he had with Mrs Hudson.

The situation is as follows. Four mother and daughter pairs went to purchase ribbon, and over the course of the afternoon, two coincidences could be noted. One was that each mother bought twice as many yards of ribbon as her daughter; the other that each purchaser acquired exactly as many yards of ribbon as the cost of that ribbon per yard in pennies. As examples of that last fact, consider that someone buying one penny a yard ribbon would have purchased one yard, or that someone buying two pence ribbon would have purchased two yards.

In addition to these two foundational coincidences, there are some other pieces of information. Rose purchased two yards more than Daisy. Lily purchased three yards less than Mrs Brown. Mrs White spent 76 pence more than Mrs Black. Daisy spent 48 pence less than Mrs Green.

If Daisy purchased ribbon at four pence a yard, what is Heather's mother named?

❋ Solution on page 393 ❋

Trout

"There's going to be a number of things on the table for lunch tomorrow," Mrs Hudson told me. "It being Easter and all. My cousin Richard managed to get hold of a lovely trout this morning, so that's going to be poached in a light cream and wine sauce, with chives. There'll be new potatoes to go with it, I'd imagine."

"Sounds very pleasant," I ventured.

"I'm sure it will be," she said. "I asked Richard how big the thing was. You know how fishermen love to boast. Well, he only went and told me that the head weighed the same as the combined weight of the tail and half the body, that the body weighed as much as the head and tail together, and that the tail came out at nine ounces. I'm sure you can see what that means."

I kept my own counsel on the implications of that statement, and nodded.

How much does the fish weigh?

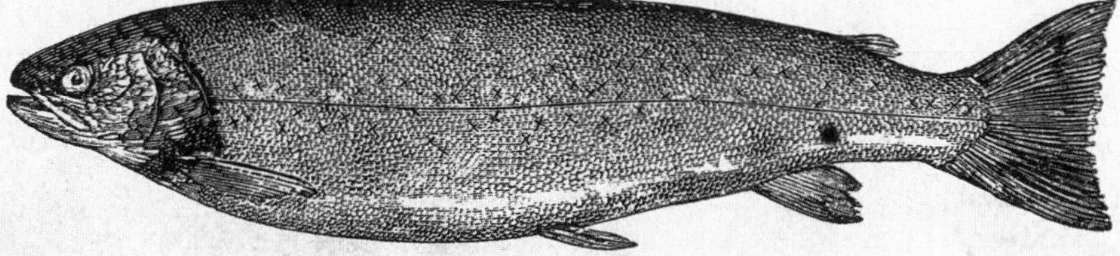

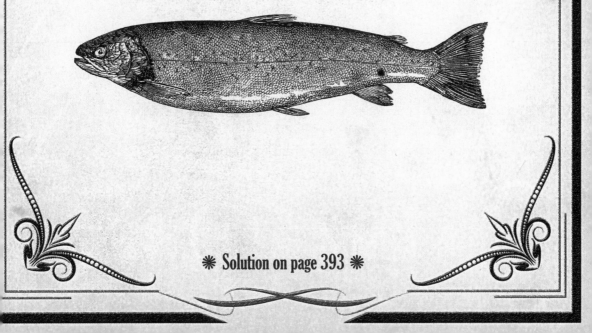

✻ Solution on page 393 ✻

Getting to Market

During our hunt for C. L. Nolan in the course of *The Adventure of the Wandering Bishops*, Holmes and I had to get from Hook, the much-decayed ancient capital town of Hookland, to Coreham, the current capital. In Hookland, they say that Coreham is a cursed city, and there were moments where I felt rather sympathetic to such superstitious claims.

To our moderate annoyance, the only vehicle available to transport us from Hook to Coreham was a mouldering trap pulled by an equally mouldering old nag. The driver was little better than his conveyance, and showed a remarkable lack of anything resembling sense. Had it not been for a heavy case that Holmes was carrying, we would just have walked. It would have been faster and less aggravating.

After twenty frustratingly slow minutes in the trap, I asked the fellow how far we'd come from Hook.

"Halfways as far as to Doglick from here," mumbled the driver.

I got him to repeat the name, just to be sure I'd heard him correctly. Doglick turned out to be a flyspeck of a hamlet every bit as unprepossessing as its name. Some five miles after we'd got clear of the place, I made the mistake of again asking the driver as to our progress, specifically, how much further it was to Coreham.

His answer, word for word, was identical.

I asked no further questions, and an hour later, we finally arrived in Coreham, which is at least a pretty place.

Can you tell how far it is from Hook to Coreham?

✵ Solution on page 394 ✵

The Tenth Wordknot

Holmes handed me my tenth and final wordknot one quiet afternoon when I was well rested and refreshed, and more than a little bored. I peered at both him and the slip of paper cautiously, half-expecting lions to leap from behind a cupboard the moment I took it from him, or some such terrifying crisis.

As it was, nothing more distressing happened than Holmes smiling at me, which of course unsettled me colossally. The slip of paper bore the following:

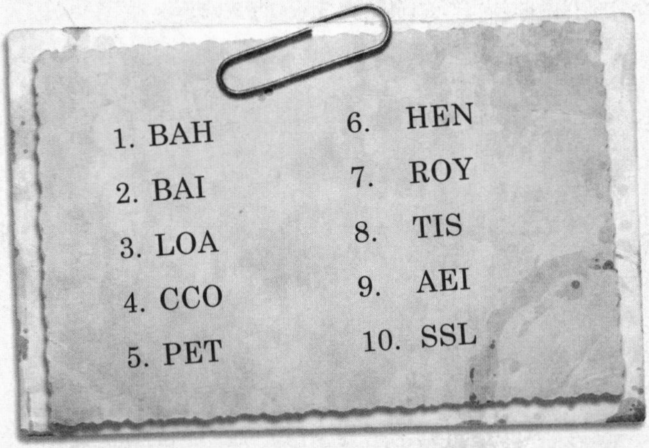

1. BAH
2. BAI
3. LOA
4. CCO
5. PET
6. HEN
7. ROY
8. TIS
9. AEI
10. SSL

The task was to unscramble the letters to find three loosely-themed ten-letter words, working from the basis that the first line of the text comprised their initial letters, the second line their second letters, and so on. It was not easy.

Can you do it?

❋ Solution on page 395 ❋

Pencils

During *The Adventure of the Third Carriage*, Holmes had the need to spend a day masquerading as a wholesaler of stationery. He returned from this outing much vexed, so naturally I asked him whether his investigations had gone well.

"Oh, yes, very useful," he said. "I got the information I was after."

"But something appears to be bothering you nonetheless," I replied.

He sighed. "The stationery business is cripplingly ineffective. It irks me to have had to pretend to approve of such ridiculous business practices."

"I see," I said. This was not strictly a true or accurate statement.

"Imagine this," Holmes said. "A box of 160 pencils, in eight rows of twenty."

"Sounds about right."

"No!" Holmes sighed again. "You could get ten per cent more pencils to a box in a heartbeat."

Can you see how?

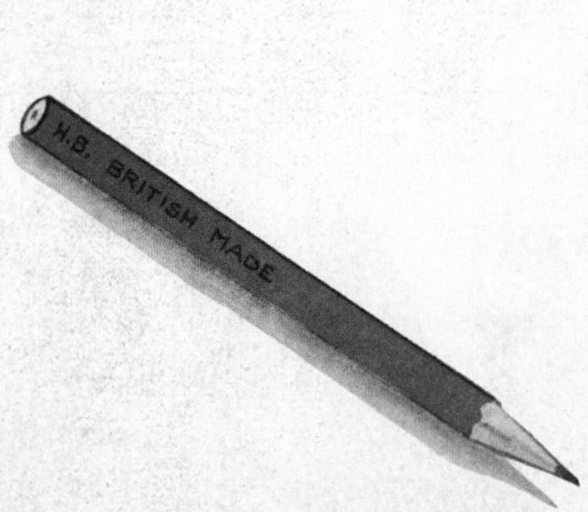

✱ Solution on page 395 ✱

Easter Spirit

Holmes gestured grandly at the coffee table. "There are four eggs," he began.

"I hate to disagree, old chap," I said. "There don't appear to be any eggs there at all."

He smirked at me. "Where's your Easter spirit?"

"Not on the coffee table, that's for sure."

"There are four eggs, Watson. If they are not physically present, they are certainly there metaphorically."

"I dare say I can accept that," I said.

"One of the four is three inches in length. The other three are smaller, and all I will tell you of them is that they collectively equal the volume of the larger egg, that they are all precisely similar in shape to their larger cousin, and that they differ from each other in length by half an inch from short to medium, and by half an inch from medium to long."

I sighed. "I suppose you want me to puzzle out their lengths?"

"Just that of the shortest of all will do."

Can you find the answer?

✻ Solution on page 396 ✻

Rufus

When Holmes and I met with Wiggins one afternoon, he was accompanied by a rather scrappy-looking mutt, who eyed me with evident suspicion.

"This is Rufus," Wiggins said. "He's a friend."

"Charmed," I said.

"He's very energetic," Wiggins told us. "Just this morning, he and I set out for a little walk."

At the word 'walk', the dog barked happily.

"When we set out, he immediately dashed off to the end of the road, then turned round and bounded back to me. He did this four times in total, in fact. After that, he settled down to match my speed, and we walked the remaining 81 feet to the end of the road at my pace. But it seems to me that if I tell you the distance from where we started to the end of the road, which is 625 feet, and that I was walking at four miles an hour, you ought to be able to work out how fast Rufus goes when he's running."

"Indeed we should," said Holmes, and turned to look at me expectantly.

What's the dog's running speed?

❋ Solution on page 396 ❋

Three Men

"I came across an interesting little exercise that might benefit you, Watson. It'll test your powers of reasoning, and nothing else."

I put down my book, and grabbed a pencil and notepad. "Fire away, old chap."

"Excellent. On a theoretical train, the conductor, driver and ticket inspector are, in no particular order, named Smith, Jones and Robinson. As luck – or, in this instance, contrivance – would have it, there are also three passengers with the same surnames, whom I will refer to as Mr Smith, Mr Jones, and Mr Robinson, in order to distinguish them from that train's staff."

"Very well," I said.

"There are several pieces of information I can give you. One, Mr Robinson lives in Brixton, whilst the conductor lives in Chelsea. Two, Mr Jones cannot do algebra. Three, Smith regularly beats the ticket inspector at billiards. Four, the passenger who shares the conductor's name lives in Tottenham. Finally, five, the conductor shares his local pub with the passenger who works as a professor of mathematical physics at University College, London."

I frantically finished jotting down notes. "I have all that," I told Holmes.

"In that case, please be so good as to let me know the name of the driver. I'll warn you now that there is insufficient information to calculate every particular of every man, but there is enough to identify the driver."

Can you find the solution?

❋ Solution on page 397 ❋

BARBA

The Tyrant

"I should warn you, Watson, that I am a vengeful, bloody-minded tyrant."

I looked round at Holmes, and deliberately kept my face straight. "I've long suspected it," I told him.

"Which is why I'm about to have you executed," he replied. "Luckily for you, my religion permits you a get-out clause."

"That's a relief," I said.

"I will present you with two identical large jars, along with 50 white marbles, and 50 black marbles. You are to distribute these marbles between the two jars however you wish, so long as all 100 are used. One of these jars will then be chosen at random, and if you withdraw a white marble from it, your life will be spared."

"That seems oddly specific for a religion."

"It's an oddly specific religion," Holmes replied. "How would you maximize your chances of escape?"

✻ Solution on page 398 ✻

The Final Camouflage

In sharp contrast to the gentle circumstances in which Holmes assigned me his final wordknot, he waited until I was actively ill with a heavy cold before tasking me with his final word camouflage. I was feeling thoroughly sorry for myself that morning, not to mention fuzzy-headed, and I did not respond particularly well. Holmes, of course, was utterly unbothered, so in the end I worked on his puzzle anyway.

The four words that he assigned me were gatecrashed, hyperboles, subceiling and godfathered. My task was to find the small words hidden with the larger, one per word, such that the four small words were grouped together by a loose theme.

Can you discover the theme?

❋ Solution on page 398 ❋

Seven Applewomen

A rather odd affair, this one. It was inspired, once again, by Hookland. Holmes said that he came across it in an old book, and felt that it would serve as an unusually stringent test of my poor, battered faculties. Like many of its ilk, it is contrived to the point of utter lunacy, but even so, it may prove interesting.

In a Hookland market, there are seven applewomen, who have the suspiciously regularised amounts of 20, 40, 60, 80, 100, 120, and 140 apples to sell. Being friends – and somewhat peculiar – they decide on a variable pricing scheme for their wares which will ensure that when each sells her entire consignment, each will come away with the same amount of money. Why they didn't just pool up all the takings and divide them equally is quite beyond me. Perhaps it's due to the same religious requirements that forced Holmes' theoretical tyranny to give the condemned a basket of marbles.

Still. Can you work out the pricing scheme?

✻ Solution on page 399 ✻

Terminus

Maxwell Perry had died in a small alley just the right side of Brick Lane, shot in the chest. His attire suggested that he'd been in something of a panic – his shoes were unlaced, his trousers belted but unbuttoned, and his jumper both back to front and inside out. Profound though his alarm had clearly been, it had just as clearly not saved him.

As investigations unfolded, it became clear that Perry was involved in the opium trade, moving his death towards natural causes. Unfortunately, he was also a distant cousin of someone of note, and poor Inspector Lestrade was on the receiving end of a considerable amount of pressure to solve the murder. Having a whole pile of witnesses and suspects didn't help.

Holmes grudgingly agreed to have a look over Lestrade's notes, mainly to get the fellow out of our rooms. When they arrived he flicked through them, making desultory comments as he went. "Brinton claims to have seen the victim running past like 'a sack of monkeys', whatever that means... Murphy heard a shot, and found the body, but didn't see anyone else, which seems short-sighted at best... Bligh remembers seeing the victim running away because of the visible jumper label... Colgate saw one man shoot another, face to face, but was too far to get even the slightest useful detail... Routledge found a pistol in a waste skip behind a pub... Oliver says the victim turned a corner and almost barrelled into him, then shrieked and dashed off..." He dropped the file. "That's more than enough, I think. It's quite blatant who killed the man."

What did Holmes mean?

✻ Solution on page 400 ✻

ANSWERS AND SOLUTIONS

PART ONE

ELEMENTARY

A MATTER OF IDENTITY

"It is vital to set aside your preconceptions if you are to think freely, Watson. It is the single most important step in accurate deduction. Make no assumptions that the evidence does not clearly support. Louise and Lisa have another sister, Lucy, likewise the product of the same pregnancy. They are not twins because they are in fact two out of three triplets."

A DIFFICULT AGE

"Our chap's birthday is New Year's Eve, Watson, and our singular day is January 1st. Two days ago, on December 30th, he was 25. The next day, he attained 26. Today is the start of the new year, and at the end of this year he will become 27. At the end of the following year, therefore, he will be 28."

THE FIRST CURIOSITY

It is possible, but it would not be wise. The house would have to be located precisely upon the North Pole. Such a dwelling would be very cold indeed, and immensely inaccessible.

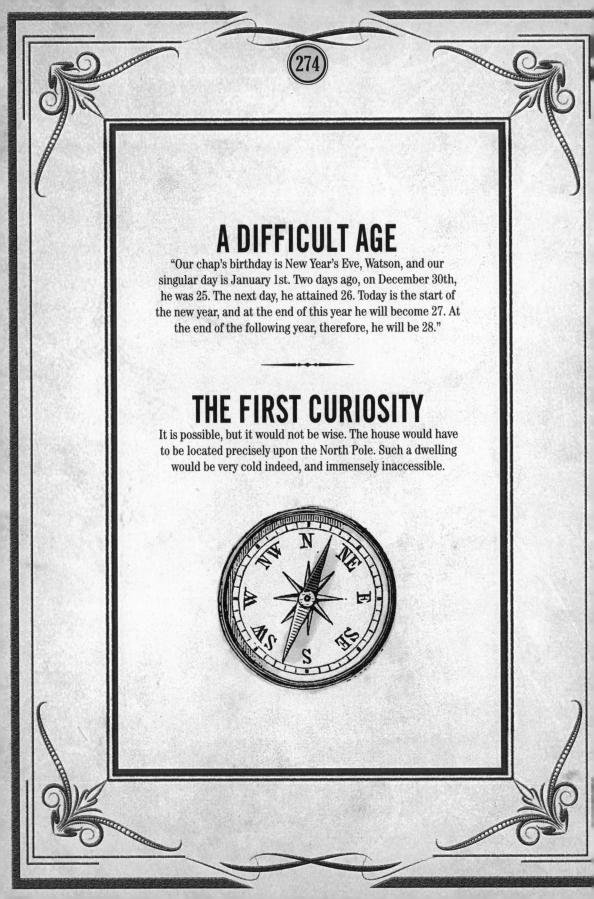

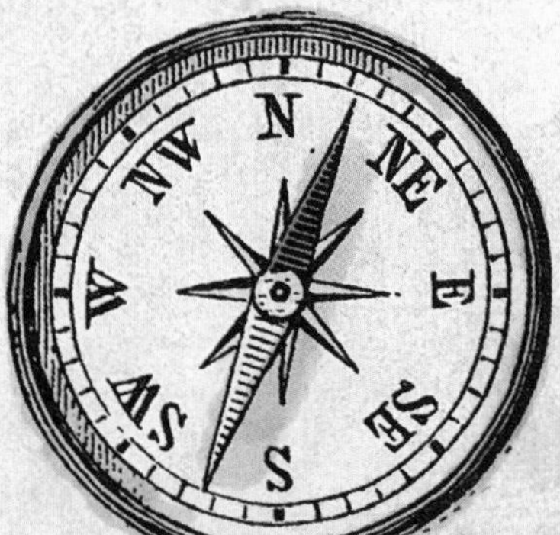

RABBIT RACE

Given the consistency of the various times involved, the first three quarters of the race took exactly ¾ of the time – and the whole race took 9 minutes.

THE BARREL

"What you need to do is to tip it on its side just far enough that the water touches the lip of the barrel," Holmes told me. "Then look inside. If any of the bottom of the barrel is visible, then it is more than half empty. If any of the side wall is obscured, it is more than half full. If the water is exactly at the join, then it is in the precise half-way state."

"And would that be half-empty or half full?" I asked.

Holmes did not deign to reply.

THE FIRST MENTAL TRIAL

Holmes was, of course, referring to my name.

ELEMENTARY GEOMETRY

You need to make the distance as effective as possible, and the means to do so is as follows. First, plot the relative positions of the warehouse and the dock entrance, which are not in your power to alter, and then put in the river. Now, extend a line from the warehouse directly to the river, so that it hits it precisely on the perpendicular, make a note of that distance, and continue the line on past the river exactly the same distance again. You may think of that as a reflection of the warehouse on the other side of the river. From that point, extend a second line directly to the dock entrance. The place at which the second line crosses the river is the point that gives the shortest route from warehouse to river to entrance.

The solution works because obviously, any spot on the river is the same distance from the warehouse as it is from it's reflected spot on the other side. A straight line from the reflected point to the dock entrance is the shortest distance – and that marks the spot on the river bank that is the most efficient. What is the shortest distance from the reflected warehouse is also the shortest distance from the real one.

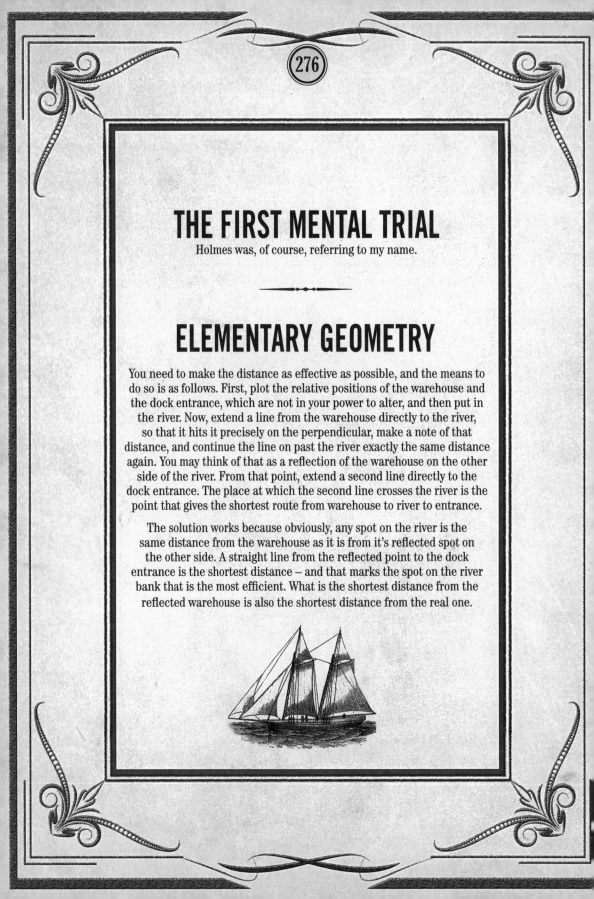

THE FIRST LITERAL ODDITY

As I'm sure you must have noticed, each word has the distinction of alternating consonant with vowel. I have since discovered that the terrible honorificabilitudinitatibus is the longest word in English to do so, with 27 letters to its count, although the others that Holmes mentioned are in joint seventh place at 15 letters in length.

THE MEAL

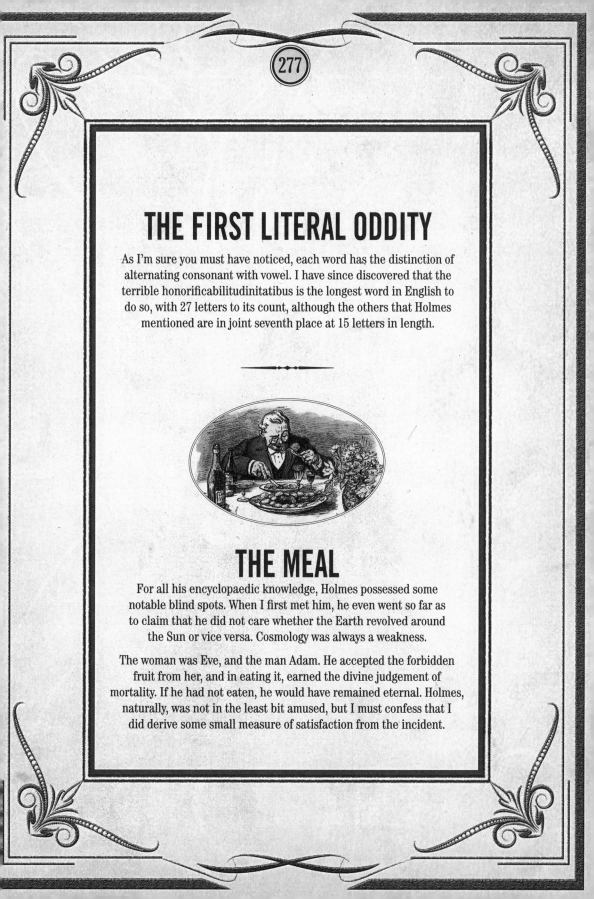

For all his encyclopaedic knowledge, Holmes possessed some notable blind spots. When I first met him, he even went so far as to claim that he did not care whether the Earth revolved around the Sun or vice versa. Cosmology was always a weakness.

The woman was Eve, and the man Adam. He accepted the forbidden fruit from her, and in eating it, earned the divine judgement of mortality. If he had not eaten, he would have remained eternal. Holmes, naturally, was not in the least bit amused, but I must confess that I did derive some small measure of satisfaction from the incident.

REGENT STREET

The tardier man painted more lamp-posts, compensating for the earlier fellow's three by completing six. So the discrepancy is three – but this must be applied to each side. The tardy fellow did three extra; the early one three too few. Therefore the tardy man painted six more posts.

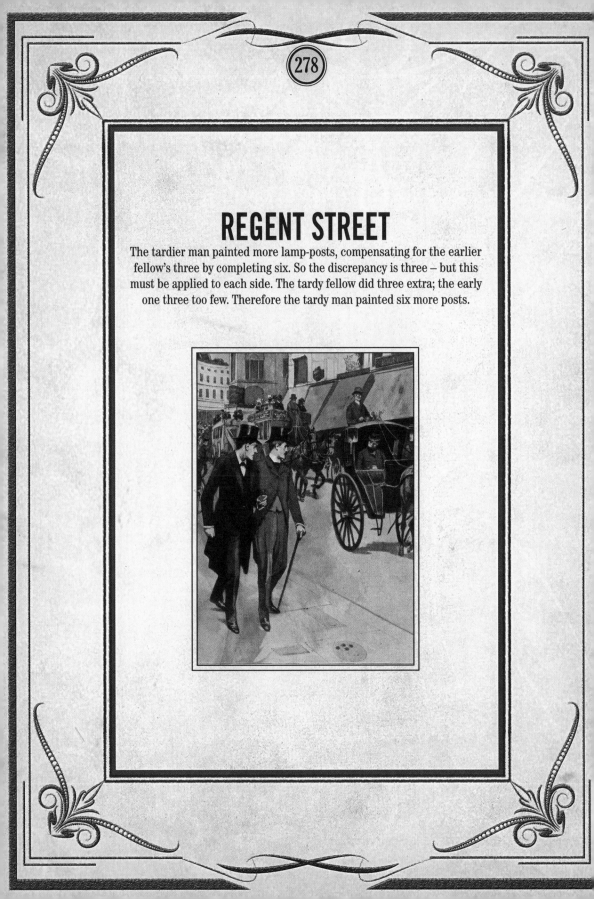

RIDER

The answer is not 10mph, although it is tempting to think it should be.

Let us say the journey is 24 miles. The outward journey, then, is 2 hours, and the return is three. The average speed then is found by adding 12+12+8+8+8, and dividing by 5, giving you a speed of nine and three fifths miles per hour.

Now consider a journey twice as long. Your average speed will be four hours at 12mph + six hours at 8mph, divided by the ten hours taken in total – or, again, nine and three fifths miles per hour.

So as you can see, the distance is irrespective. You take longer at the slower speed, and this skews the average below the more intuitive even division between the two.

THE SECOND MENTAL TRIAL

Holmes was right, it was fairly elementary. The midpoint around the clock between 3am and 3pm is 9am. Three hours after 9am is midday.

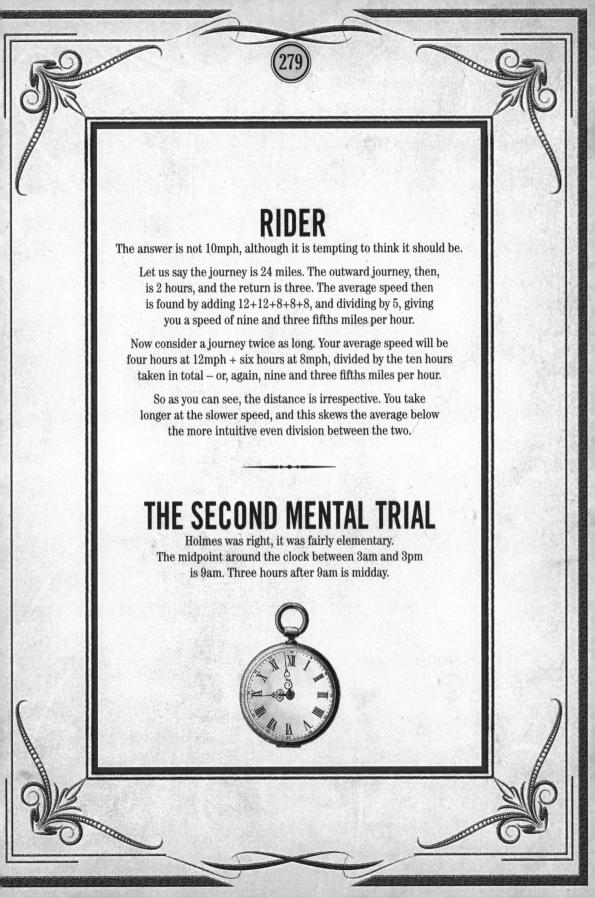

THE GANG

"I assume," Holmes said, "that you took no action because no laws had been broken."

"Well..," began Lestrade.

"Tell me, were the firemen rescuing a pet or a child? I suspect the latter, since they handed the unfortunate to the wife."

Lestrade gave up. "An infant."

THE FIRST PORTMANTEAU

The location in question is Her Majesty's Royal Palace and Fortress, famed worldwide as the Tower of London. The heart of the place is the White Tower, a square moated keep, although the moat is now dry. The Tower is guarded by Yeoman Warders, known popularly as Beefeaters, and contains the Queen's Crown Jewels. Ravens also guard the tower, and it is said, Heaven help us, that if they ever fled, the British monarchy would collapse.

THE THIRD MENTAL TRIAL

Alfie sat only in the second half of the journey. In that section, he had to get up when he had half as far to go as he had already travelled – or, in other words, he had sat for two parts of that half of the journey, with one remaining. So he was seated for 2/3 of the second half of the journey – or 1/3 of the whole thing.

CATFORD

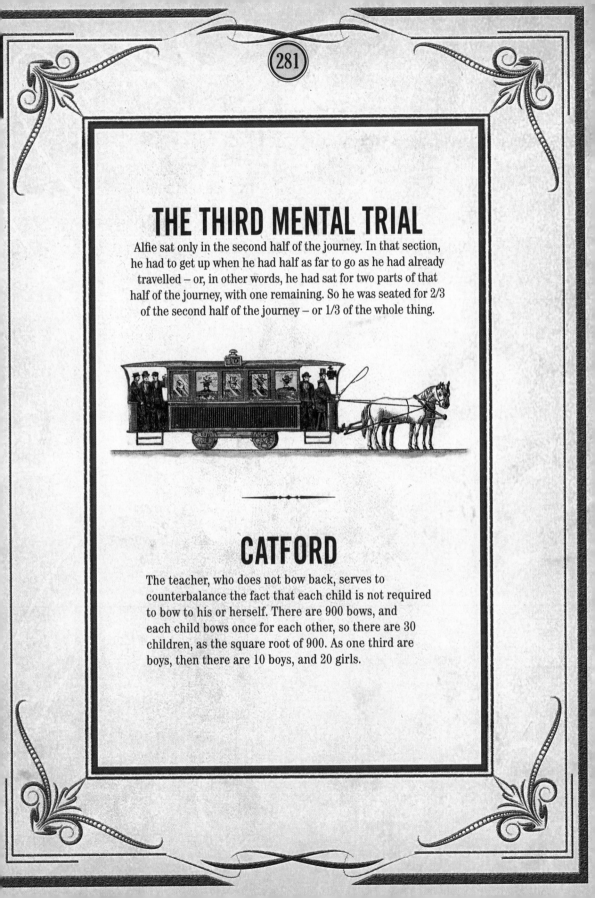

The teacher, who does not bow back, serves to counterbalance the fact that each child is not required to bow to his or herself. There are 900 bows, and each child bows once for each other, so there are 30 children, as the square root of 900. As one third are boys, then there are 10 boys, and 20 girls.

THE SECOND CURIOSITY

The obvious truth, of course, is that the distance between England and France varies quite wildly. Between Dover and Calais, it is just 21 miles, but the island of Guernsey, which is undeniably twixt the pair, is 26 miles from the English shore.

TRAINS

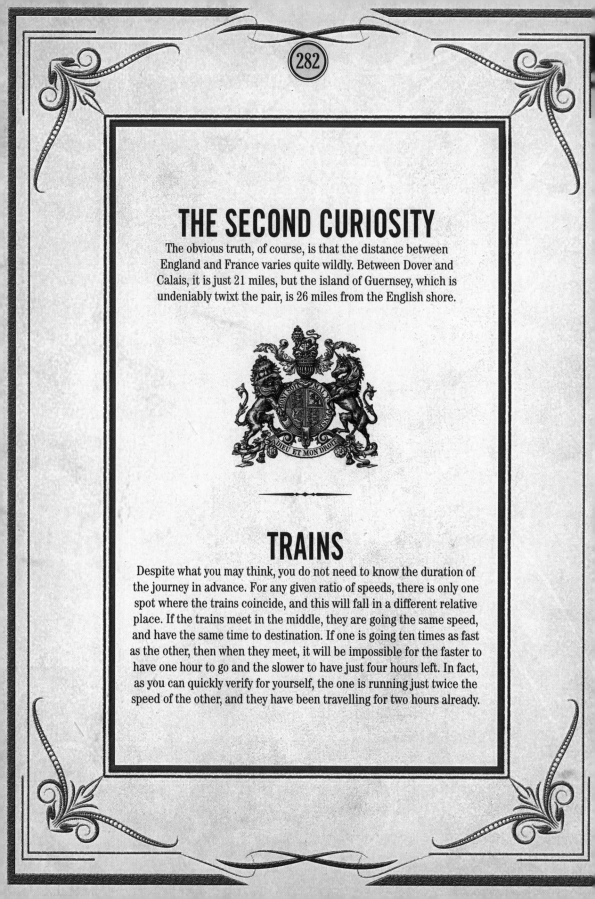

Despite what you may think, you do not need to know the duration of the journey in advance. For any given ratio of speeds, there is only one spot where the trains coincide, and this will fall in a different relative place. If the trains meet in the middle, they are going the same speed, and have the same time to destination. If one is going ten times as fast as the other, then when they meet, it will be impossible for the faster to have one hour to go and the slower to have just four hours left. In fact, as you can quickly verify for yourself, the one is running just twice the speed of the other, and they have been travelling for two hours already.

GLOUCESTER

Whatever the exact amounts of the liquids, provided that there is sufficient of each to complete all three steps, the answer will be the same. The fellow is halving the amount of milk in the first step, by doubling it with water, and then doubling the remaining water with the half-strength blend. The final step does not affect the contents of the larger barrel. The liquid is just one-quarter milk.

WIGGINS

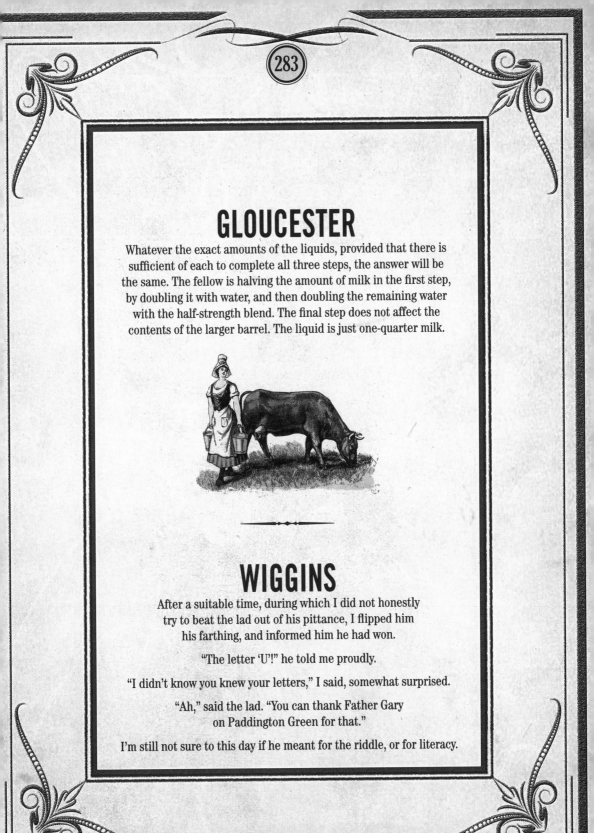

After a suitable time, during which I did not honestly try to beat the lad out of his pittance, I flipped him his farthing, and informed him he had won.

"The letter 'U'!" he told me proudly.

"I didn't know you knew your letters," I said, somewhat surprised.

"Ah," said the lad. "You can thank Father Gary on Paddington Green for that."

I'm still not sure to this day if he meant for the riddle, or for literacy.

TO CATCH A THIEF

For every five strides of Holmes', the thief was taking eight, but those eight were equivalent to just three and a fifth of the taller man's. So Holmes was gaining one and four fifths of one of his strides for every five he took. The burglar's 27-stride lead is equivalent to ten and four fifths of Holmes' strides, and it will take exactly six gains of one and four fifths strides for Holmes to catch his quarry.

So Holmes has to take just 30 paces to catch the villain - who, in that time, will have run a total of 75 steps.

THE SECOND LITERAL ODDITY

Consisting solely as they do of the first seven letters of the alphabet – they are in fact the joint longest words in English to do so – both cabbaged and fabaceae are words that can be played as a sequence of notes upon a musical instrument.

CHEAPSIDE

There are two possible answers to the question. The fellow could have been either Holmes' uncle or his father.

THE THIRD CURIOSITY

The answer is, of course, £13,212.

SWINGING PENDULUMS

"Nothing," Holmes said. "It wouldn't make the slightest bit of difference. The mass of the bob has no effect on the swing, as the whole thing is driven by gravity, which treats all objects as completely equal. Resistance from the air might play a part, if the experiment were not being conducted in a vacuum.

AN ISSUE OF AGE

To keep the difference in their ages down to as small a fraction as an eleventh of the total, the two digits of each age must be close together. Furthermore, the total age must be divisible by 11. As it transpires, the total has to be 99, and the couple's ages 54 and 45, the latter being the lady's age.

THE BOARD

The meeting comprised of eighteen individuals. If three people mark the difference between half and two thirds, then the total is six times that number.

ALMONDS

With a little calculation, you can see that in each cycle, the youngest received nine almonds, the middle one got twelve, and the oldest had fourteen. The sum of these totals, 35, goes into 840 some 24 times. 28/35 is four-fifths, which means that the ages of each child are four fifths of the number of almonds each gets in a round. So the youngest is 7 and one fifth years old, the middle one is nine and three fifths years, and the eldest is 11 and a fifth years.

ON THE STRAND

The teacher and the tailor were both women, and therefore vanishingly unlikely to be named Hugo.

GRANDDAD

As Holmes has often said, "Once you eliminate the impossible, whatever remains, no matter how improbable, must be the truth." The highwayman married late in life, and the grandfather in question was her mother's father, not her father's father.

HOOKLAND

The minimum number to meet those conditions would be seven moles – 3 of them totally blind, 2 blind in the right eye, 1 blind in the left eye, and 1 with normal vision. You'll note that seven left eyes (4 blind, 3 sighted) and seven right eyes (five blind, 2 sighted) are specifically mentioned. The maximum, of course, would be fifteen, 5 + 4 + 3 + 2 + 1.

THE WATCHMEN

As it turned out, it was rather obvious, yes. Picture the route as a circle, and imagine the guards setting off both clockwise and anti-clockwise simultaneously. There inevitably comes a moment where the two guards will meet. That is the time (and place) where the guard will have to be every hour, whichever way he is walking.

THE PRISON

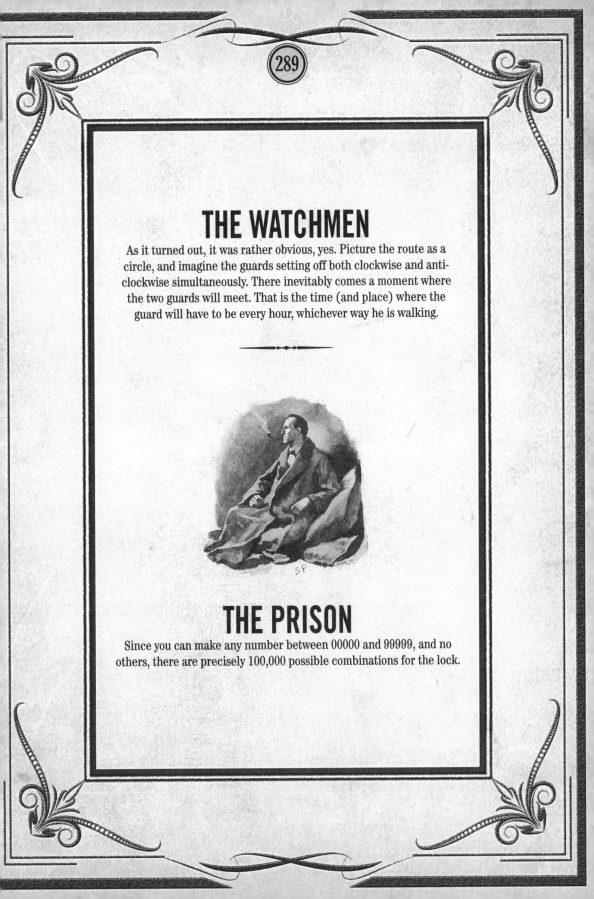

Since you can make any number between 00000 and 99999, and no others, there are precisely 100,000 possible combinations for the lock.

THE FIRST WORDKNOT

The words are *chocolates*, *delicacies* and *peppermint.*

WHISKY

Seven shillings is 84p. If the brandy is worth 80 pence more than the glass, and the glass is worth x, then (80+x) is the value of the brandy, and x+80+x = 84. So the glass is worth tuppence, or 2 pence.

COUSIN TRACY

3. As both Tracy and Albert have six children, and the children of their marriage must be counted for both of them, they must have had the same number of children before they were married. There are only four possibilities, from 1 child together and 5 each separately (a total of 11) to 5 children together, and 1 each separately (a total of 7). We know the total is nine children, so both Tracy and Albert had 3 children each before marrying, and then 3 more together.

TRILOGY

If the former officer died without regaining consciousness, there is no way anyone could know what he had been dreaming about. The story has to be a fabrication.

THE CANDLES

There are lots of numbers that are difficult to get to, but 100 can be achieved with two boxes of 16 candles, and four boxes of 17.

BUCKETS

The weights would be identical. An object floating in water displaces an amount of water such that the weight of the water displaced is precisely equal to the weight of the object.

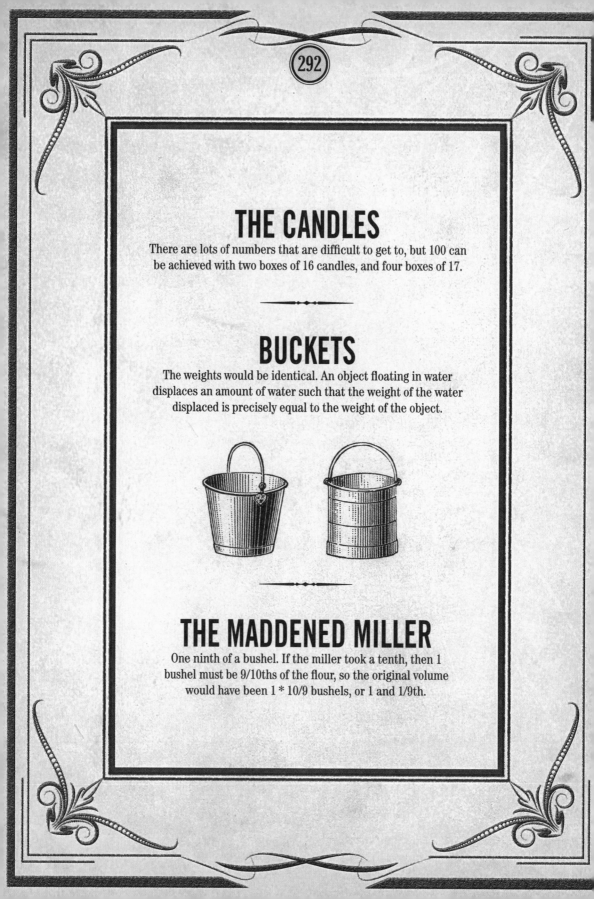

THE MADDENED MILLER

One ninth of a bushel. If the miller took a tenth, then 1 bushel must be 9/10ths of the flour, so the original volume would have been 1 * 10/9 bushels, or 1 and 1/9th.

THE FIRST CAMOUFLAGE

The words are *ant*, *bee*, *bug* and *moth*, and they are all types of insect.

FABULOUS

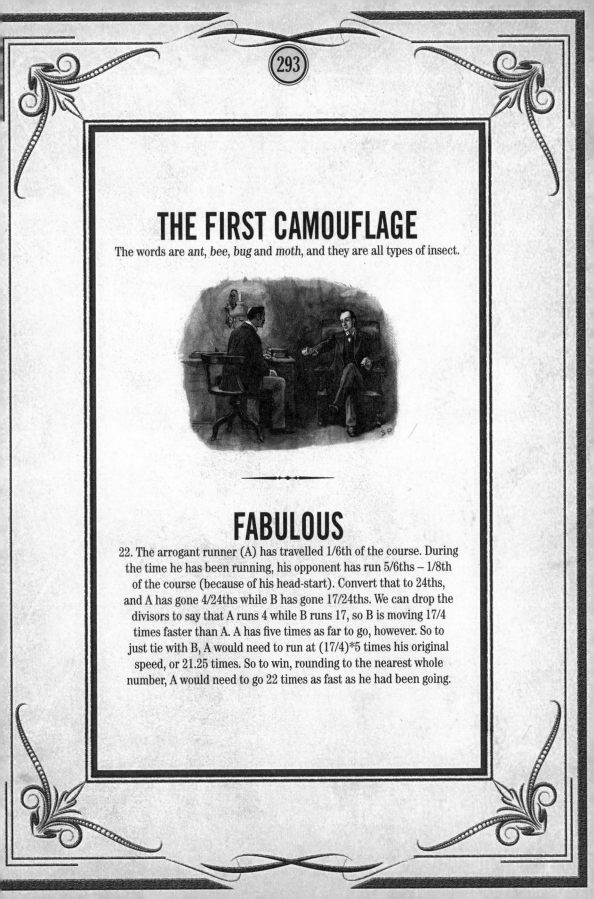

22. The arrogant runner (A) has travelled 1/6th of the course. During the time he has been running, his opponent has run 5/6ths – 1/8th of the course (because of his head-start). Convert that to 24ths, and A has gone 4/24ths while B has gone 17/24ths. We can drop the divisors to say that A runs 4 while B runs 17, so B is moving 17/4 times faster than A. A has five times as far to go, however. So to just tie with B, A would need to run at (17/4)*5 times his original speed, or 21.25 times. So to win, rounding to the nearest whole number, A would need to go 22 times as fast as he had been going.

OUT EAST

60%. The same number of men and women must have been married, so whatever number that is, it represents 2.1% of men and 1.4% of women. Simplifying those numbers, we see that the ratio of male to female inhabitants must be 2:3. So 3/5ths of the population – 60% – are female.

THE SUICIDE

There was no source of liquid anywhere in the room. Whilst not strictly impossible that our client's uncle had forced himself to dry-swallow a score of large pills, it did seem an unlikely inconvenience to inflict on oneself during one's last moments. In fact, he'd been poisoned, and although the killer staged the pills and removed the poisoned beverage, he totally forgot to replace the latter.

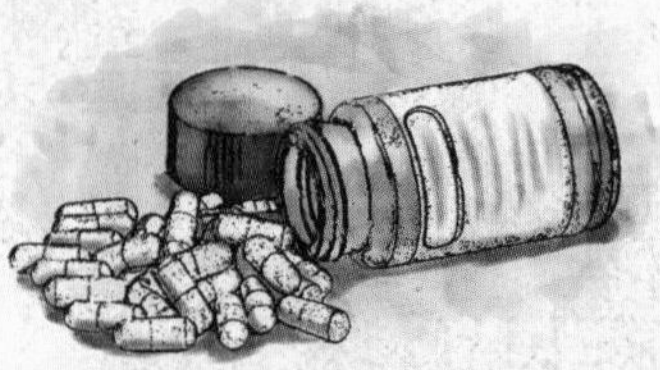

SCARVES

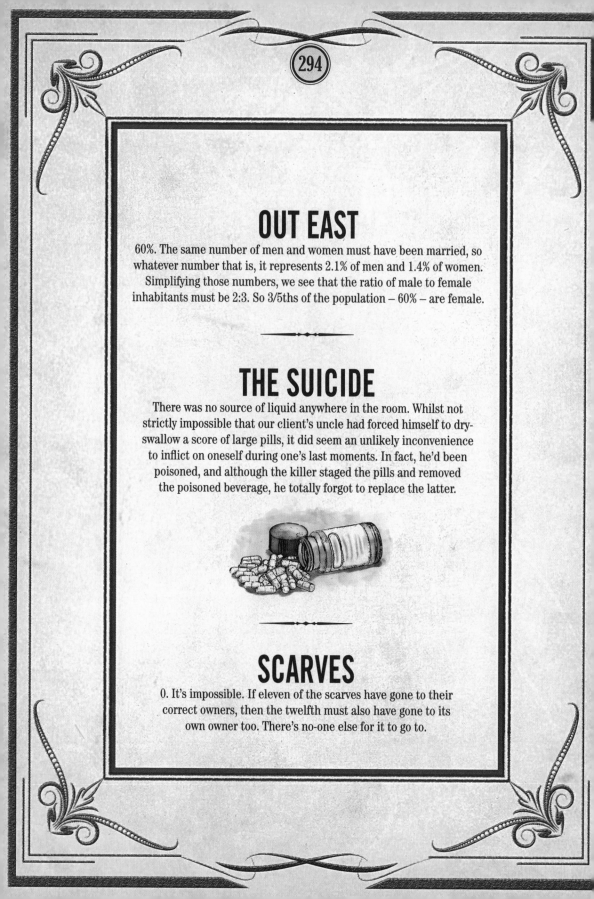

0. It's impossible. If eleven of the scarves have gone to their correct owners, then the twelfth must also have gone to its own owner too. There's no-one else for it to go to.

JOE

Joe is 10 and Ruth is 4. The only time when relative ages move so swiftly is when one of the people is very young. If you try 1 as Ruth's initial age, you'll quickly see that all the ratios pan out – 1 and 7, 2 and 8, and 3 and 9, which makes them currently 4 and 10.

THE WENNS

33. Since there are more patrons than numbers of pennies, and no sum of pennies can be duplicated, the number of pennies each patron has must be represented by a continuous arithmetical distribution of rising 0, 1, 2, 3, etc. With both duplicate amounts and 33 pennies being forbidden, a theoretical 34th patron would have no possible number of pennies to be allocated. So the most people that there can be is if there are 33 patrons ranging from 0 to 32 pennies.

MAIDA VALE

10 miles. James is going twice as fast as Gerry, and so will catch up to him in 1 hour, at the 4 mile point. The dog is thus running at 10 miles per hour, continually, for 1 hour.

SHEEP

960. David gets 1,200 sheep, as 200 is 20% of 1000. Now, x+25% = 5x/4, so to find x, we must divide by 5/4, or multiple by 4/5, which is 0.8. As 1,200 * 0.8 = 960, Caradog gets 960 sheep.

THE SECOND WORDKNOT

The words are *tourmaline*, *aquamarine* and *rhodolites*.

THE PARTNER

£800 to Gerry, and £200 to James. If a third of the business is £1,000, then the whole business must have been worth £3,000. Of this, 60% belongs to Gerry, and 40% to James. After the deal, both James and Gerry will own 33.3% of the business, so James is losing 6.6% while Gerry is losing 26.6%. Expressing those lost percentages in thirds for simplicity will give us James's loss at 20/3, and Gerry's at 80/3. So the money should be shared between James and Gerry in the ratio 20:80. Thus James should get £200, and Gerry £800.

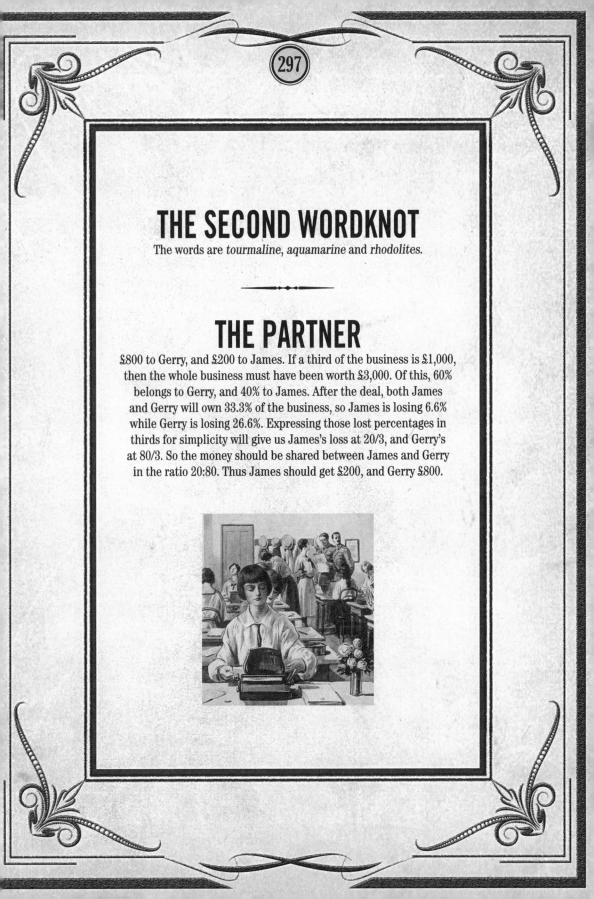

FRUITY

7. The pear = 1 apple + 6 plums. We know that 3 apple + 1 pear = 10 plums, so replacing the pear with 1 apple + 6 plums, we get 4 apple + 6 plums = 10 plums. That means apples and plums have the same weight. We know that the pear = 1 apple + 6 plums, so since 1 apple = 1 plum, the pear weighs 7 plums.

HANDS

It will be even. Two people are required for a handshake, so the total number of people shaking hands from any subset of total handshakes must always be even.

A SENSE OF URGENCY

Anything multiplied by 0 is 0.

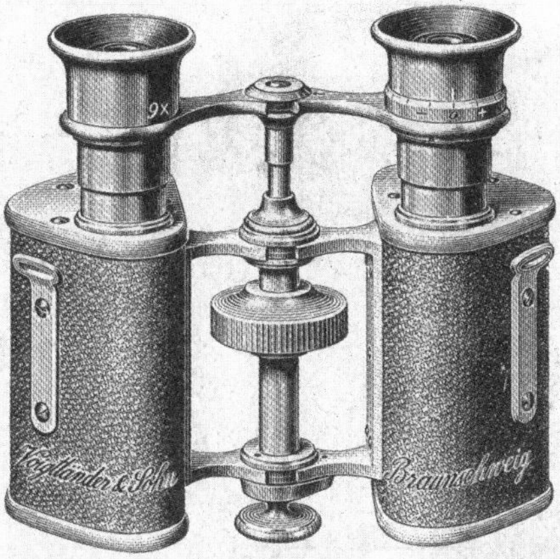

HOT AND COLD

Hot air rises, so we warm things above heat sources. Cold air thus of necessity sinks. Your best option is to place the ice on top of the cube, where it can cool your metal both with physical contact, and with the cold air flowing down from the ice.

ON THE BUSES

18 miles. Smith's walking speed is a third of his riding speed, so he spends 75% of the time walking. 75% of 8 hours is 6 hours, and 6x3=18.

HOOKLAND KNIGHTS

The number 16 belongs with the second knight. On the first knight, the pairs of numbers are all made up in their entirety of curved lines. On the second knight, the pairs of numbers contain both curved and straight lines. On the third knight, the numbers are entirely made up of straight lines.

THE THIRD WORDKNOT

The words are acrobatics, daredevils, and tightropes.

THE PAINTING

The price drops to 5/8ths of its previous amount each time. I purchased it for 25/64ths of £250, which to the nearest pound is £98 – £97.65625, to be exact.

DANIEL

The corpse is on top of the rope coils. Boutros was at the bottom of the rope, and since we know he was being belayed from above, the rest of the rope was above him. Wherever the rope fell, if it had snapped – or even been let go – the rope would be next to or above the body, not beneath it. Dickey must have thrown Boutros off the top of the cliff, after one of the two of them sent the rope over (whether deliberately or accidentally).

PART TWO

STRAIGHTFORWARD

WATER INTO WINE

Consider first the large glass. It contributes a third of its size of wine, and two thirds of water. The smaller glass is equal to a half of the large one, so it contributes an effective quarter-glass of wine, and a quarter-glass of water. Therefore we have a third plus a quarter of wine, and two thirds plus a quarter of water. Multiply these values out so that they are measured in equal twelfths. That is then 4 + 3 twelfths of wine, compared to 8+3 twelfths of water – or seven eighteenths of wine, to eleven eighteenths of water. We end up totally in eighteenths rather than the twelfths we converted to because there is a glass and a half of liquid.

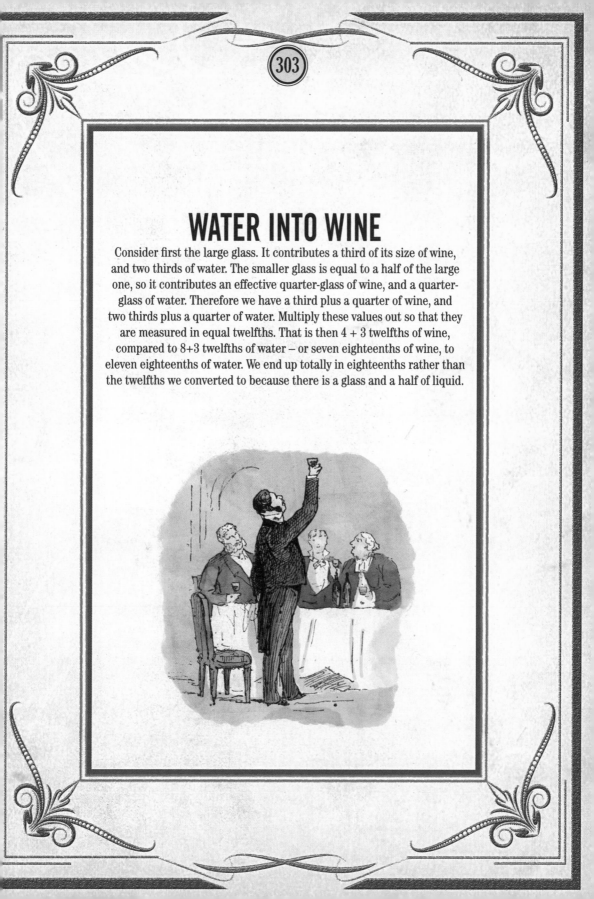

ALBY

Holmes considered the matter carefully for a moment. "It is clear that your cousin is an exemplary employee, so obviously he is not at work during his daytime rest. I assume therefore that he works the night-shift, and lives in a converted cellar or some similar basement abode that he has to walk down to get in to."

Mrs Hudson seemed genuinely delighted to have her riddle seen through so swiftly.

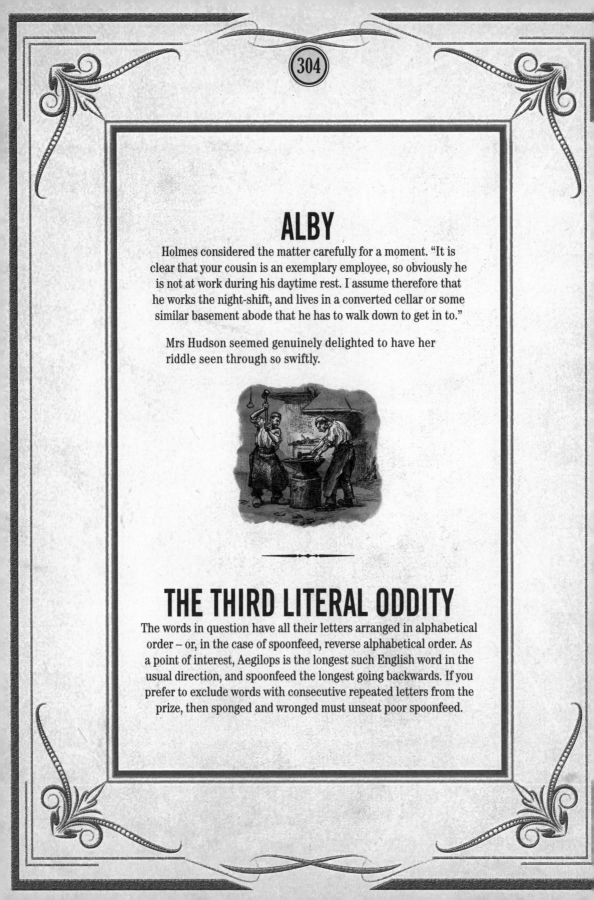

THE THIRD LITERAL ODDITY

The words in question have all their letters arranged in alphabetical order – or, in the case of spoonfeed, reverse alphabetical order. As a point of interest, Aegilops is the longest such English word in the usual direction, and spoonfeed the longest going backwards. If you prefer to exclude words with consecutive repeated letters from the prize, then sponged and wronged must unseat poor spoonfeed.

THE TIME

Regula Falsi, the technique of trying various solutions on a speculative basis, works nicely for this puzzle. Say it's 8pm. Then a quarter of the time from noon is 2hrs, and a half of the time to the following noon is 8hrs. The total is 2hrs too much. Try 9pm, giving you 2.25hrs before and 7.5hrs after. That's 9.75hrs, or 45 minutes too much. So an hour extra is worth 1.25hrs. You need to decrease the gap by .75 hrs. 0.75/1.25 is 0.6, or 36 minutes. The time is 9.36pm. A quarter of the time from noon is 2h 24m, and half the time to next noon is 7h 12m, or 9h 36m when added together.

THE FOURTH CURIOSITY

Of course, it does nothing of the sort. If you have three fourths, then a fourth is one third of that amount, not a quarter.

A VERY HUDSON CHRISTMAS

The smallest party that fits that description is just seven people – a married couple, the father's parents, and the couple's three children, two girls and a boy. Mrs. Hudson needs to set eight places, including herself.

DRIFTS

The answer lay in the passage of the wind. A large, flat surface such as the side of a house is going to divert the wind quite considerably. It has to break quite some distance before the house, in order to flow around it, and this prevents a reasonable percentage of the snow from being flung against it. This is not the case with something as small – and rounded – as a telegraph pole, so the pole gets proportionately more snow driven onto it.

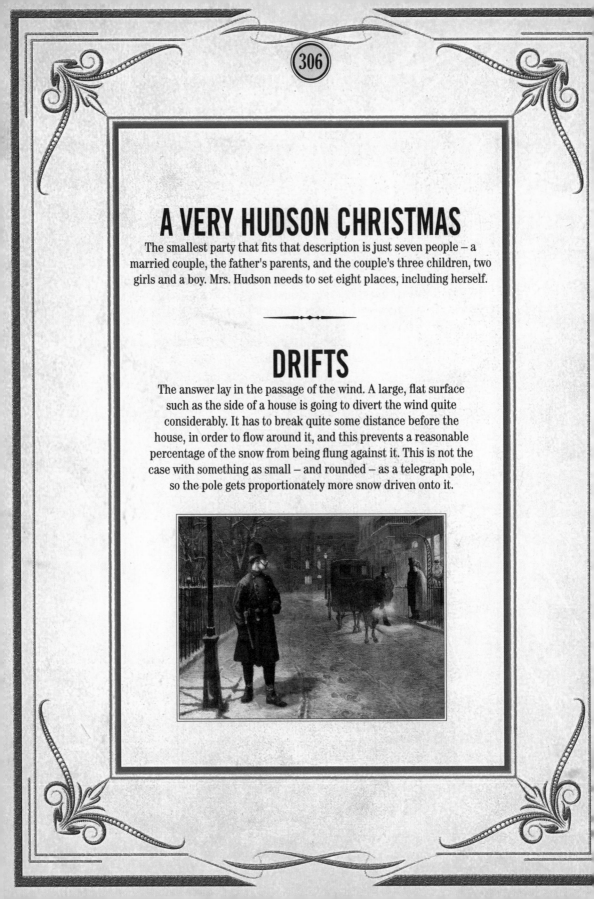

THE FOURTH MENTAL TRIAL

Alfie is 44. His age plus six years is equal to five fourths of his age minus five fourths of four years. Therefore, his age plus six years is equal to five fourths of his age minus five years. Add five to each side, and his age plus 11 is five fourths his age. Remove his age from either side, and one quarter of his age is 11. Therefore, he is 44 years old.

SUFFOLK

By judicious use of Pythagoras's theorem, and the observation that the direct line from Gosbeck to the Crowfield-Hemingstone road cuts the route into a pair of right-angled triangles, the puzzle will quickly fall to our analysis. The direct line from Gosbeck to the road I should have taken is 12 miles, forming the longer line of the triangle with Crowfield, and the shorter line of the triangle with Hemingstone. The sum of the two hypotenuse values is 35, and from this, it is rapidly clear that the distance from Crowfield to Hemingstone is 25 miles.

THE FIRE

After I finally conceded that I would probably be burnt, Holmes pointed out that the correct course of action was to set another fire, a short way down from the unburnt end. Because the wind is blowing in a fixed direction, the new conflagration will be driven in the same direction as the current one. In its wake, the new fire will leave burnt ground. As it proceeds, I would be able to follow it onto the charred area, and when the larger flame front arrived, it would be unable to get purchase in this space. Thus I would create for myself an island of safety – from the flames, anyway.

MODESTY

With 21 years between the eldest and youngest sibling, the girl must be 24, and her brother just 3.

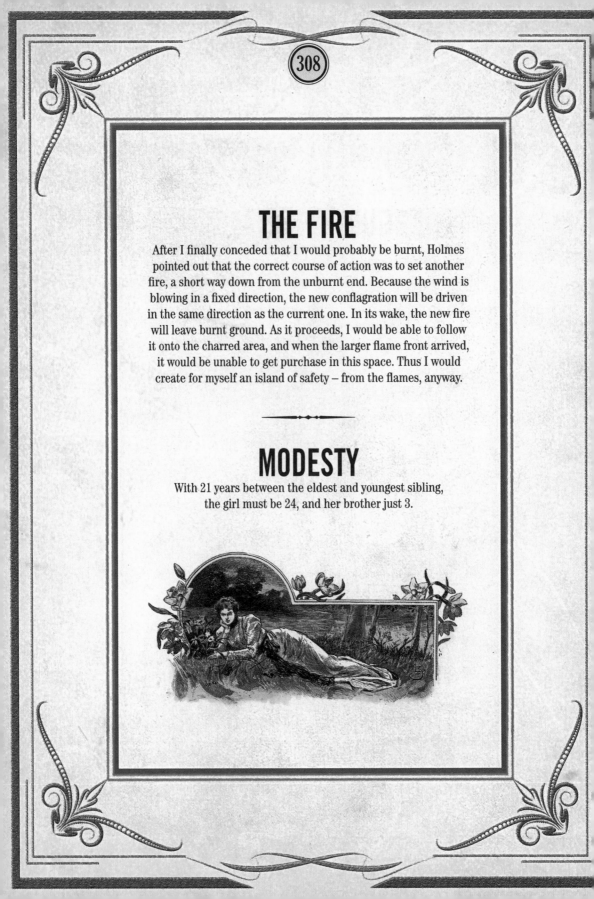

THE SEVENTH SWORD

Given the distances between the villages, the application of Pythagoras' theorem will quickly establish the height of the triangle they form, treating any one of the lines as the base. If Rushock to Chaddesley is the base, the height of the triangle to Shenstone is one and one fifth miles. This makes the area of the triangle twenty-one twenty-fifths of a square mile. Then multiply the three sides together and divide by four times the area to get the distance to the central spot, and you'll discover that the distance is thirteen sixteenths of a mile.

THE HOUSE

As it transpired, the young woman had been hired chiefly for her similarity of appearance to her employer's daughter. The unfortunate girl had begun a romance with the small fellow, a sailor, and the father was violently opposed. Whilst his daughter remained unmarried, he had the use of her inheritance from her deceased mother – the lady of the house was therefore the girl's new stepmother.

The father decided to send the sailor a dismissive message, and then confine his daughter in a small room at the top of the house. Holmes' client was there to provide the false appearance of all being as usual. Apart from our client's original hair style, the two young women were of a type, and the activities the couple had her perform were such as to give the daughter's beau the impression that life without him went on pleasantly. He didn't believe a word of it, of course.

It all ended well enough, with the lovers free of interference and married, and our client gratifyingly unmolested.

THE WOOD MERCHANT

When Holmes told me what the police were missing, I found it unbelievable that it had not occurred to me as well. The wood-merchant was well tanned. It takes months to grow a big beard, during which time the skin of the face is shielded from the sun. If he had shaved such a facial adornment off so recently, his mouth and neck would be several shades lighter than the rest of his face.

THE DARK MARRIAGE

Holmes explained to me that the man had married a woman who had died. Afterwards, he married her sister. When he himself died, the sister was left a widow – making his original wife his widow's sister.

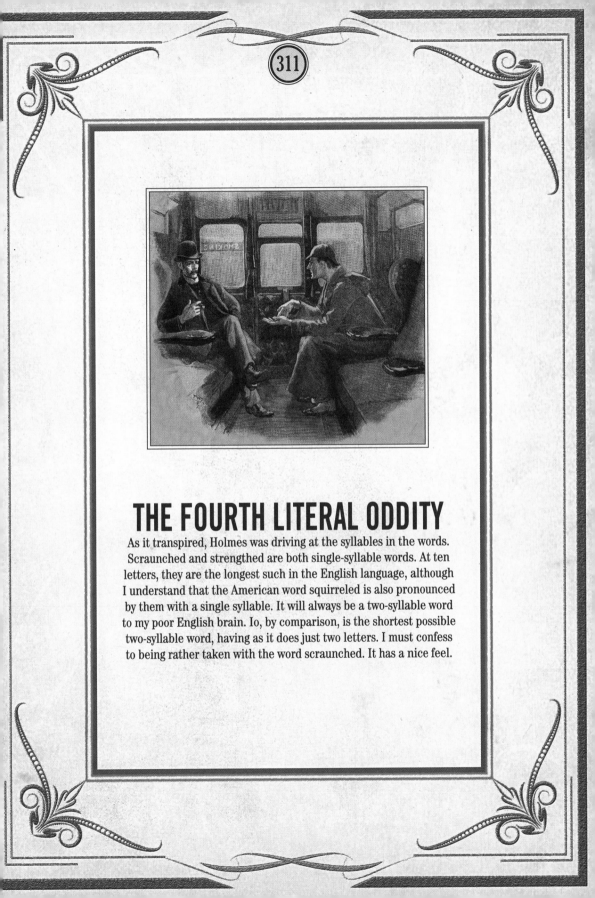

THE FOURTH LITERAL ODDITY

As it transpired, Holmes was driving at the syllables in the words. Scraunched and strengthed are both single-syllable words. At ten letters, they are the longest such in the English language, although I understand that the American word squirreled is also pronounced by them with a single syllable. It will always be a two-syllable word to my poor English brain. Io, by comparison, is the shortest possible two-syllable word, having as it does just two letters. I must confess to being rather taken with the word scraunched. It has a nice feel.

PORT AND BRANDY

I was busily trying to juggle percentages and the such when Holmes pointed out that the two decanters would both contain exactly as much liquid as when they started. This meant that however much port had gone into the brandy would be exactly offset by the amount of brandy added to the port.

I tried his blend, and as he suggested, it was in fact a very engaging drink, albeit a potent one.

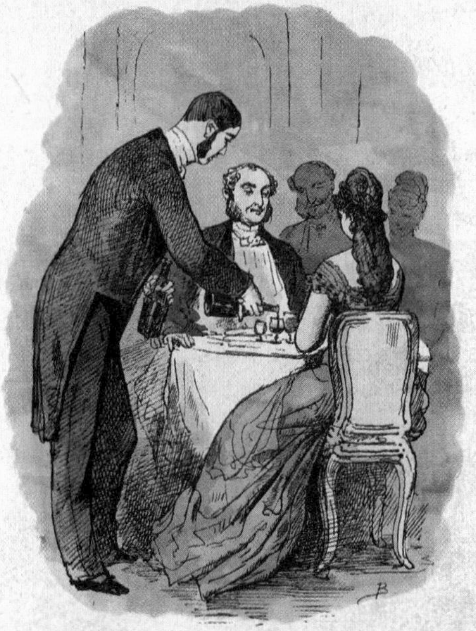

THE FIFTH MENTAL TRIAL

I managed to formulate an answer. If Holmes had less than the average number of coins, he had to bring the total average down. The average of sixty farthings across the three boys is twenty farthings each. There could not be a part-coin, so as Holmes' three coin deficit brought the average down exactly, and there were three boys, his contribution was effectively the same as removing one coin from each boy. So the average between the four was one less than it had been, or 19, and Holmes had 16 coins in his pocket.

I forestalled him before he could flip me a thrupenny bit too.

STAMINA

It was the sweat that gave him away. In such temperatures, one single half-pint of water is not enough to keep a man sufficiently hydrated to permit such luxuries as sweating. Had I been less fatigued on arrival, I would have immediately recognised that my own perspiration had long since dried up. I'm not sure whether the chap ahead of me had cut out a large chunk of the course, or obtained a surfeit of water somewhere along the route, but either way, he'd broken the terms of the exercise.

THE FIFTH CURIOSITY

It is obviously bunk. The designation 'B.C.' was not even invented until the year 532 A.D., and when Henry I was the monarch, he was known simply as Henry. He did not gain his appellate 'I' until Henry II took the throne.

THE SHOREDITCH BANK JOB

"They are writers, old friend. This is a copy of their previous crime caper." Holmes tossed a lurid-looking novel onto the table. "They wanted the details of their story to be plausible. Their book was accepted for publication last week, and the constable who had assisted them with knowledge of proper procedure was fairly paid for his time and expertise."

THE SECOND PORTMANTEAU

The image refers to none other than Windsor Castle, Queen Victoria's preferred home when engaging in Royal entertainments. The Queen herself is shown sitting in a most comfortable chair, indicating that she is both at home and at ease in this location. That alone is enough to narrow the location down considerably. The castle is sited on a small hill above the village of Windsor, and apart from its own architecture, perhaps its best-known feature is the Long Walk, a leafy parade as illustrated, which stretches south for some three miles from the castle gate.

THE DAY OF THE BOOK

During Shakespeare's lifespan, England used and kept the Julian calendar. Spain, however, changed to the Gregorian in 1582. The date of Shakespeare's death is recognised in accordance with the Julian calendar which he lived under, but if it is adjusted to the Gregorian calendar, it would actually fall on May 3rd. Cervantes died on April 23rd by the Gregorian calendar, 11 days before Shakespeare did.

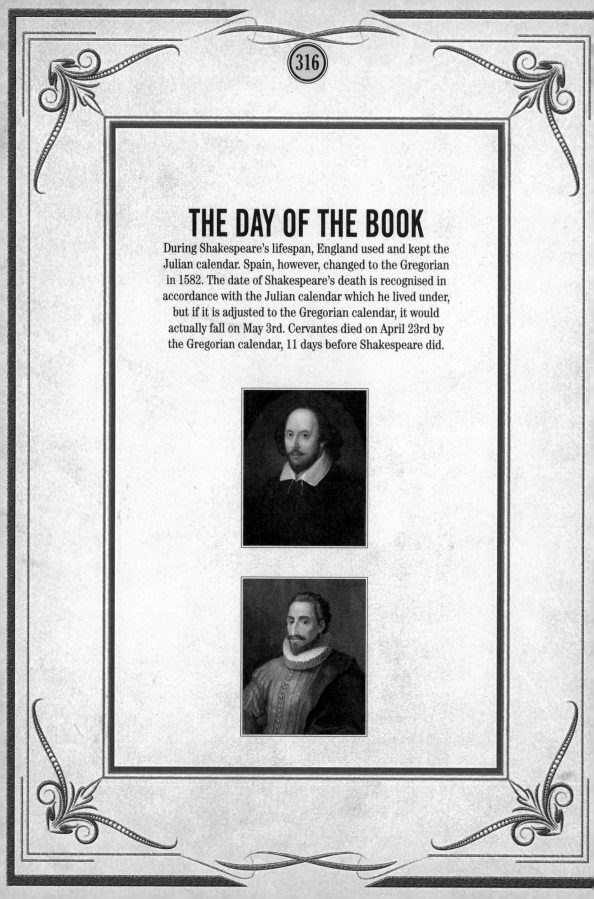

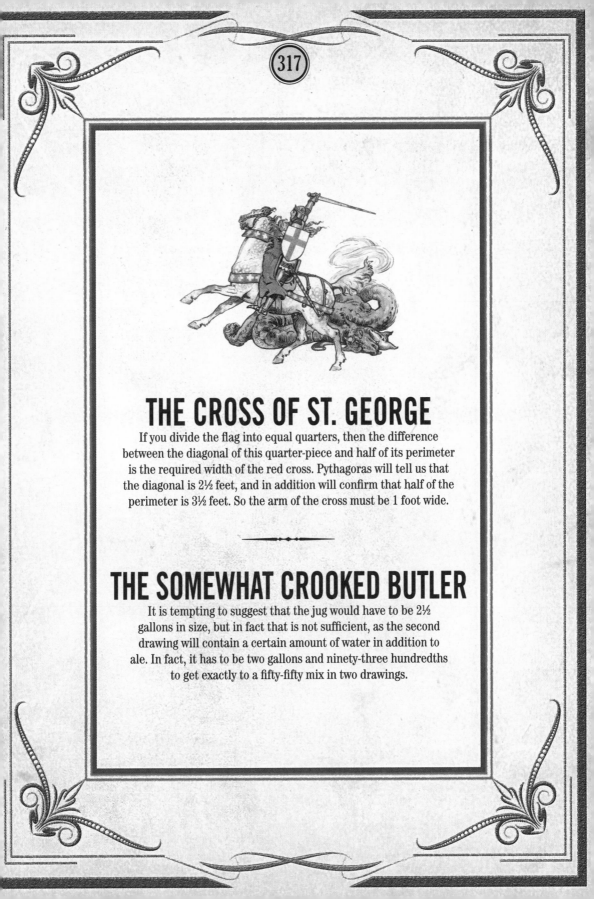

THE CROSS OF ST. GEORGE

If you divide the flag into equal quarters, then the difference between the diagonal of this quarter-piece and half of its perimeter is the required width of the red cross. Pythagoras will tell us that the diagonal is 2½ feet, and in addition will confirm that half of the perimeter is 3½ feet. So the arm of the cross must be 1 foot wide.

THE SOMEWHAT CROOKED BUTLER

It is tempting to suggest that the jug would have to be 2½ gallons in size, but in fact that is not sufficient, as the second drawing will contain a certain amount of water in addition to ale. In fact, it has to be two gallons and ninety-three hundredths to get exactly to a fifty-fifty mix in two drawings.

C

There is a solution which requires just three operators.

If you do not have it yet, you might like to take this chance to look away.

No?

Still with me?

Very well. The answer is brilliant in its simplicity.
123 - 45 - 67 + 89 = 100.

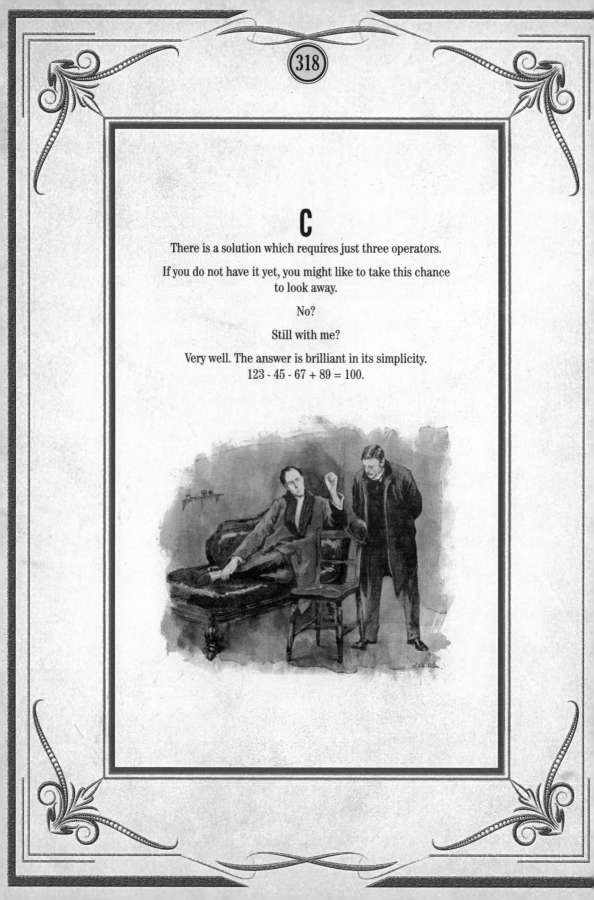

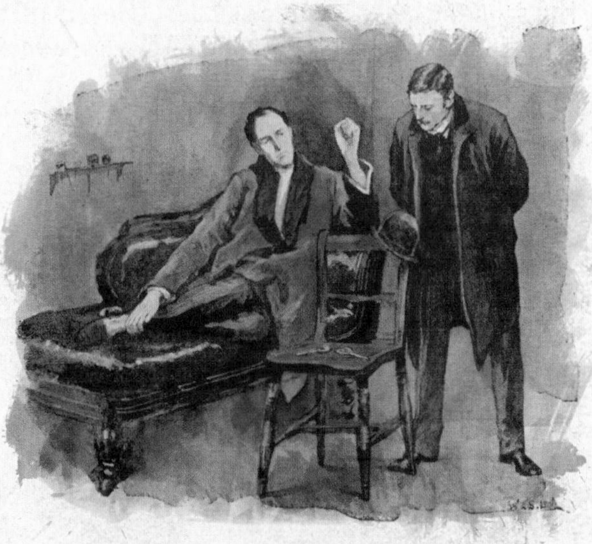

THE HUDSON CLAN

Sally is Mrs. Hudson's third cousin once removed. This means that Mrs. Hudson's great-grandmother was the sister of Sally Shaw's great-great-grandmother. Sally's grandmother – Mary, as it transpired – would thus have been a second cousin to Mrs. Hudson's mother Ada, as their grandmothers were sisters. So moving back down the generations, Mary was second cousin once removed to Mrs. Hudson, and second cousin twice removed to her son. Holmes was able to set her straight, but we were neither of us any clearer on why she needed to know.

COUSIN JENNIFER

It took me a moment or two, which tickled Mrs. Hudson greatly, but the answer did come to me eventually. Cousin Jennifer was newly born, so naturally could not do a thing for herself, nor walk out of the hospital at the tender age of seven days.

THE FIFTH LITERAL ODDITY

Both of the primary words Holmes mentioned contain the six vowel letters once and once only, in ascending alphabetical order, without any repetition. It is my belief that facetiously, at eleven letters, is the shortest such word. Subcontinental, on the other hand, has all five major vowels in reverse order, again once and once alone.

I believe it to be the longest such, provided that one discounts the noble efforts of uncomplimentary because of the out of place 'y' at the end.

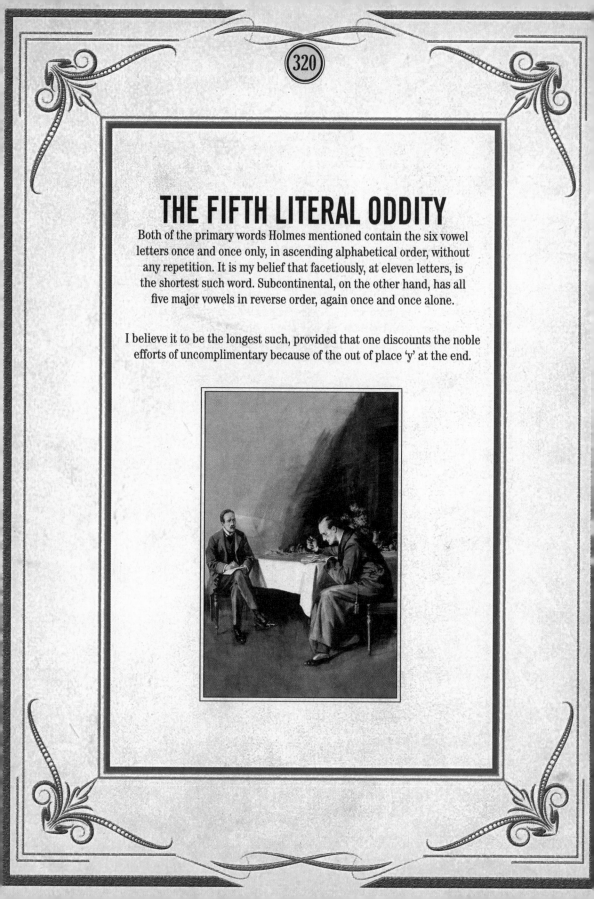

THE PLEASANT LAKE

The missing letter is "E", and the inscription says "Persevere, ye perfect men; Ever keep these precepts ten."

SLICK

It transpires that ice is not actually slippery, no more than stone is. However, its melting point is dependent on pressure. When you put weight on it, it melts (provided that the temperature is not way below freezing), and it is the water that is slippery. It refreezes when you move on. When you walk on rough ice, you have fewer points of contact between ice and shoe, and so your weight is concentrated, increasing the pressure, the amount of water, and the slipperiness. Walking on very smooth ice spreads your weight out, and minimizes the melting.

THE SECOND CAMOUFLAGE

The words are *ear*, *eye*, *lip* and *nose*, and they are all parts of the face.

FORTY-FIVE

One of the numbers has to be a quarter of one of the others, so the larger must be divisible by 4. Together, these two must add to a little more than the sum of the other two numbers, so the largest must be a small amount less than half our target. 24 and 6 both give us 12 when operated on according to instructions, but would mean the other two had to be 14 and 10, which do not sum to 15. But 20 and 5 both give 10 when adjusted, and 45–25=20, which fits with 8 and 12. So the numbers are 8, 12, 5 and 20, and 8+2 = 12–2 = 5*2 = 20/2 = 10.

ST MARY AXE

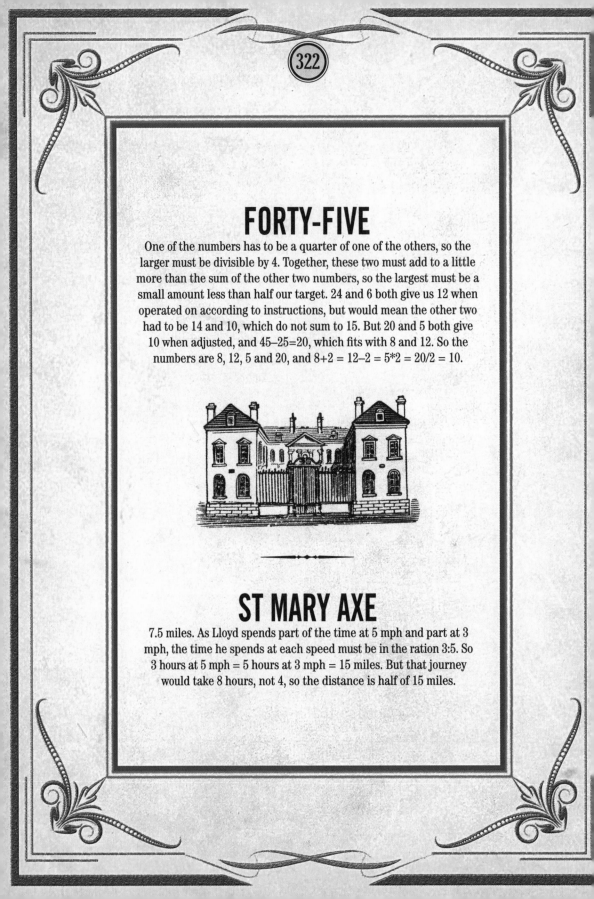

7.5 miles. As Lloyd spends part of the time at 5 mph and part at 3 mph, the time he spends at each speed must be in the ration 3:5. So 3 hours at 5 mph = 5 hours at 3 mph = 15 miles. But that journey would take 8 hours, not 4, so the distance is half of 15 miles.

RONNIE

£556. Where x is the cloak's value, x+500 = 12 (months), and x+60 = 7. Combining those, we can say that x+60 = 7*(x+500)/12. Thus 12x + 720 = 7x + 3500, so 5x = 2780, and x = 556. A modest year's salary does seem rather a staggering amount for a cape, unless it was a hand-me-down from Good Queen Bess herself, or made from overlapping scales of solid gold.

FEBRUARY

1928. There are only five of anything in February during a leap year, and then only one day, so it follows that each day of the week must get a fifth February appearance every 28 years. However, centuries are only a leap year if they are divisible by four, which rules 1900 out. The next five-Wednesday February after 1888 thus has to be 1928.

ISAAC

The trick is to obtain a pair of objects that will present an identical profile to the air, but which you can contrive to give different weight to. You then drop them, and observe them falling simultaneously. We settled on a pair of matchboxes, one with matches in and one filled with coins, but there's no end of possibilities. A pair of bottles, one empty and one full, dropped onto a cushion, perhaps.

THE CODE

Since you know the word is English, the simplest way of finding it is a matter of discovering the one-word anagrams of GAUNTOILER. The only one in common usage is REGULATION. If you prefer to attack the matter mathematically, consider the position of the numbers in the sum given. With two 5-figure numbers adding to a 6-figure one, the first digit of the answer, R, can only be "1". For the start of the 5-digit numbers, we see that G+O leave G in the units again. If either G or O was 0, the answer would be 5-digit not 6, so there must be 1 carrying over from the next column along, and O must be '9'. Similarly, A+I >= 10, in order to give the number to carry over. At the end, we see T+R=I, but R is 1, so we know I must be one greater than T. N+E=E means N must be 0. U+L must equal 9. I don't have the room here, but keep pressing the matter on this basis, and the puzzle will fall. The sum, incidentally, is 36,407 + 98,521 = 134,928.

THE TRACK

9 minutes 20 seconds. Blue is moving 4/7 the speed of red, and red needs to have run blue's distance plus one whole lap in order to pass him. After one lap of red's, blue is 3/7 of a lap behind. After two, he's 6/7 down. It should be obvious that red is closing the distance at exactly 3/7ths of a lap for each lap of his own. He has 1/7th to go, so that will take him a third of a lap. So the total distance is 2 and 1/3rd laps, which at 4 minutes a lap is 9 minutes and 20 seconds.

THE FENCE

If the length of the fence is y feet, and the number of posts is x, then x + 150 = y = 3(x – 70) = 3x – 210. So we can say that 2x = 360, or x = 180 (and, by the by, y = which would give an area of around 6,806 sq ft if made into a square enclosure, or, maximally, an area of 8,666 sq ft as a circular area of radius 52.52ft).

A CHELSEA TALE

It turned out that Jez (short for Jeremy, apparently) is a window-cleaner. He was on the outside of the building, and when he panicked, he jumped into the room in front of him.

THE FOURTH WORDKNOT

The words are *underscore*, *subheading* and *typesetter*.

THE BISCUITS

It was Stephen. Only one of the statements is true. Since Will and Stephen's statements are mutually exclusive, the true statement must be one of them. Now, assume Stephen's statement is true, and he is innocent. In this instance, the opposites of the other statements do not give a definite solution – it could still be either Mary or Gwen, neither of whom are wrongfully accused (and thus given an alibi when their accusations are negated). Since Wiggins had an immediate solution, the statements must give a firm answer. Thus Will is telling the truth, and Stephen stole (and ate) the biscuits.

DANGEROUS LADIES

30AD. Since the ladies had a total lifespan of 69 years over the course of 129 years, there must have been sixty years when neither were alive. So Boadicea was born 60 years after 30BC – in 30AD.

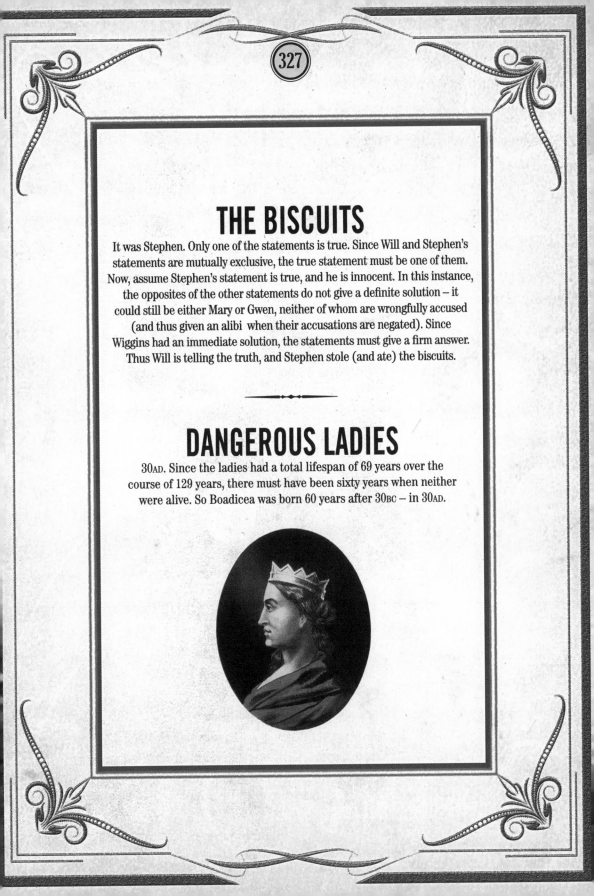

SQUARE SHEEP

12. What I finally remembered is that a circle is the most perfectly compact expression of any given area, so it follows that for any given perimeter length – ie, number of matches – the closer your shape gets to a circle, the bigger the area it contains. In this instance, a perfectly regular 12-sided shape (a dodecagon) with sides of length 1 will give you an area of 11.19y2, since the area of a dodecagon is 0.5 * 12 * side-length * distance from centre to the middle of any side (which is 1.865 * side-length). Similarly, a perfectly regular 11-sided shape (an endecagon) with sides of length 1 works out at 9.365y2. So you can make a 10y2 space with 12 yard-long fences.

MR ANDREAS

£14,315. To calculate simple compound interest of this sort (that is, where the interest is calculated once per designated time unit), you can calculate the 55% manually, add it to the base sum, and repeat a series of times. But it is simpler and more efficient to use the formula A = P * (1+r)^t, where A is the accrued wealth, P is the principal (or initial) capital, r is the rate of interest as a fraction, and t is the number of iterations. So in this instance, A = 1600 * (1+0.55)^5, or 1600 * 8.9466.

DAVEY

The only possible answer is that when Wiggins turned around and started walking towards Davey, Davey started walking backwards at the same pace. Peculiar behaviour, to be sure.

THE WATCH

Jim worked 00:00 – 06:00 and 10:00 – 16:00.

Dave worked 04:00 – 10:00 and 16:00 – 22:00.

Peter worked 12:00 – 18:00 and 22:00 – 04:00.

Mike worked 06:00 – 12:00 and 18:00 – 00:00.

THE FIFTH WORDKNOT

Twittering. Chattiness. Volubility.

THE LEASE

45. From Archie's statement, $4x/5 = 2y/3$, and $x+y = 99$. So $12x=10y$, or $x=10y/12$. Now substitute, so $10y/12+y = 99$, or $10y + 12y = 1188$, or $22y=1188$, so $y=54$. Then, $x+54 = 99$, or $x=45$. There are 45 years left.

TEA

9. First, place the 5lb and 9lb weights in different pans, so that 4lb of tea will balance them. Weigh four such 4lb lots, leaving (of necessity) 4lbs in the bale. Then take each 4lb lot in turn, remove the weights from the scales, and divide each lot so that it is perfectly balanced. This will add five weighings to the four previous, for a total of nine.

LOOSE CHANGE

I started out with 220p, which is of course just tuppence short of nineteen shillings. The trick is to start at the end and work backwards. So 6+9+6 = 21*2 = 42 + 10 = 52*2 = 104 + 6 = 110*2 = 220.

HOW MANY COWS

121,393. The Fibonacci sequence is a famous mathematical model describing exponential growth of precisely this kind, such that each number in the sequence is the sum of the two numbers preceding it. It runs 0, 1, 1, 2, 3, 5, 8, ..., where in this instance, the terms of the sequence would indicate the number of calves produced in that year. It is useful here to note that the sum total of all numbers up to any Nth term in the sequence is equal to the (N+2)th term minus one. Further more, as N = (N–1) + (N–2) – the basic definition of the sequence – then also (N+2) = 2*(N) + (N–1). So from those two, it follows that if we know two sequential terms, N and N–1, then the total of all the values in the sequence up to N is equal to 2*(N) + (N–1) –1. The 24th and 25th terms of the sequence are 48,368 and 28,657, so the black woodland cow would have a total of 2*(48,368)+(28,657)–1=121,392 descendants in that time. She, of course, is still active, for a total 121,393 cows. That's a lot of cows behaving quite oddly, so I can see Mr Podge's concern somewhat.

ODD

My eventual answer was to combine two 1s to make 11, so that 11 + 1 + 1 + 1 = 14. You could do it other ways if you added in other mathematical operations – 1/1 + 9 + 3 + 1, for example.

DRAFT

As the window cools, the air in the room next to it gets colder. Cold air sinks, so the warmer air of the room gets pulled down to fill the space. Then it too chills. This effect produces a circular draft from fireplace to window, with warm air running along the ceiling, and cold air along the floor. We feel this as a draft. This is part of the reason why Mr San Galli's excellent heating radiators are often placed below windows.

THE SEAMSTRESS

When it's dark, it's very hard to see anything outside from a lit room. This is particularly true when it's raining, no matter how lightly. Since the house is in a rural environment, there would have been nothing in the way of extra light to illuminate the fellow. She must have made up the intruder to prepare the way for some other mischief to take place.

BEES

Just 15 bees, which seems to me to be a low estimate by a factor of 1,000, even for a small hive. Still, we must tackle the situation as expressed by Holmes's correspondent. We know that two of the factions of bees represent 1/5th and 1/3rd of the workers. Expressing those figures in a common denominator makes for 3/15ths and 5/15ths. The difference between these amounts is 2/15ths, which multiplied by 3 gives us 6/15ths. These bees account for 3+5+6=14/15ths of the workers. The remaining 1/15th of the workers is 1 bee, so 1*15 = 15.

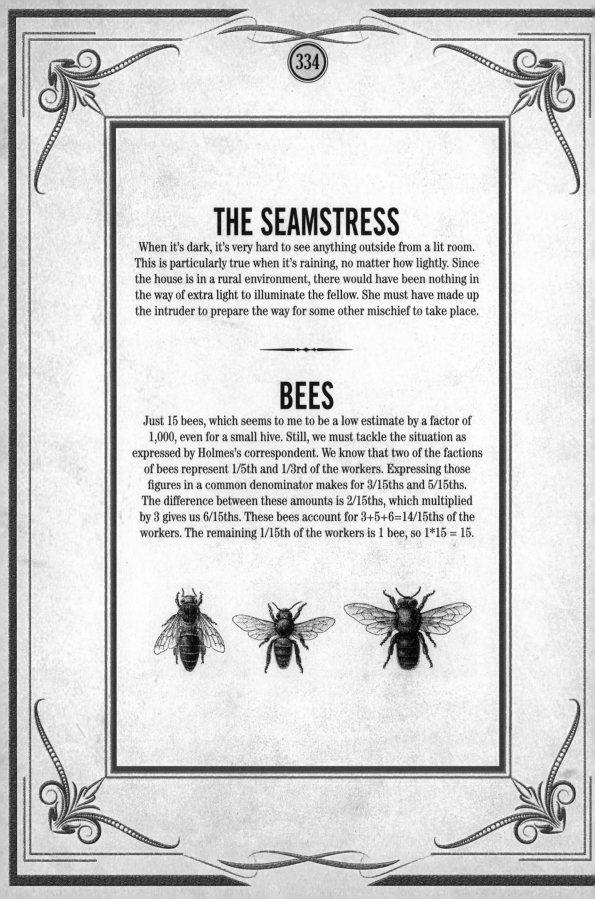

FRUITFUL

It is just three pieces of fruit, one of each type, as a moment's thought will swiftly make clear.

THE THIRD CAMOUFLAGE

The words were *bill*, *fund*, *loss* and *sell*, and the theme was business.

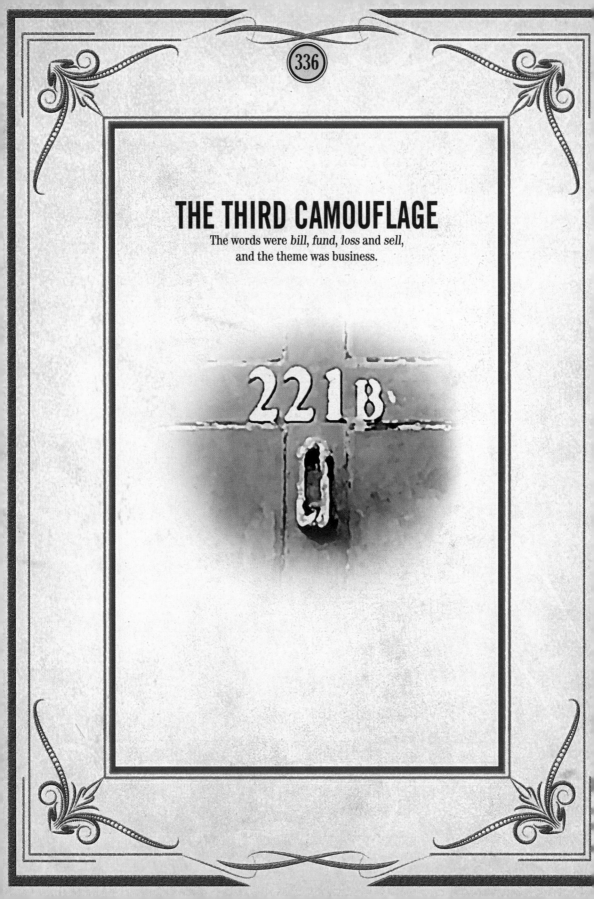

SPEED

Sid won again. In the previous races, Ray ran 90y whilst Sid ran 100y. So in the last race, Ray and Sid would be neck and neck at the 90-yard point, Ray having run 90y and Sid 100y. In the remaining 10y, Sid continued outpacing Ray and won.

PART THREE

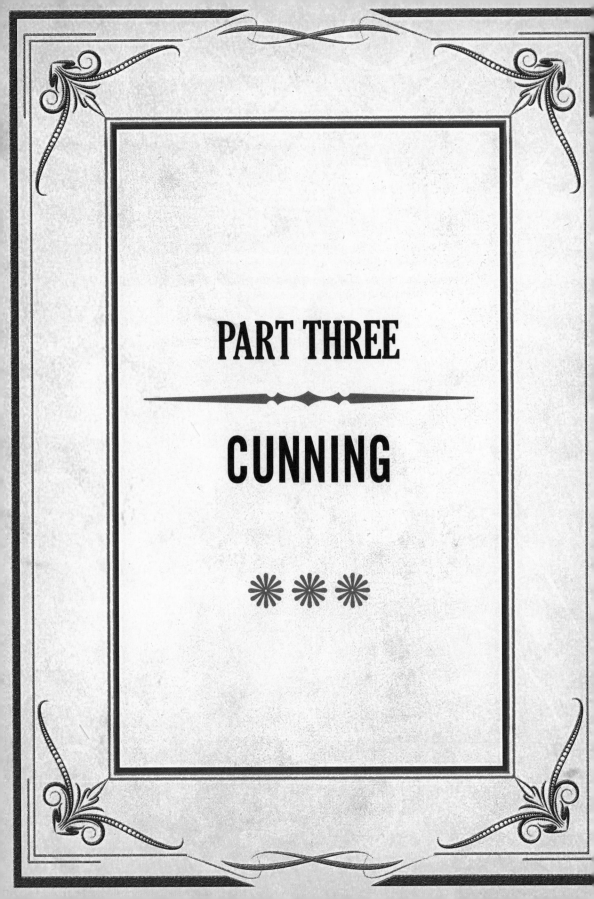

CUNNING

THE STATUETTE

"Watson old chap, you'd best stick to medicine," Holmes said. "The two men were in cahoots. The pair pick a likely item. One buys it and talks up the value of its twin, and then the other sells it back again to the same dealer, at great profit. They split the proceeds, and when the poor dealer comes hoping to sell what he thinks is the companion piece, his original client has moved on. Instead of making £800, he has lost £200. The pair were only caught in their deception because they became greedy, and tried two such stings in London in too short a space of time."

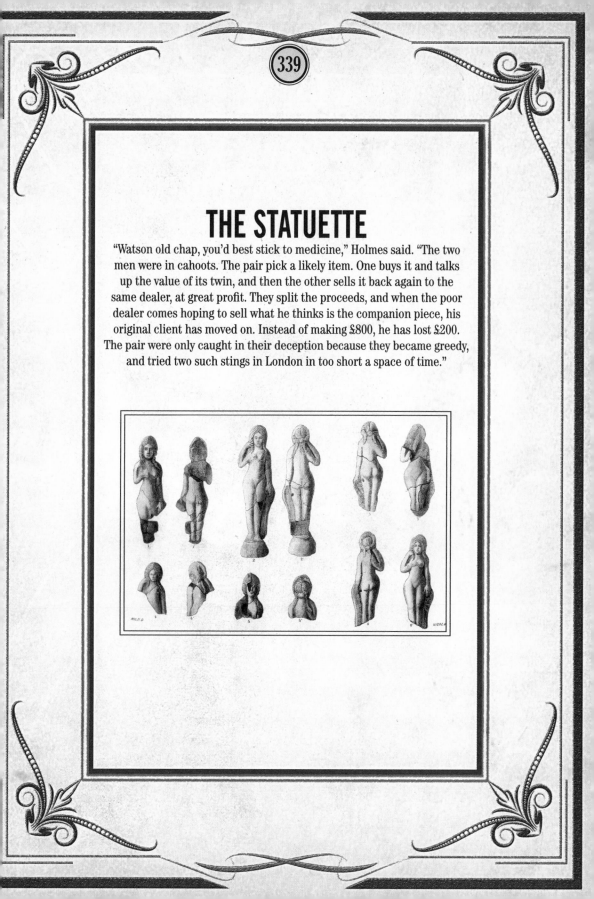

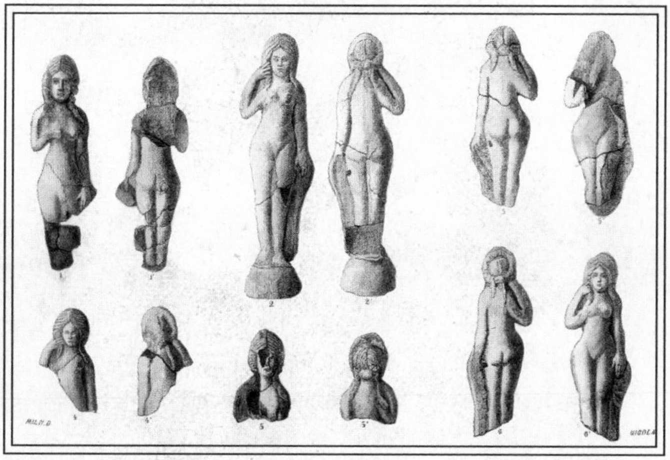

DEDICATION

I am, of course, talking about clocks - ranging in number of components from hourglasses, with their myriad of sand grains, down to the good old sundial. Grandfather clocks can be far larger than a man, whilst some truly miniscule hourglasses are available.

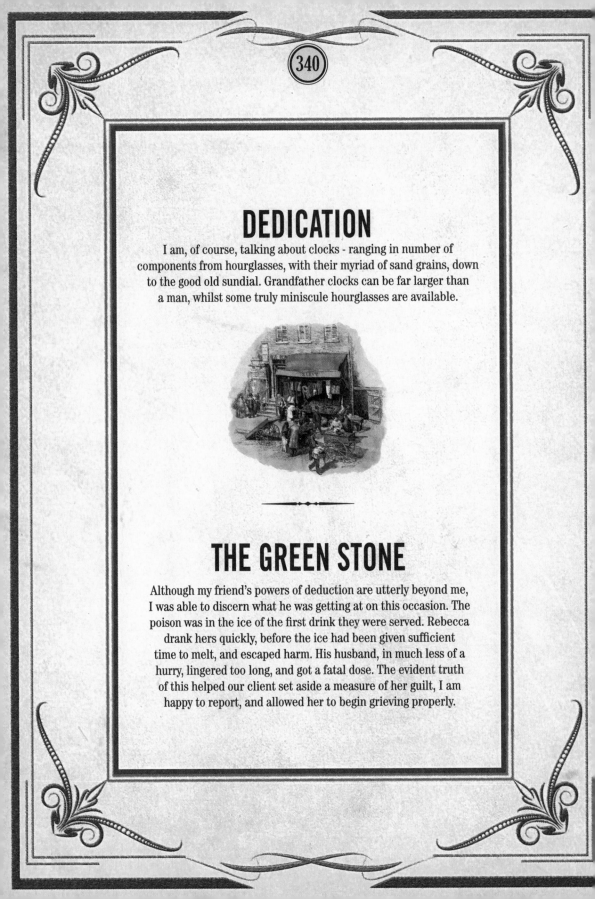

THE GREEN STONE

Although my friend's powers of deduction are utterly beyond me, I was able to discern what he was getting at on this occasion. The poison was in the ice of the first drink they were served. Rebecca drank hers quickly, before the ice had been given sufficient time to melt, and escaped harm. His husband, in much less of a hurry, lingered too long, and got a fatal dose. The evident truth of this helped our client set aside a measure of her guilt, I am happy to report, and allowed her to begin grieving properly.

THE SIXTH CURIOSITY

Upon reflection, no, it is in fact a wild bilking. Two 6" circles together are half as large as one 12" circle. Mrs. Hudson should have paid half her usual sum.

THE CULT OF THE RED STAR

It turns out he was referring to the same man by each of those relationships. The victim's mother was the murderer's sister (father's brother-in-law). The victim had a brother, who had married the murderer's daughter (brother's father-in-law), and he himself had married the daughter of the murderer's brother (father-in-law's brother).

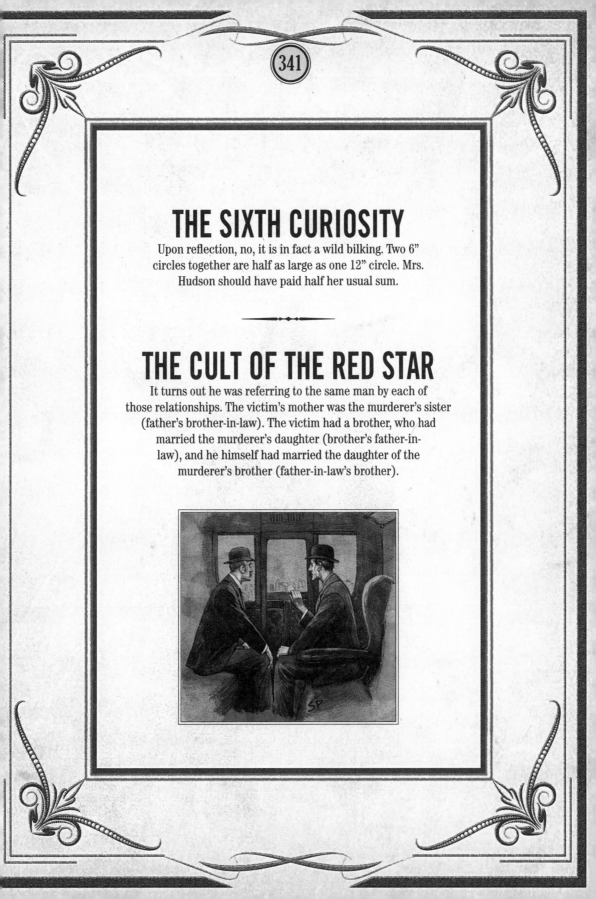

AFTERNOON

It can only be twenty-six minutes to six.

THE SIXTH LITERAL ODDITY

They are all words which have no repeated letters. Being fifteen letters long, they each make use of more than half of the alphabet. I was amused to note that despite this, there are six letters which none of the four encompasses.

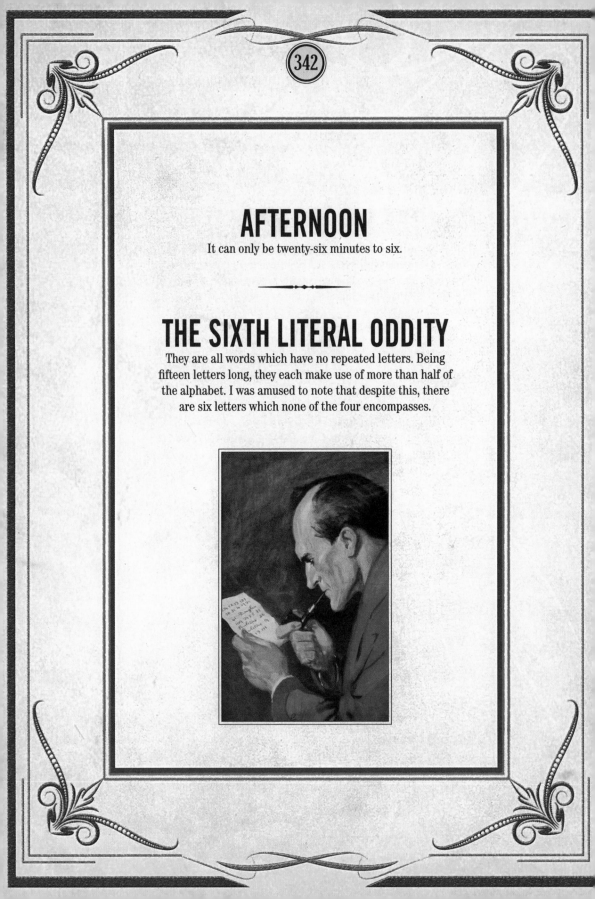

SUFFOCATION

The question that Holmes asked was: "Did you see the time reflected in the hall mirror?" The poor maid gasped, and went as white as a sheet, because of course that was exactly what she had done. The nephew had left at 6:11, not at 5:49, and eventually the murderous fool confessed that he'd killed his aunt in desperation, as she was about to write him out of her will.

THE SIXTH MENTAL TRIAL

The four are descended from each other in a straight line. It is the only way to order the switching around. George is Alfie's father, Fred is Alfie's son, and Harry is Alfie's infant grandson.

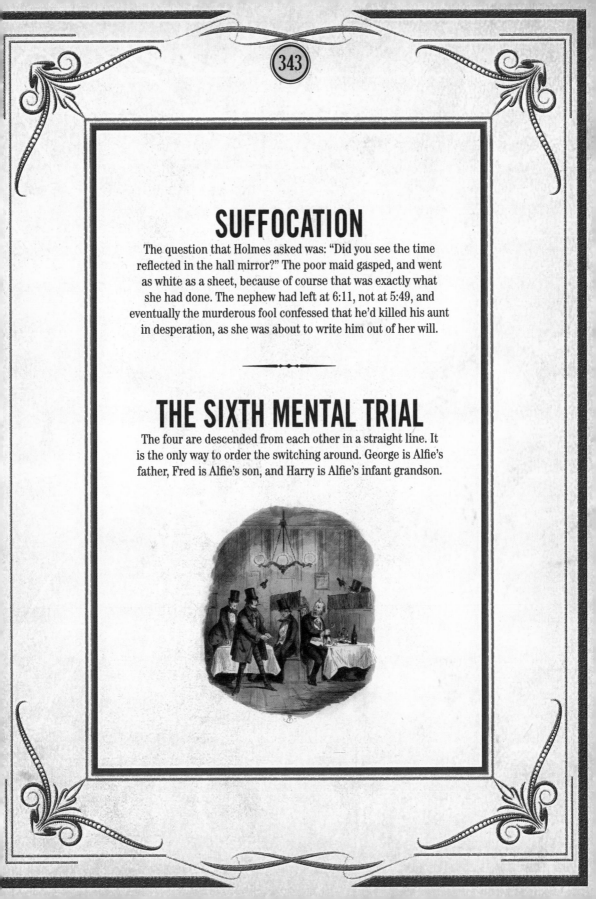

WATCH OUT

"It's the difference in air pressure," Holmes informed me. "Higher up, the air is thinner. Makes it harder to breathe, but it also means that the air gives less resistance to the watch spring. This makes it run faster."

THE DINNER TABLE

There is only one pair of solutions that will give each man new partners every time, and yet still keep George 3 seats away around the table, and Bill just two seats distant. These are as follows: Alfie, Fred, Bill, Don, George, Eric, Charlie; and Alfie, Eric, Bill, George, Charlie, Fred, Don.

THE BICYCLE

If you process through the years and consider the ratios, the answer will quickly become apparent. Three times 13 is 39, seven years out; a year later, three times 14 is 42, five years off the mother's new age of 47. So for each year that passes, the time to close the gap shortens by two years. If you stick with jumping whole years however, the gap will go from 1 year to -1 year, so you need to use a half-year to get the gap to exactly zero. At 15, it is 3 years difference, at 16 it is 1 year, so at 16½ the girl will be exactly a third of her mother's age, which will be 49½. The girl has to wait 3½ years.

HIGHLAND FLING

"It's as plain as the hairs on your head, Watson. The supposed witch packed the bell with snow before her dramatic entrance. It stopped the bell sounding, and then either shook loose thanks to the exertions of the bell-ringer, or melted away in the intervening time. I'd need to check in person to see which, and I have no intention of doing any such thing. Either way, the addled locals failed to notice the obvious explanation, turning instead to the most arrant foolishness."

BIG SQUARES

You will discover that the smallest possible nine-digit square number which makes use of each of the digits once and once alone is 139,854,276.

THE SEVENTH LITERAL ODDITY

To my surprise, it turns out that there are just three words ending in -bt, doubt, debt and redoubt. Their commonality fooled me into the assumption that if I could think of three off the top of my head there had to be many more, but it is not the case. Likewise, there are just three standard words ending with -gry – angry, hungry, and the reasonably obscure puggry, the latter being a light head-scarf worn over a hat as additional solar protection.

THE CIRCUS

The murdered performer had taken the magician's assistant as a sweetheart, but he had a lethally jealous rival – the musical conductor. The trapeze act used the musical score to provide the necessary split-second timing. Holmes had heard the conductor change the timing of the music, speeding it up just enough so that when it came to make his dashing leap, the trapeze artist was out of position. He leapt too soon, trusting the music, and crashed to his death.

URCHINS

Every lad will walk next to every other lad once, so will form eight pairs. Four of those pairs will be formed two at a time, when he is in the middle of the three, and the other four singly, when he is on the end of a group. Therefore he will require six outings to walk with everyone once.

THE THIRD PORTMANTEAU

The solution is that the image points to the Palace of Westminster, commonly referred to as the Houses of Parliament. The elegant building represents the House of Lords, our parliament of inherited peers. The rougher one represents the House of Commons, our elected representatives, although I must hasten to point out that our parliamentarians are to be considered common only in the sense of not being Peers of the Realm. The two Houses are ineluctably intertwined in the government of Britain, as the rope indicates. The arguing men indicate the political divisions in British public life, which ever invite raucous debate – often, I'd wager, such disagreements are more for the look of the thing than from any great variance of principle, but still, disagreements they remain. The pole with the carriage clock represents the mighty St. Stephen's clock tower which so characterises the view of central London. In the image, this is overshadowed by the bell; this reflects the fact that the tower itself is overshadowed by Big Ben – its most famous occupant, the great bell which rings out the hour.

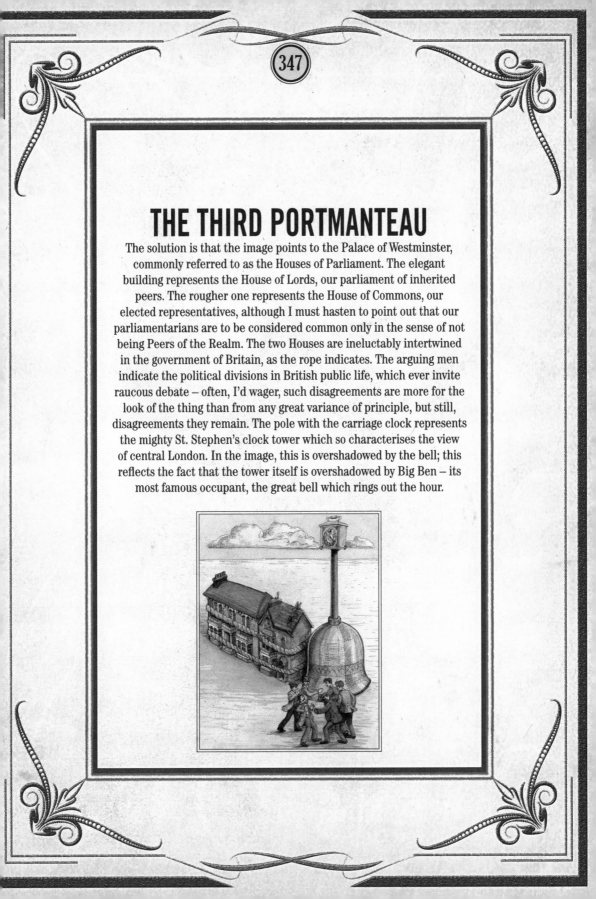

THE MEADOW OF DEATH

As Holmes pointed out, the lack of any signs of human agency in the couple's demise suggested some sort of environmental factor. We know that they were not poisoned, so toxic gas is ruled out. The lack of broken limbs, the proximity to the village, and their being hand in hand together all suggest that they were not in notable distress prior to their deaths, so that whatever killed them was very sudden. By Holmes' confession, he had made no mention of the length of time that they had been dead. As it transpired, they had been out walking in the winter, and had been completely buried in a sudden slide of snow. They had remained there, hidden, all winter, only to be discovered after the thaw had come.

THE EGG

Holmes proposed that the answer lay in Mr. Darwin's theory of natural selection. Birds, Holmes observed, habitually breed in lofty places – trees, cliffs, and the like. In such a situation, an egg which was able to roll any great distance would surely be at a disadvantage. By contrast, the oddly unbalanced shape which is so familiar to us all will roll on a swiftly curving path, making it a safer design.

THE EIGHTH LITERAL ODDITY

The two are amongst the longest English words which are anagrams of each other. Furthermore, and even more impressively, they do not share any letter-pairs in common, neither is any letter in one of the words in the same position in the other. That is quite a feat, in a fourteen-letter anagram pair.

This may be compared to the admittedly longer anagram pair of conservationalists and conversationalists, which at eighteen letters, are the longest non-scientific English anagram pair, but where the only difference is the rather trivial transposition of the 's' and the 'v'.

GOLD

The box is 100x100" square, and 11" deep. The floor of the box contains layers of eight by nine slabs, leaving a one inch gap on the side. Eleven of these layers will fill the box to the top, accounting for 792 of the slabs. That leaves eight slabs to go in on their edge in a space 100 inches by 11 inches – one exact row of eight slabs lengthways.

STONES

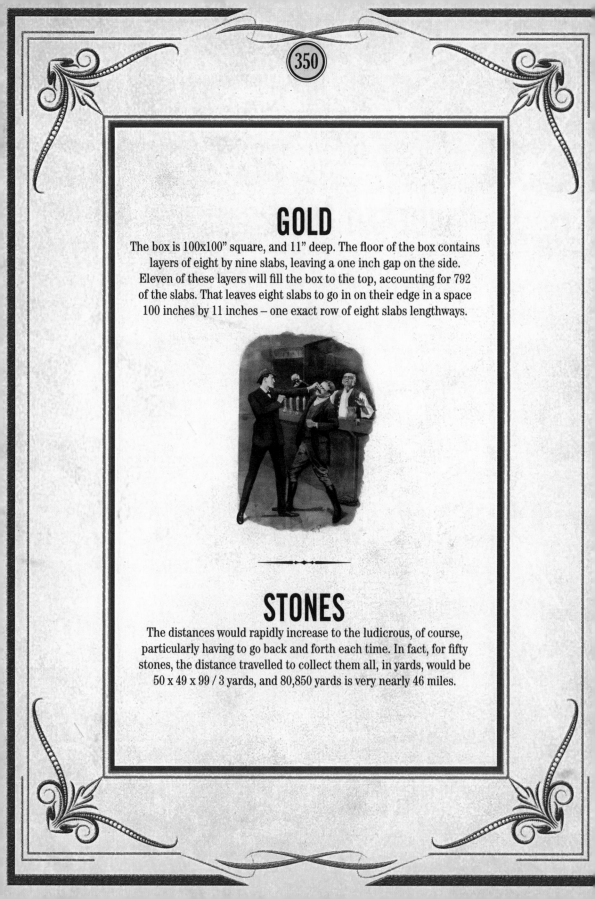

The distances would rapidly increase to the ludicrous, of course, particularly having to go back and forth each time. In fact, for fifty stones, the distance travelled to collect them all, in yards, would be 50 x 49 x 99 / 3 yards, and 80,850 yards is very nearly 46 miles.

THE SEVENTH CURIOSITY

It took me a long moment to recollect t hat Herod had ordered only boy children slain. All the feet would have belonged to boys.

FENCING

"That sort of tone can only be caused from a flat, dull noise by broken reflections of sound," Holmes explained. "You would need to be near a set of railings of some sort, or something of a similar structure with many small bars close together in parallel. Each one reflects a tiny fraction of the sound, but at a precisely staggered interval, being slightly further away than the last. It is this effect which causes the apparent ringing."

THE SOHO PIT

The man is going twice as deep as he has done so far, so when finished, the hole will be a total of three times its present depth. The current depth of the hole has to be less than his height, and, when finished, greater than his height but less than twice that. Within those bounds, the only solution is that the hole is currently 3ft 6 deep, and when finished, will be 10ft 6.

THE SEVENTH MENTAL TRIAL

Alfie has two brothers, and four sisters. With three men and four women, each woman has three of each sex of sibling, and each man has two brothers and four sisters. Bill, by comparison, is from a family of five. Each of the brothers has one brother and three sisters, and each of the sisters has two of each. So Alfie, with two brothers, has one more than Bill does.

THE HANGED MAN

As Holmes was so fond of saying, when the impossible had been discounted, the improbable, no matter how unlikely, had to be the truth. It was impossible that the killer had left the room so securely fastened, so he had to still be in the room, and that meant the death was a suicide. Holmes' fingers were wet after touching the carpet because the artist used a block of ice to stand on when fastening his noose to the ceiling, wearing boots against the cold. Then he kicked the block down flat and died, determined to leave one last riddle. The ice later melted, but the carpet was still damp.

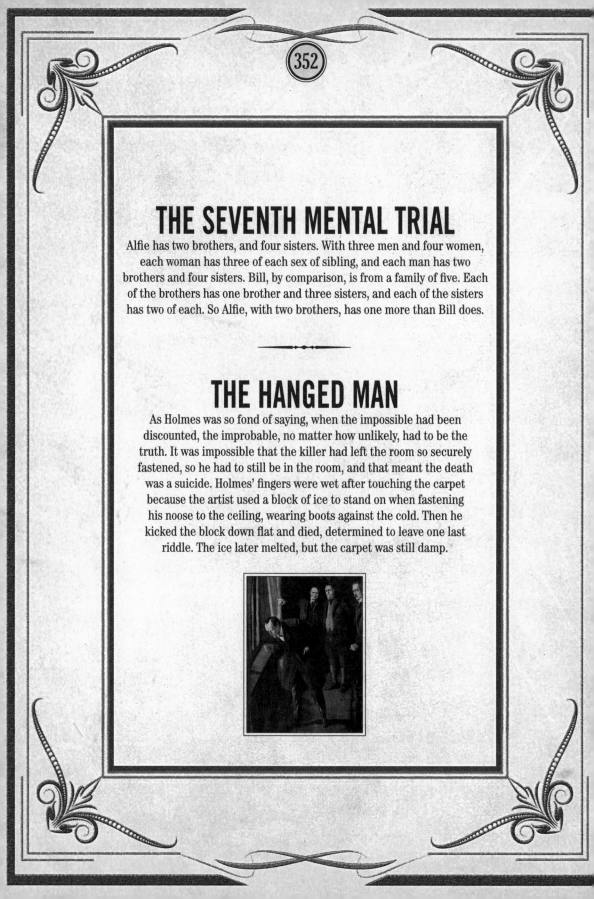

A HEARTY DROP

The first action is to fill the pail, and then fill the jar from the pail. Alfie then quaffs the contents of the pail. There are now 7 pints in the barrel, 3 pints in the jar, and 2 pints in Alfie.

Next, the contents of the jar are poured back into the pail, and the jar is filled again from the barrel. That leaves 4 pints in the barrel, which Bill grabs happily, and three pints in each vessel.

The jar is poured into the pail until the pail is full, leaving 1 pint inside the jar, and five in the pail. Charlie drinks the pint in the jar. Then the jar is filled again from the pail, leaving two pints inside it. Charlie takes the jar, for his four pints in total, and Alfie gets the pail, with his remaining two pints. The men can then take more time over their remaining drinks, although Bill has some catching up to do.

THE BARN

"I'll put you out of your misery, Inspector. It is a simple enough matter. Your fellow rode to the barn during the snowstorm. The snowfall obliterated the signs of his passing. He then turned the shoes round on his horse, so they were pointing in the wrong direction.

"Without inspecting the barn myself, I cannot say whether he found the tools he needed on site, and was struck by inspiration, or whether he brought them with him with confusion in mind all along. If the latter, he may have removed the horse's shoes before the evening's escapade began. Either way, it is no great matter to put them on back to front.

"Then, with his horse suitably attired, he waited until the snow stopped, and rode off, boldly leaving a clear trail that would be sure to fox his pursuit."

SOLARIS

Since the Sun appears to rise in the east, the Earth revolves counterclockwise on its axis. So at true midnight by local time, the Earth is spinning you in exactly the same direction as it is moving around the Sun, and at true midday, it is spinning you in exactly the opposite direction. Therefore you are going faster at midnight. A a point near the equator (less as you move towards the poles), your speed varies by about 0.3 miles per second either way from Earth's base speed of around 18 miles per second around the Sun. But don't worry, the Sun itself (with our solar system, obviously) is moving at up to 500 miles per second through the universe, so your variation in speed is quite minor.

A WORSHIP OF WRITERS

Tomkins. From the information given, Squires must the playwright, Appleby the historian, Whitely the humorist, Archer the poet, Gardner the short story writer, and Tomkins the novelist.

LOGGERS

360ft cubic feet of wood, which works out at a little over 2.8 cords. The relative amount of time Doug and Dave spend sawing and splitting must match the ratio of how much of each job they can perform in one day – that is, they must divide their day by 6:9, or 2:3. Thus they must spend 3/5ths of the day sawing, which is slower, and 2/5ths of the day splitting. 3/5ths of 600 is 360 cubic feet of wood (as is 2/5ths of 900).

THE SIXTH WORDKNOT

The words were violinists, trumpeters, and pianoforte.

DUCK DUCK GOOSE

4 shillings. Starting with 1 for a chicken gives you 2 for a duck, which, in the second equation of 3c + d = 2g would mean that 3*1 + 1*2 = 2*goose = 5. But we can't have 2.5 shillings for a goose. So double the chicken and duck prices. 3*2 + 1*4 = 10, giving 5 for a goose. Try that in the third equation of 3g + 1c + 2d = 25. 3*5 + 1*2 + 2*4 = 15 + 2 + 8 = 25. So 5s, 4s and 2s are the correct prices, and a duck is 4s.

THE JEWELLER

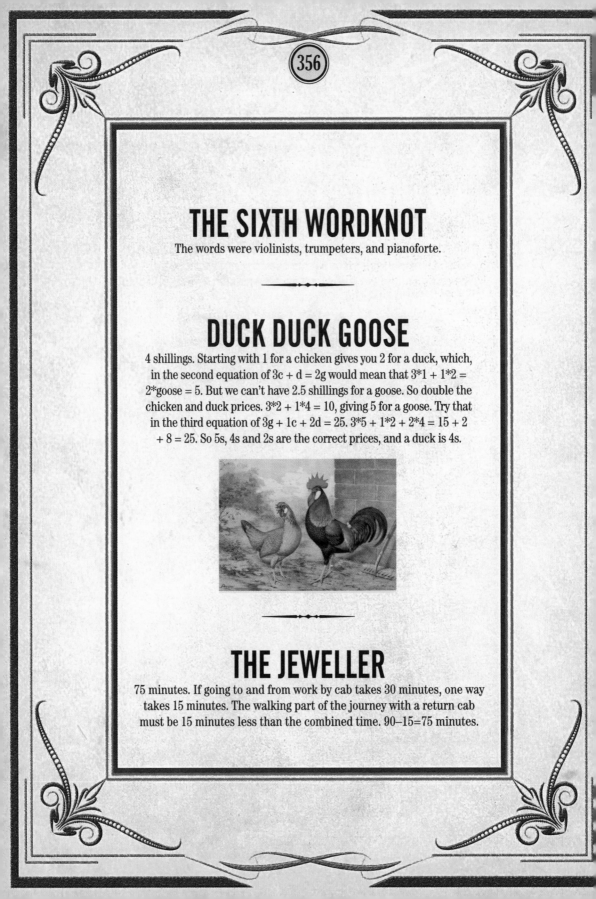

75 minutes. If going to and from work by cab takes 30 minutes, one way takes 15 minutes. The walking part of the journey with a return cab must be 15 minutes less than the combined time. 90–15=75 minutes.

THE NOTE

13 21 13 21 32 21 12. Speak the digits aloud, and it will become clear that each line is described by the numbers in the following line – so "One 2"; then "One one, one two"; then "Three 1s, one 2," and so on.

THE LEGACY

£24. We know that $x + y = 100$, and that $x/4 - y/3 = 11$. Multiply out the divisors in that second equation (i.e. *12), and you get $3x - 4y = 132$. Now $x=100-y$, so $3*(100-y) - 4y = 132$, and $300 - 3y - 4y = 132$, or $7y = 300 - 132 = 168$. So $y = 168/7 = 24$. (And x, Frederick's bequest, must be £76).

CHILDREN

3 of one and 1 of the other is more likely. There are 16 possibilities (2 options, 4 times = 2^4 = 16), all equally likely. Of those, 2 are single-gender, BBBB and GGGG. Eight are 3–and–1: BGGG, GBGG, GGBG, GGGB, and their opposites. Six are two of each – BBGG, BGBG, BGGB, and their opposites. So there's a 8/16 (or 50%) chance of three children of one gender, a 6/16 (or 37.5%) chance of two of each gender, and a 2/16 (or 12.5%) chance of all the children being the same gender. As an aside, do note that about 1 human pregnancy in 90 produces twins, which may somewhat complicate a more precise calculation, and in practice, the chance of a male birth is very rarely exactly 50%, so the terms of this question are not rigorous reflections of reality.

THE TRUNK

35 yards. We don't know the tractor's speed, but it moves a certain distance – Y – for each pace Holmes takes. So when he has moved 140 yards, the front of the tree has moved 140Y yards. Holmes has walked that distance plus the length of the tree, x, in that time, so in yards, 140 = x +140Y. In the other direction, Holmes has walked 20 paces, so the tip of the tree has moved 20Y yards. Since they're going in opposite directions, their combined distance equals the length of the tree, and x = 20 + 20Y. So now we have x = 20 + 20Y, and x = 140 – 140Y. So 20 + 20Y = 140 – 140Y, and 1+Y = 7–7Y, thus 8Y=6, or Y=0.75. Since x=20+20Y, then x=20+15 = 35 yards.

THE REVENGE

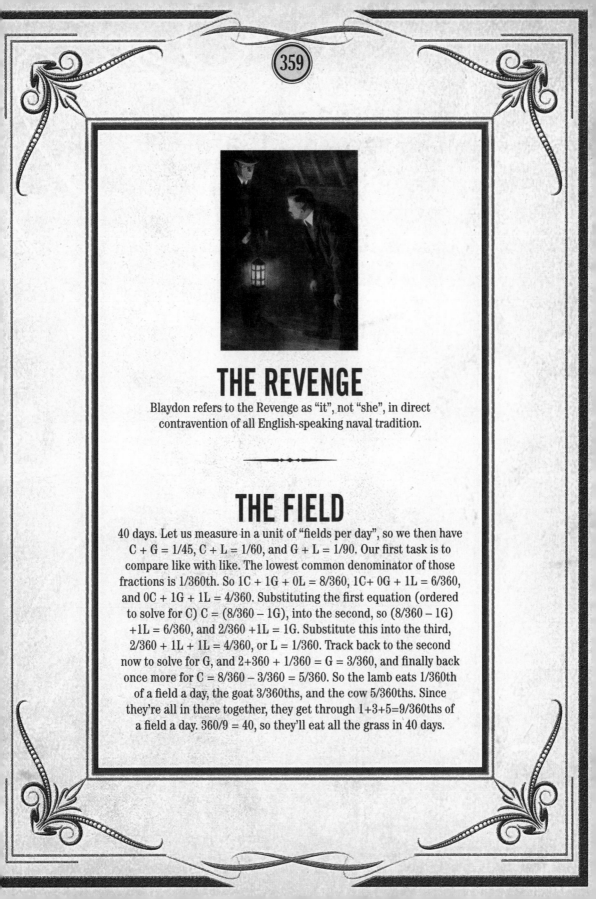

Blaydon refers to the Revenge as "it", not "she", in direct contravention of all English-speaking naval tradition.

THE FIELD

40 days. Let us measure in a unit of "fields per day", so we then have C + G = 1/45, C + L = 1/60, and G + L = 1/90. Our first task is to compare like with like. The lowest common denominator of those fractions is 1/360th. So 1C + 1G + 0L = 8/360, 1C+ 0G + 1L = 6/360, and 0C + 1G + 1L = 4/360. Substituting the first equation (ordered to solve for C) C = (8/360 – 1G), into the second, so (8/360 – 1G) +1L = 6/360, and 2/360 +1L = 1G. Substitute this into the third, 2/360 + 1L + 1L = 4/360, or L = 1/360. Track back to the second now to solve for G, and 2+360 + 1/360 = G = 3/360, and finally back once more for C = 8/360 – 3/360 = 5/360. So the lamb eats 1/360th of a field a day, the goat 3/360ths, and the cow 5/360ths. Since they're all in there together, they get through 1+3+5=9/360ths of a field a day. 360/9 = 40, so they'll eat all the grass in 40 days.

THE TYPE

27. In order to be able to form each month in full, you need the following twenty-seven letters – AA, B, C, D, EEE, F, G, H, I, J, L, M, N, OO, P, RR, S, T, UU, V, and Y.

STABBING

The butler. He claims to have tripped over the body in the darkness, and yet to have seen the victim lying on the floor from outside the room. He's clearly lying.

THE MANAGER

36. Go back x years, and the deputy was half the manager's current age, making him 24, and the manager the deputy's current age, y. So $y - x = 24$, and because the difference between ages will stay constant, $y + x = 48$. Thus $2y = 72$, and the deputy is 36.

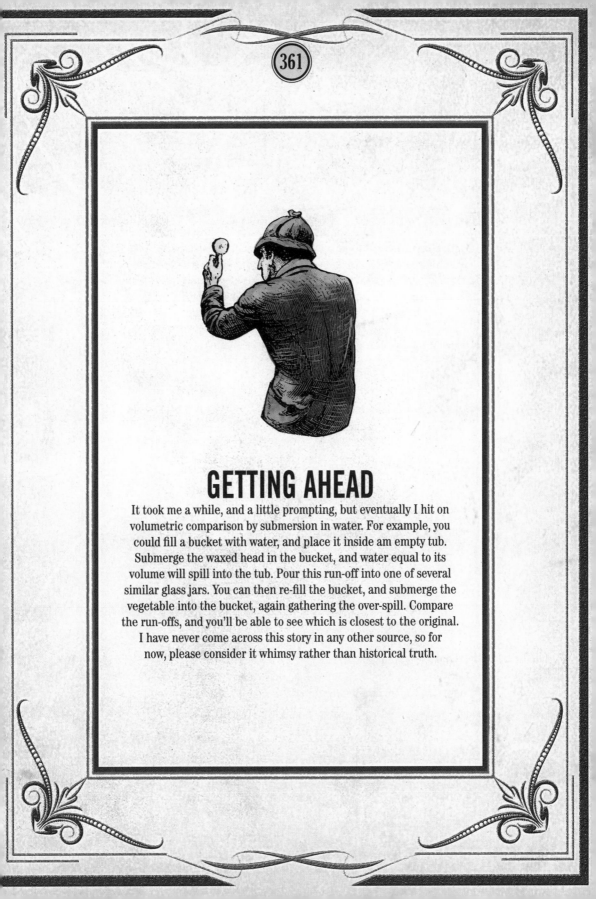

GETTING AHEAD

It took me a while, and a little prompting, but eventually I hit on volumetric comparison by submersion in water. For example, you could fill a bucket with water, and place it inside am empty tub. Submerge the waxed head in the bucket, and water equal to its volume will spill into the tub. Pour this run-off into one of several similar glass jars. You can then re-fill the bucket, and submerge the vegetable into the bucket, again gathering the over-spill. Compare the run-offs, and you'll be able to see which is closest to the original. I have never come across this story in any other source, so for now, please consider it whimsy rather than historical truth.

BICYCLE

The trick is to divide our journey by the ratio of our comparative speeds – 5:4, in this instance. So as the faster walker and slower rider, Holmes would ride for 4/9ths of the way, and I, in the opposite situation, would ride 5/9ths of the way. If we each do our riding in one stint, it doesn't make any difference who goes first. Either Holmes could ride eight miles, then leave the bicycle for me to pick up, and walk; or I could ride ten miles, leaving the bicycle for Holmes to pick up. The trip will take 3 hours, with each of us riding for one hour and walking for two, and the bicycle waiting for an hour in the middle.

THE CANVAS

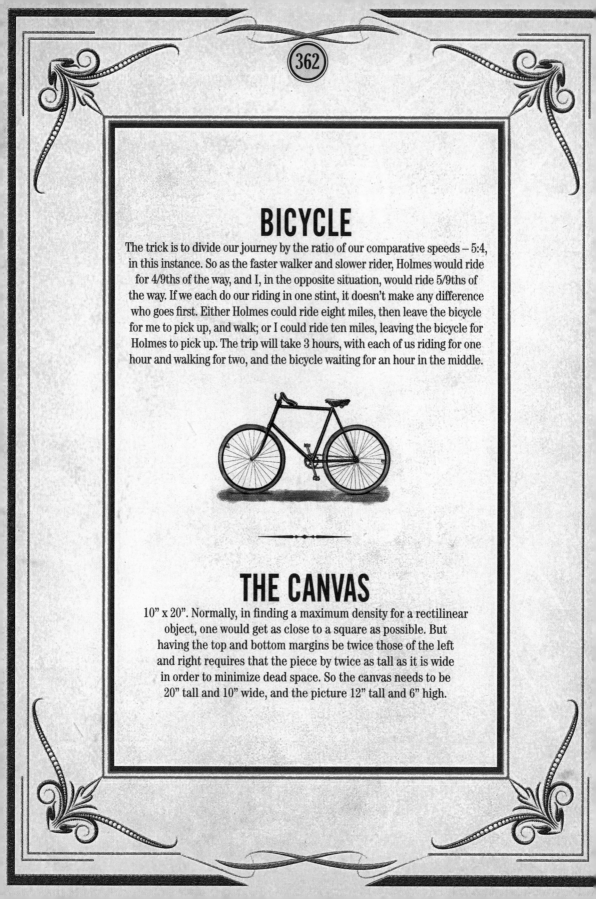

10" x 20". Normally, in finding a maximum density for a rectilinear object, one would get as close to a square as possible. But having the top and bottom margins be twice those of the left and right requires that the piece by twice as tall as it is wide in order to minimize dead space. So the canvas needs to be 20" tall and 10" wide, and the picture 12" tall and 6" high.

PIG

15. Either you found this easy, or you need to hold on to your hats, my friends. It is genuinely straight forward, but it requires several steps. We know that 95x+97y = 4238, and that the numbers of both pigs and sheep must be non-zero integers. Indeterminate equation theory allows a solution. First, solve our equation for x, where x = (4238/95) – (97y/95), and reduce the right-hand side into integers and fractions as far as possible: x= 44 + 58/95 – y – 2y/95, which simplifies to x = 44 – y + (58–2y)/95. Now, since x is an integer, the right-hand term also must be an integer. As 44 and y are both integers as well, that last bit (58–2y)/95 must also be an integer, albeit one we are utterly unsure of. Let's call that value "2i" just for now. We can then rearrange our new definition of 2i = (58–2y)/95 in terms of y as y = 29 – 95i. But y is an non-negative integer, so 0 <= 29 – 95i, and i <= 29/95. We now have a term for y that we can substitute back in the equation for x, so x = 44 – (29 – 95i) + (58 – 2* (29 – 95i))95, and although that looks ugly, a lot of it cancels out, and it simplifies down to x = 44 – 29 + 95i + 2i, or x = 15 + 97i. Again, x must be an integer, so 0 <= 15 + 97i, and –15/97 <= i. So now we have a range where –15/97 <= i <= 29/95, and since i also has to be an integer, in this case it must be 0. Finally, we have equations for both x and y expressed in terms of i, so x = 15 + 97*0, or 15, and y = 29 – 95*0, or 29. Pigs were x, so he bought 15 pigs. You can approach any indeterminate equation using this method, although equations with more unknowns require commensurately more steps. If the equation is insoluble, your range for i will be impossible.

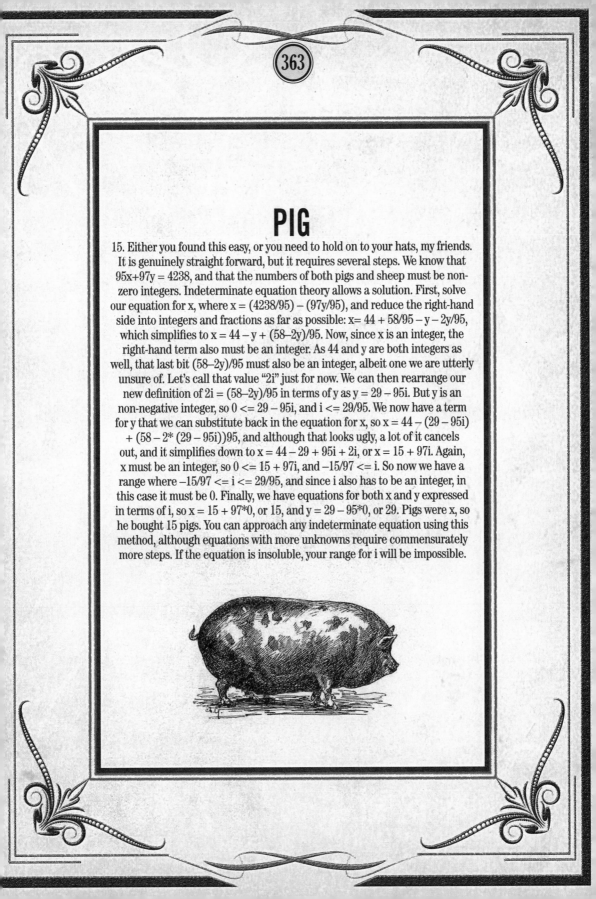

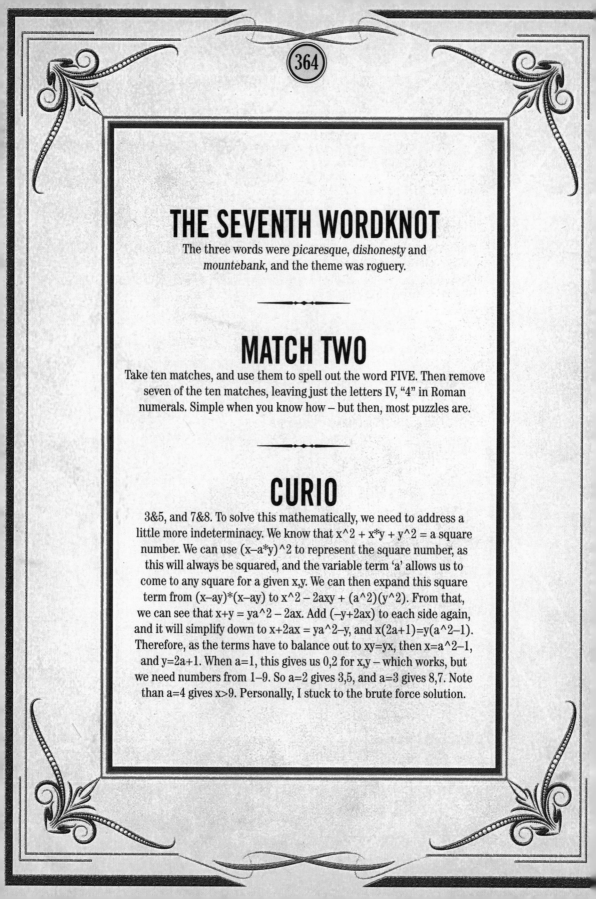

THE SEVENTH WORDKNOT

The three words were *picaresque*, *dishonesty* and *mountebank*, and the theme was roguery.

MATCH TWO

Take ten matches, and use them to spell out the word FIVE. Then remove seven of the ten matches, leaving just the letters IV, "4" in Roman numerals. Simple when you know how – but then, most puzzles are.

CURIO

3&5, and 7&8. To solve this mathematically, we need to address a little more indeterminacy. We know that $x^2 + x*y + y^2$ = a square number. We can use $(x-a*y)^2$ to represent the square number, as this will always be squared, and the variable term 'a' allows us to come to any square for a given x,y. We can then expand this square term from $(x-ay)*(x-ay)$ to $x^2 - 2axy + (a^2)(y^2)$. From that, we can see that $x+y = ya^2 - 2ax$. Add $(-y+2ax)$ to each side again, and it will simplify down to $x+2ax = ya^2-y$, and $x(2a+1)=y(a^2-1)$. Therefore, as the terms have to balance out to xy=yx, then $x=a^2-1$, and $y=2a+1$. When a=1, this gives us 0,2 for x,y – which works, but we need numbers from 1–9. So a=2 gives 3,5, and a=3 gives 8,7. Note than a=4 gives $x>9$. Personally, I stuck to the brute force solution.

ENGINE TROUBLE

200 miles. Say x is the distance from the spot where the engine fault developed to the destination, and y is full speed. We then know that the normal time "t" to complete the journey is t=x/y, that at 3/5ths of y, the time is t+2 = 5x/3y, and that if we'd gone 50 miles further we'd have arrived 1 hour 20 minutes late, so t+4/3 = 50/y + 5(x–50)/3y. Substitute t=x/y through the second equation, and you'll quickly find that t has to be 3, and x=3y. So we would normally have had 3 hours left to go, making a typical four-hour journey, and the distance left would have had to be 3 times the normal top speed in miles per hour. Now we know the third equation gets us there 2/3 of an hour sooner than the second, so substitute t+2 = 5x/3y into the third equation, and 5x/3y – 2/3 = 50/y + 5x/3y – 250/3y, so 5x – 2y = 150 + 5x – 50, and 2y = 100. Thus full speed is 50mph and, finally, our full distance takes four hours at 50 mph to travel, so must be 200 miles.

RECALL

28. Start at the back and work forwards, reversing the operations as you go, and it is easy. 2*10 = 20, –8 = 12, *12 = 144, +52 = 196, sq rt = 14, * 3/2 = 21, * 7 = 147, * 4/7 = 84, / 3 = 28. Note that *4/7 reverses +75% because 4/4 + 3/4 = 7/4.

MORAN

Yes, actually. You need to remember that the first shot marks the start of the time count, and so counts as t=0, not t=5s. To meet his boast precisely, the gun would have had to shoot 60 rounds in 4 minutes and 55 seconds. The same principle is why if you put two points on a piece of paper, one line segment connects them rather than two.

THE EIGHTH WORDKNOT

The words are *hoodwinked*, *handcuffed* and *restrained*.

BARNABAS

2 half-crowns. We know the work-rate of both people is consistent between the two tasks. Wiggins can shovel as quickly as Barnabas can dig, but he can dig four times faster than Barnabas can shovel. There are two steps required in comparing Wiggins digging to Barnabas digging, but as the work-rate is same in both steps, Wiggins' work rate is 2 to Barnabas' 1. So however they broke down the jobs, and however long it took, Wiggins was twice as good a worker as Barnabas, and the money should be split 2:1.

THE FORTY-FOUR

20 and 64. You could use trial and error to find two plausible ages 44 years apart that multiply to 1280, but there is also an algebraic solution. We have x*y=1280 and x–y=44. So x=44+y. This gives us 44y+y^2 = 1280, or reordering into a standard quadratic, y^2 + 44y – 1280 = 0. From the quadratic formula, y = (–b +– sq root (b^2 – 4ac))/2a, where a, b and c are the multiples of each term in order. Note that +– means you have to solve twice, once adding the square root, and once subtracting it. In our case, a is 1 (for just y^2), b is 44, and c = –1280. So we have (–44 +– sq rt (44^2 – (4*1*–1280))) / 2, which once you sort out the arithmetic, breaks down to (–44 +– 84) / 2 = –64 and +20. We're just looking for magnitudes for the ages (the single minus arrives since we were given the difference between the two ages, not the sum), so Michael is 64 and Minnie is 20.

THE MURDER OF MOLLY GLASS

Mrs Glass had lit the fire in her bedroom before going to sleep. Once she was slumbering, her husband turned off the gas line to the house. The fire duly went out. Then he switched the gas back on again, so that it built up unhindered in her bedroom, and asphyxiated her.

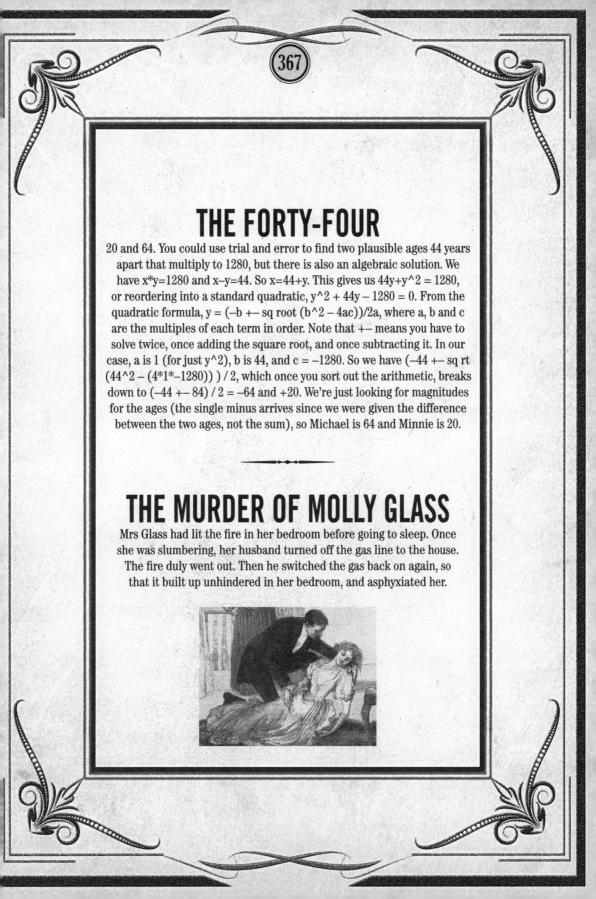

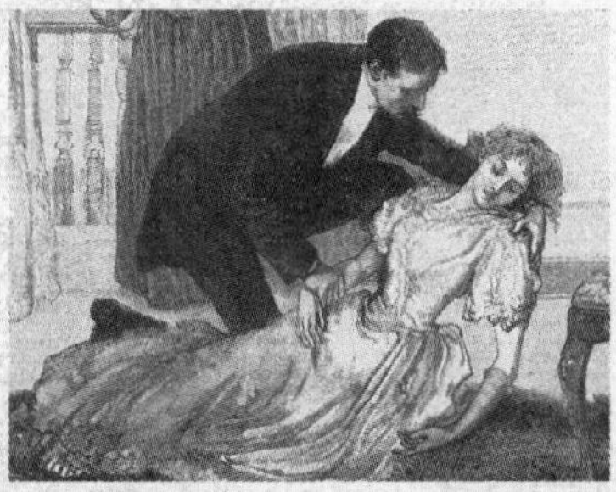

PART FOUR

FIENDISH

THE EIGHTH MENTAL TRIAL

It might be tempting to divide the money up according to the amount of oil each man had before the operation, 8 and 5 farthings, but that would be unfair to Alfie. Thirteen pints of oil are split between the three men. That leaves each man with 4 and 1/3 pints. Bill has lost just 2/3 of a pint of oil; the bulk of the donation has come from Alfie, who has lost 3 and 2/3.

To discover a fair breakdown, first think of the entire donation in terms of thirds of a pint. 3 pints is 9 third-pints, as any publican will tell you, so Alfie has lost 11 thirds to Bill's 2. The fair division of the money then is 11 farthings to Alfie, and 2 to Bill.

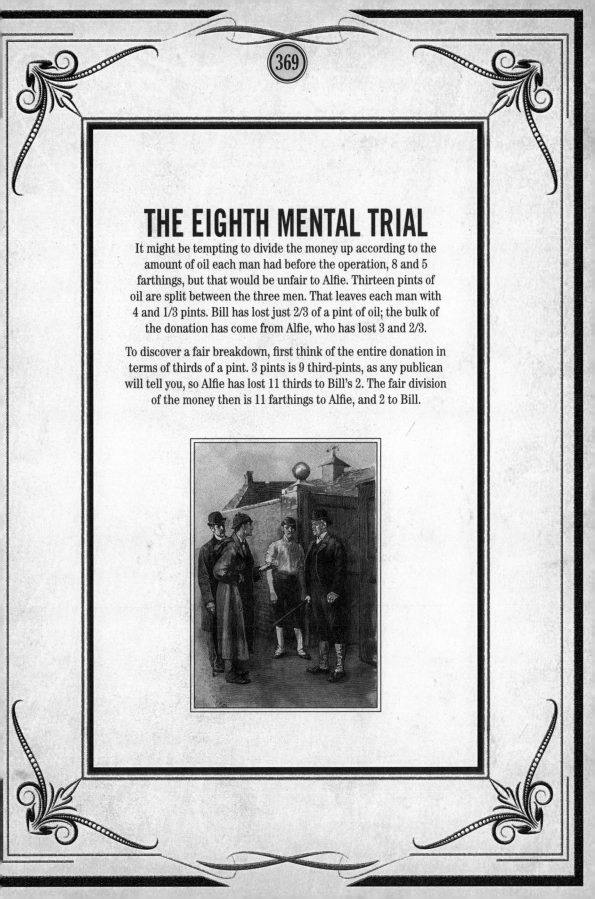

IN PARIS

As Holmes eventually pointed out, the only two rational possibilities were either that the woman was demented, or that the entire hotel staff were colluding against her. The former option, whilst neat, would hardly have occasioned his presenting the matter to me in such a manner.

As it happened, the staff were indeed colluding. The brother had been diagnosed with severe typhoid fever during the night, and was immediately whisked away to a small, quiet hospice outside the city. Terrified that news of the lethally infectious disease might panic the World's Fair visitors and lead to a scandalous financial disaster, the manager had the room sealed and disguised, and briefed all the staff to remain resolute in the face of the lady's questioning.

SIX-SIDED DICE

Consider 1 die first of all. The 4, 5 and 6 can be discounted, as their positions are fixed by the earlier numbers. Then the 1 can be marked on any of 6 faces. That leaves 4 faces for the 2 to occupy, and 2 faces for the three. Multiplying these out, there are 48 options for marking one die. Each subsequent die can be marked independently of the other two, so the grand total of possible marking schemes for three six-sided dice is 110,592.

THE NINTH LITERAL ODDITY

I must admit that I was unable to find an answer until Holmes suggests that I write the words down using only capital letters, to wit CHECKBOOK and EXCEEDED. Then it became clear that they were composed entirely of letters that possessed horizontal symmetry as capitals. If you placed a mirror over the top half of the word and reflected the bottom half with it, it would be unchanged. I dare say you could contrive the word 'COOKBOOKED', or some similar chimera, but I personally feel that would be something of a dodge.

THE EIGHTH CURIOSITY

I was astounded to hear that it would raise the girdle by very nearly a full yard – approximately 19/20ths, if you wish to be more precise.

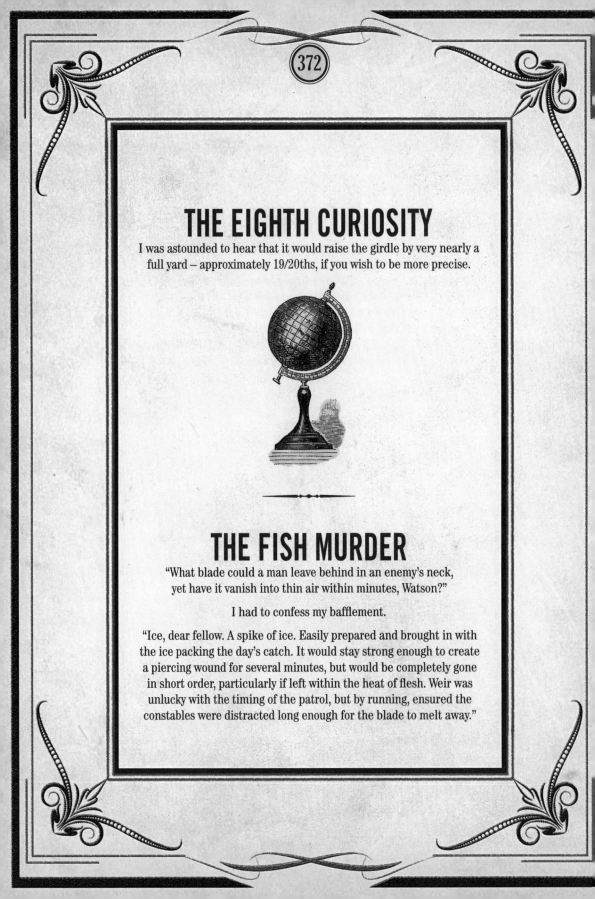

THE FISH MURDER

"What blade could a man leave behind in an enemy's neck, yet have it vanish into thin air within minutes, Watson?"

I had to confess my bafflement.

"Ice, dear fellow. A spike of ice. Easily prepared and brought in with the ice packing the day's catch. It would stay strong enough to create a piercing wound for several minutes, but would be completely gone in short order, particularly if left within the heat of flesh. Weir was unlucky with the timing of the patrol, but by running, ensured the constables were distracted long enough for the blade to melt away."

SHEEP

"At no point did I tell you that the pens had to be empty before you began, Watson. If one of the pens contains a sheep already, the matter is trivial. I do not present this problem to make sport with you, but to highlight that it is vital to look for solutions which are beyond the obvious."

GET A HAT

It should be clear that one person with one hat to choose can never be mistaken, two people can get it wrong in just one manner, and three people in just two. In fact, the general rule is that for each increase in the number of people, you need to multiply the previous result by the new total of persons. When that new total of persons is even, you must add 1 to your product, and when it is odd, you must remove one, to make allowance for the fact that an odd number of people have their options slightly restricted.

By calculating through, it will be found that seven men can get the wrong hats in 1,854 different ways. If you wanted to know just the number of all possible different ways the hats could be distributed, that would be 1 x 2 x 3 x 4 x 5 x 6 x 7, or 5,040.

THE FOURTH PORTMANTEAU

As I eventually managed to deduce, the image refers to Hyde Park. The river Serpentine is the dominant feature of the park, hence the coils of water ending in the head of a snake. The park was the site of the first World's Fair in 1851, the Great Exhibition, which was housed in the great Crystal Palace, which was later rebuilt, in modified form, in Penge. The park is also host to Speaker's Corner, where by tradition any man or woman may go to freely speak his mind, represented by the wild-tempered fellow on the box. It is perhaps an irony that Speaker's Corner is just a few yards away from the site of the infamous Tyburn Tree, the three-beamed gallows which took the lives of London's condemned for so many centuries.

NEPHEWS

"It's quite elementary, my dear fellow. If two men each marry the (possibly widowed) mother of the other, and both father a son upon their new wives, then those sons will be both uncle and nephew to each other, as each will be the brother of the other's father. There are other ways to achieve the relationship too, but that is the most straight-forward."

THE NINTH MENTAL TRIAL

After I had pondered the matter for a while, Holmes came to my rescue. "You can do it in just two operations," he assured me. "Divide the coins into three piles of three. Place two upon the scales and compare them. If one side is lighter, that pile contains the fake; if the two are equal, the set-aside pile holds it. Clear the scale, and take the pile with the fake. Now place any two of the coins upon the scales and again compare. If one is lighter, it is the fake; if they are the same, it is the held-over coin. The method is infallible."

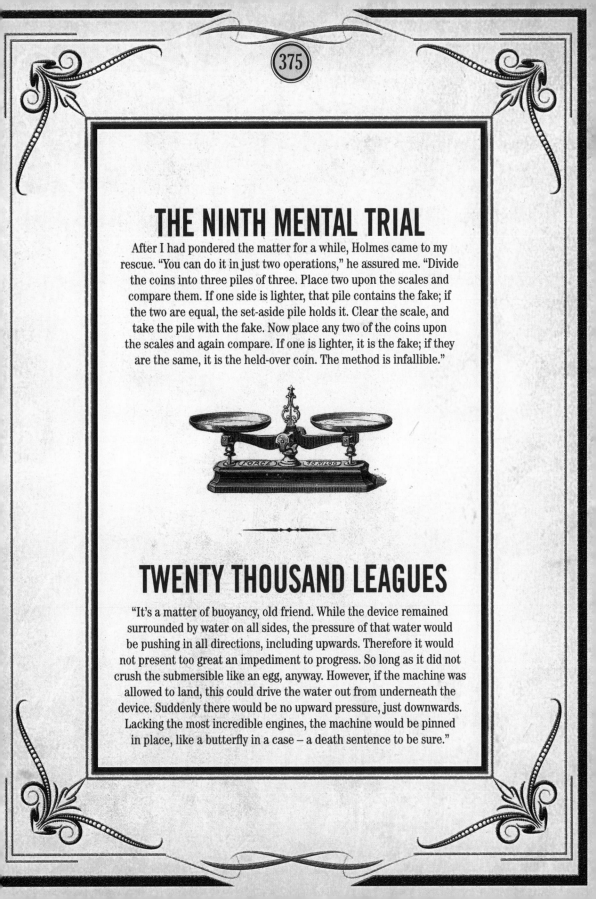

TWENTY THOUSAND LEAGUES

"It's a matter of buoyancy, old friend. While the device remained surrounded by water on all sides, the pressure of that water would be pushing in all directions, including upwards. Therefore it would not present too great an impediment to progress. So long as it did not crush the submersible like an egg, anyway. However, if the machine was allowed to land, this could drive the water out from underneath the device. Suddenly there would be no upward pressure, just downwards. Lacking the most incredible engines, the machine would be pinned in place, like a butterfly in a case – a death sentence to be sure."

THE SHOREDITCH BANK

The reason for the apparent lapse in security was clearly obvious as soon as we entered the office. The clever villains had prepared an accurate depiction of the safe, somewhat larger than the real thing, and propped it up so as to appear, from the door, as if nothing was wrong. They were then able to work on opening the safe, and when the guards came past and looked in, everything appeared to be in order. The deception would have been more obvious if the office had been brightly lit, but as it was, it was more than sufficient to buy the thieves the time they needed. Even Holmes seemed a little impressed by their ingenuity.

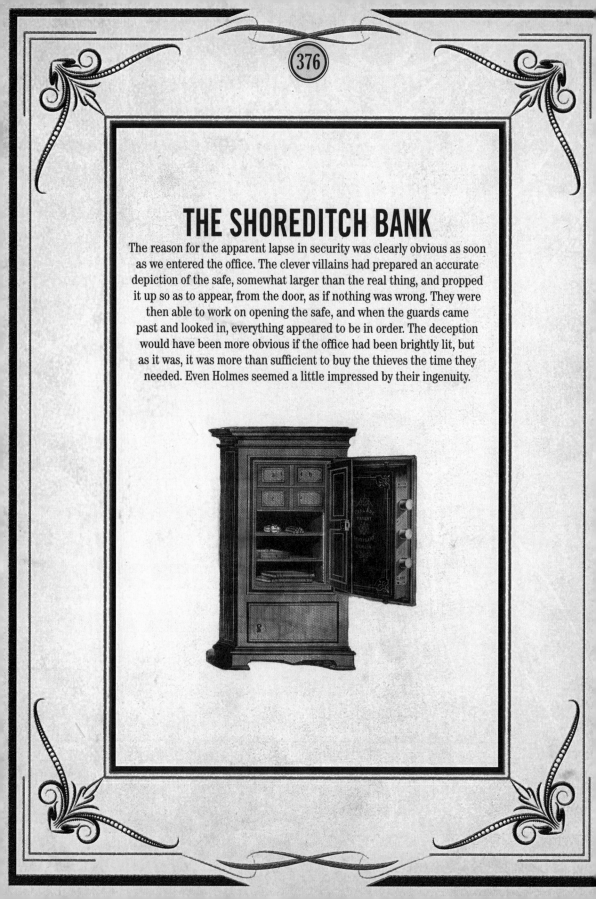

MARKHAM

"There are two lines of approach to solving this problem. One is the elliptical. You may notice, on the side table, a bottle of pills near to the decanter of Scotch. Markham was ill, and as the widow did not mention it, we can assume she did not know. Furthermore, it bespeaks a certain bleakness of outlook when a man keeps his medication next to his hard liquor.

"The other approach is more direct. The room was sealed from the inside, and we are told it is impossible that the intruder escaped unseen. It is within reason that both widow and maid may be in cahoots, but if they allowed an assailant to escape, how did they seal the room back up without being caught within it?

"No Watson, the matter is far more straightforward. If it is impossible that anyone escaped, then the unlikely must be true, and the killer is still in there – dead. Markham's prognosis must have been stark enough that he could not bear to suffer through it. He locked the room, staged the argument, and took his own life. If you look through his paperwork, I have no doubt you'll find a life insurance policy that pays handsomely in case of murder, but not at all when it comes to suicide. Let the police seek their unlikely suspect however. I see no need to burden the widow any further."

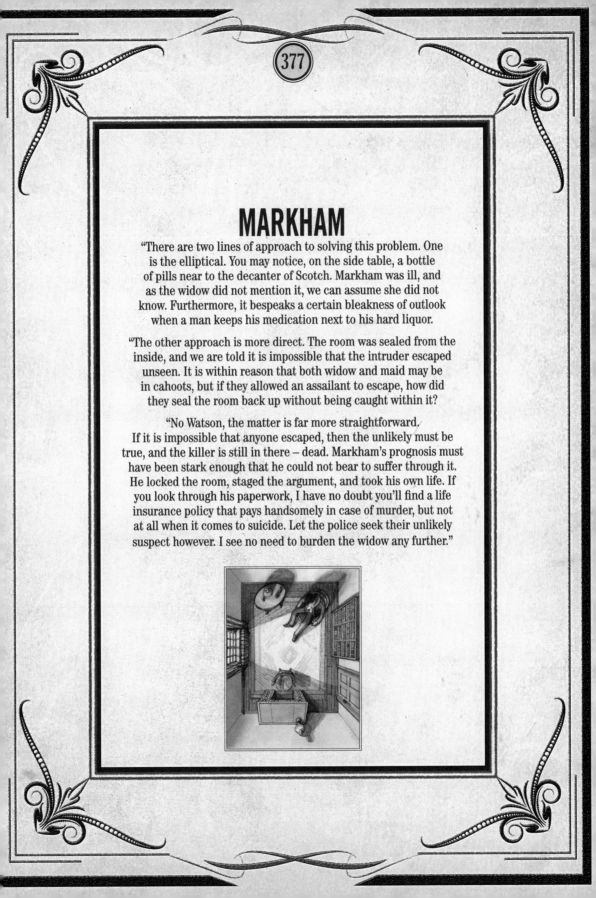

MONTENEGRO

The suitable pairs would be 5 and 9 for one player, and 13 and 15 for the other. You can make 5 in six ways, and 9 in twenty-five, for a total of 31 chances; and you can make 13 in 21 ways, and 15 in 10 ways, also for 31 chances. In any given throw with these numbers, there will be a 1/7th chance of attaining victory.

WIMBLEDON COMMON

The cabbie reacted so violently because his passenger gave his own home address as a destination. He had long suspected his wife of being engaged in an illicit affair, so when a perfect stranger asked to be taken to his own home, at a time when he himself ought to be safely out of the way, the man snapped. Instead of taking the visitor to his home, he took him out into the park and slaughtered him. Under French law, it is sometimes permissible for a jealous lover to be treated leniently for murder due to a temporary fit of insanity inflamed by the passions.

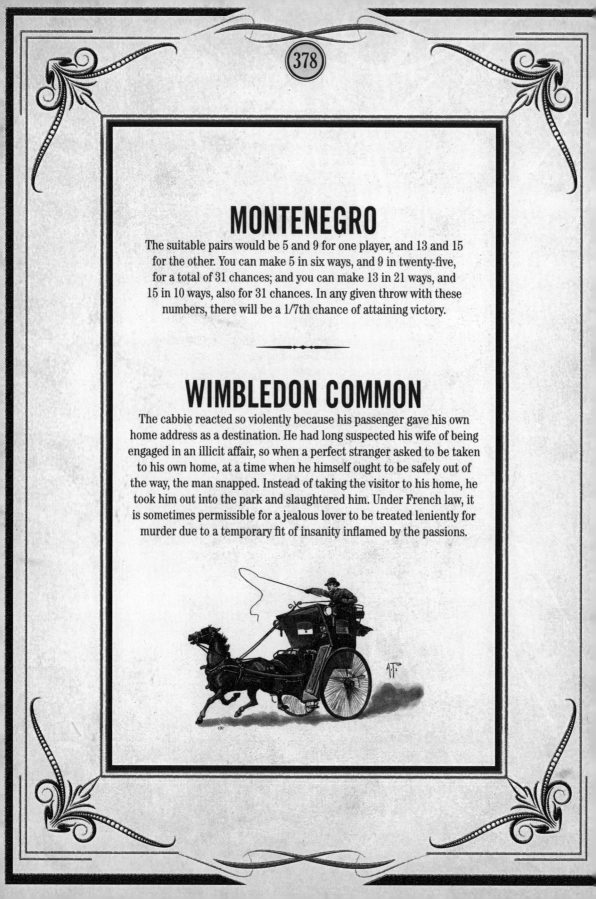

THE TENTH MENTAL TRIAL

"Your sign is white. If any man saw both of the black signs – Bill, let us say – he would know his own had to be white, and he would immediately step forward. Because he does not do so, Alfie can thus be certain that you and he do not between have both the black signs. So far, so good. Now, if you had a black sign, Alfie could be sure that his sign was white, because he knows you are not both wearing black, so he would be able to step forward. However, he does not do so. This can only mean that he sees a white sign on your back as well. Of course, any of the three of you could use parallel logic to arrive at the same conclusion, so it becomes a race of the wits as to which of you gets there first."

CARL BLACK

"Arson is a mark of desperation in an otherwise sober man," Holmes said. "I believe the root cause to be the kidnapping. Black had always been a flamboyant spender, and given the state of the company, it seems likely he had been embezzling. The partner, Robbins, would have needed a lever to move Black with, so I suspect he had discovered the embezzlement. Either way, between them they hatched a kidnap plot, and staged that business with the supposed Serbians. The insurance paid a hefty sum, Black departed quietly – and without scandal. The company finances improved markedly, which I assume was the combined benefit of the end of the embezzlement and the surreptitious slow feeding back in of the ransom money. All was well until Black got himself killed. Robbins felt that he couldn't take the risk that Black might have retained some sort of incriminatory document regarding the kidnapping amongst his effects, and panicked. It will all come out as the arson trial proceeds, mark my words."

A MATTER OF TIME

"The trick, dear fellow, is to make sure the two sticks are not touching, and light both ends of one, and just one end of the other. The stick burning from both ends will burn out in 30 minutes, whilst the second stick is still half-way through. At that point, light the other end of the second stick, and it will burn out in 15 minutes, for a total of 45 minutes."

THE LADIES OF MORDEN

To get an answer which works effectively, you have to go through the players cyclically. Once that is understood, it becomes a matter of finding suitable starting places for each column at the beginning, and descending from there.

1.	A B vs I L	E J vs G K	F H vs C D
2.	A C vs J B	F K vs H L	G I vs D E
3.	A D vs K C	G L vs I B	H J vs E F
4.	A E vs L D	H B vs J C	I K vs F G
5.	A F vs B E	I C vs K D	J L vs G H
6.	A G vs C F	J D vs L E	K B vs H I
7.	A H vs D G	K E vs B F	L C vs I J
8.	A I vs E H	L F vs C G	B D vs J K
9.	A J vs F I	B G vs D H	C E vs K L
10.	A K vs G J	C H vs E I	D F vs L B
11.	A L vs H K	D I vs F J	E G vs B C

THE FINAL PORTMANTEAU

A pretty riddle, this one. It was the trees and plants that first set me on the right track. They are all different, and arranged with precision. Where would you find a wide variety of both trees and plants, precisely arranged? The most obvious answer would be to look in a herbarium. With that decided, it was only a matter of time before my mind turned to the Royal Botanic Gardens at Kew, and all the pieces fell into place.

Occupying 120 hectares of gardens and glasshouses, Kew Gardens holds the largest herbarium on Earth, as well as a vast collection of living specimens. Their habitats include the impressive Palm House and Temperate House, respectively the first and largest wrought-iron glass-houses in existence. The former's beguiling curves are hinted at in the glass-house shown picture, as is the scale of the latter. The Alpine House provides a cold environment for chill-weather plants. The Great Pagoda is one of the Gardens' more impressive follies, and for some time was the largest Chinese-style building in Europe.

The last piece of the puzzle is the 'farmer King' - King George III, God rest his soul. 'Farmer George' was a passionate agriculturalist, and he carried out several trials and adjustments at Kew. This even included a brave plan to strengthen British sheep by crossbreeding them with stolen specimens from Spain's famous, and well guarded, Merino flocks.

THE FINAL CURIOSITY

Although the effect is vanishingly small for a billiard table, to remain perfectly level for the players, it would have to follow the curvature of the Earth. If it were perfectly level, it would be closest to the Earth at its centre point, and the balls would all roll to the middle.

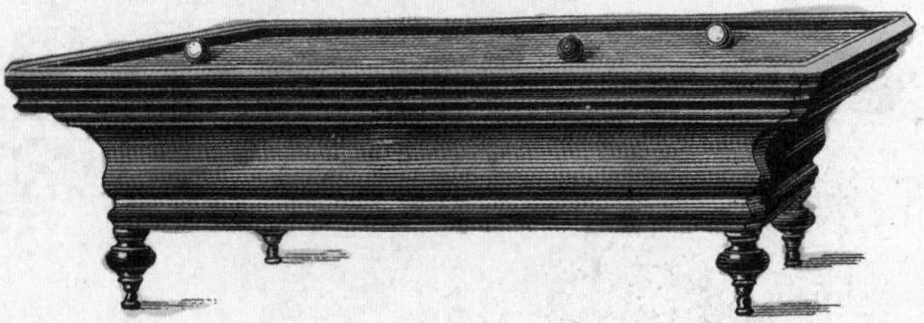

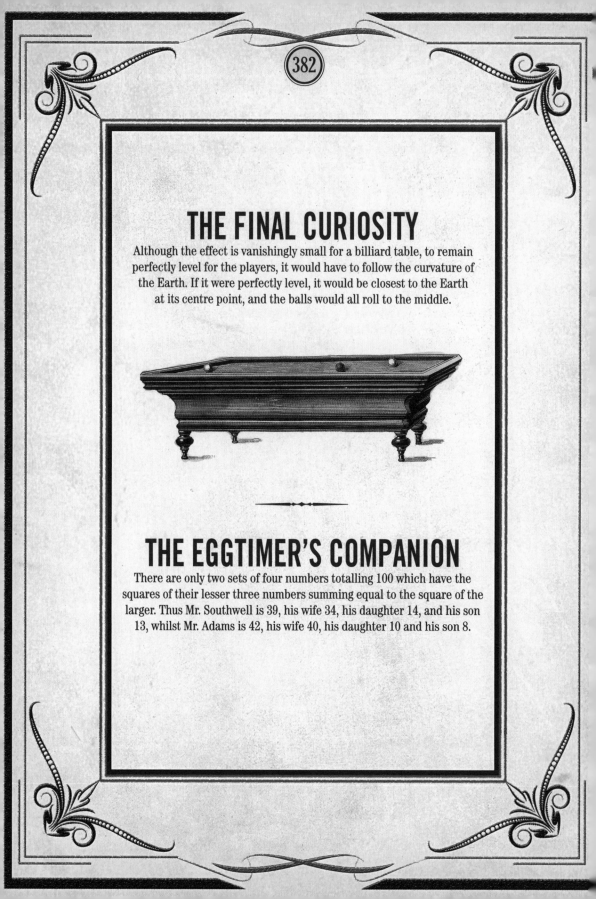

THE EGGTIMER'S COMPANION

There are only two sets of four numbers totalling 100 which have the squares of their lesser three numbers summing equal to the square of the larger. Thus Mr. Southwell is 39, his wife 34, his daughter 14, and his son 13, whilst Mr. Adams is 42, his wife 40, his daughter 10 and his son 8.

THE FINAL MENTAL TRIAL

The answer is 17. As I finally realised, the numbers are in increasing length when spelled out fully as words. Two has 3 letters, five has 4, and so on, up to fourteen with eight digits. The only number with nine digits that is less than twenty is seventeen.

DOWN ON THE FARM

The injuries were consistent with a fall from a significant height, and as Holmes pointed out, this would be consistent with the lack of any trail or drag-marks near the body's original site. The peculiarly heavy clothing further suggested that the man would have expected to be in cooler air. Together, Holmes took this to mean that he fell from an aeronautic balloon. This mode of transport would suit a spy who wished to depart from England's shores without the risk of alerting any authorities.

The clincher, for Holmes, was the half-match. He suggested that a group of spies had been attempting to escape the country, possibly in advance of an impending arrest. Taking to a Montgolfier balloon, they were above West Sussex when it became obvious that they had to lighten their load beyond the capacity of ballast to correct, or else risk being grounded and captured. They drew lots, and the unfortunate wretch before us happened to obtain the shortened matchstick. Rather than endanger the mission, he emptied his pockets and leapt to his death.

BOARD

As it turns out, the number of rectangles (including squares) enclosed by such a square board of squares is equal to the (mathematical) square of the triangular order equal to the number of (physical) squares on the board.

In this case, the board is 8 units long. The 8th triangular number is 36 – 1+2+3+4+5+6+7+8. Square 36, and you'll arrive at the correct answer, 1,296. The formula for deriving the exact number of these which are squares is slightly more complex, but if you are curious, 204 are squares and 1092 are non-square rectangles.

THE NIGHT WATCHMAN

As the hands meet every 65 and 5/11 minutes, there are eleven occasions in twelve hours where the hands are together. The hands are together exactly at twelve o'clock, of course. So the first occasion after that when the hands coincide is 1.05 and 27 3/11th seconds. Keep adding the sum, and you will discover only one occasion when the second hand would be near 49 – that is at 4.21 and 49 1/11th seconds. So that was the time of the robbery.

THE FINAL LITERAL ODDITY

It took me a long time, but I did finally manage to find Holmes' word – sestettes. These are the second divisions of Italian-style sonnets, possessing six lines and generally marking the emotional turning point of the poem.

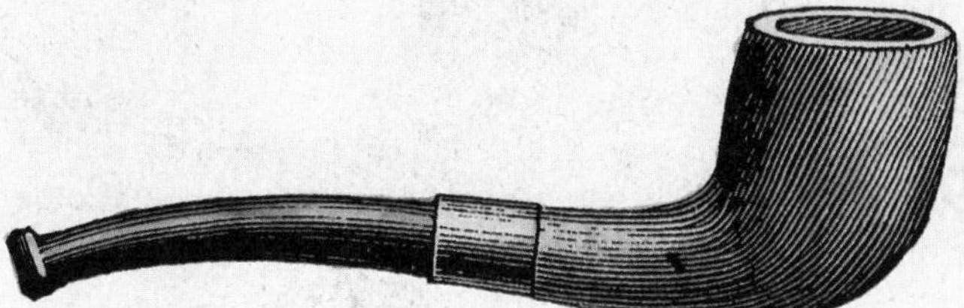

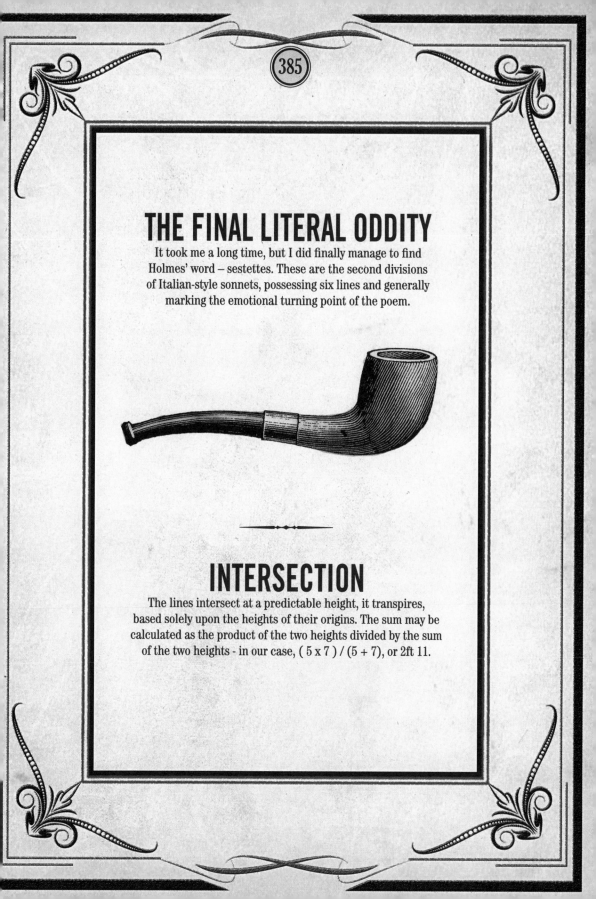

INTERSECTION

The lines intersect at a predictable height, it transpires, based solely upon the heights of their origins. The sum may be calculated as the product of the two heights divided by the sum of the two heights - in our case, (5 x 7) / (5 + 7), or 2ft 11.

PIPE DREAMS

Definitely not in one generation, no. Roughly half of pregnancies produce boys, so initially, half of the mothers would stop producing children. Of those that remained, again roughly half would produce boys, and stop. This pattern would continue indefinitely. At each stage, the expectant mothers remaining would produce as many boys as girls, so the gender balance would not change, but the number of children would plummet, and the population contract. It is not impossible that some women might have a genetic predisposition to produce more girls that boys, and this genetic trait would become highly selected for, but it takes an average of 75 generations or more for a mutation to spread through the population. Even a strongly selected pressure like this would still require hundreds of years to have a noticeable effect.

THE OLD ONES

The murderer was in the process of robbing the pub, and shot the victim to eliminate him as a witness. In fact, he had already murdered the landlord and the cook, at which point one more body would hardly matter. The fellow was eventually apprehended at Portsmouth docks, and duly hung.

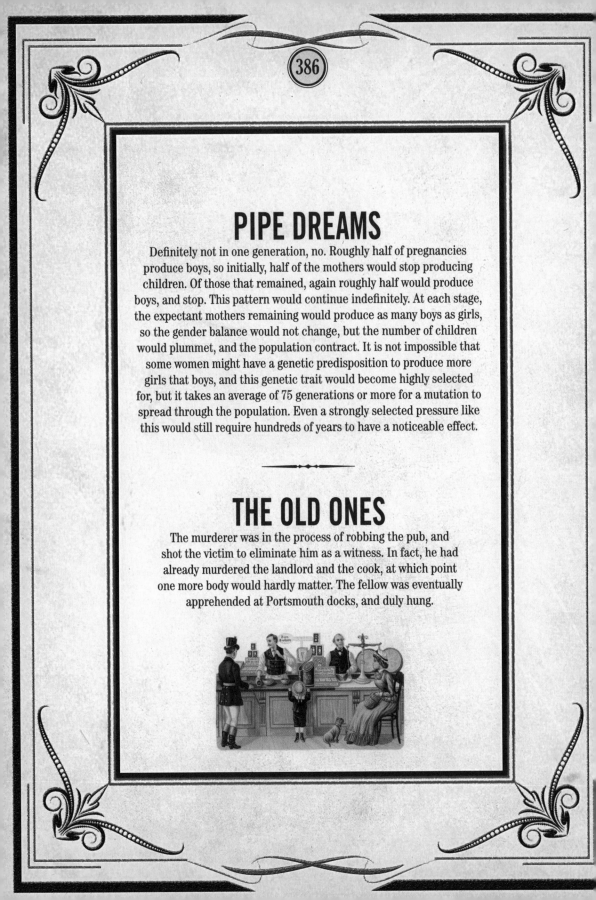

THE PLEASANT WAY

18 miles. As a general rule for this sort of problem, triple the distance of the first meeting place, and subtract the distance of the second meeting place. So 10*3 – 12 = 18.

FASHION

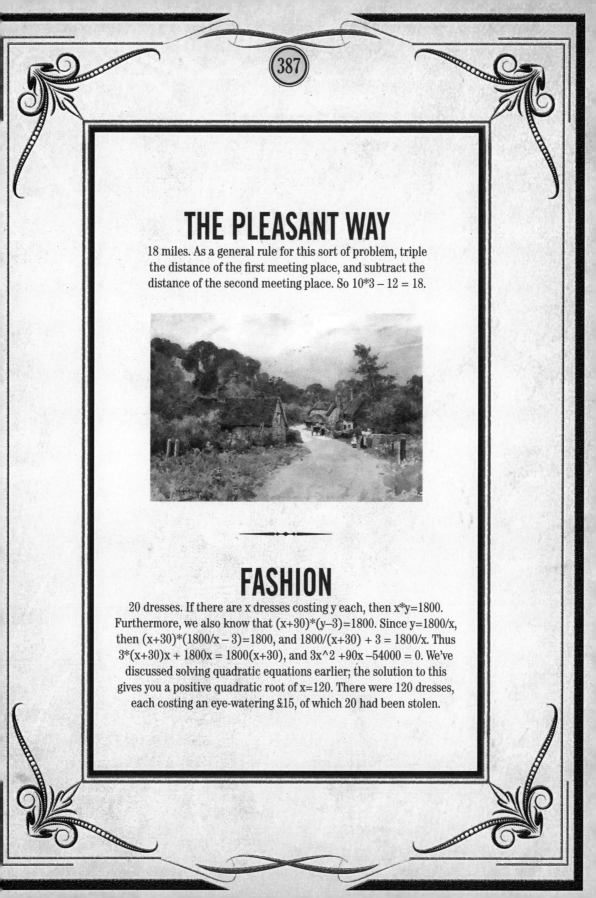

20 dresses. If there are x dresses costing y each, then x*y=1800. Furthermore, we also know that (x+30)*(y–3)=1800. Since y=1800/x, then (x+30)*(1800/x – 3)=1800, and 1800/(x+30) + 3 = 1800/x. Thus 3*(x+30)x + 1800x = 1800(x+30), and 3x^2 +90x –54000 = 0. We've discussed solving quadratic equations earlier; the solution to this gives you a positive quadratic root of x=120. There were 120 dresses, each costing an eye-watering £15, of which 20 had been stolen.

THE FOURTH CAMOUFLAGE

The words are *cut*, *dig*, *sow* and *trim*, and their unifying theme is gardening (or, more generally, agriculture, I suppose.)

THE APPLE MARKET

The truth is that the two sales methods are only directly equivalent when the number of apples sold at three a penny is in the proportion of 3:2 with the apples sold at two a penny. However, that is not the case here; the proportion is 1:1. If the first woman had had 36 apples, and the second 24, then they would have been due 12 pence each, whether they'd sold them themselves or via the friend. In this case, the three-a-penny lady would have earned 10 pence from her apples, and her friend 15 pence, so by splitting the money into two lots of 12 pence, the first woman gets 2p extra, and the second woman 3 pence less. 9.5 pence and 14.5 pence would have been a fairer division.

A PAIR OF FOURS

In the end, it took me a lot of time, not a little. However, I did find the solution – sq rt (sq rt (sq rt 4) ^ 4!). 4! is 1*2*3*4, or 24, and sq rt 4 is obviously 2, so the equation becomes sq rt (sq rt 2)^24, and you can write sq rt as ^0.5. Roots and powers of this sort cancel out, so it becomes 2^0.5^0.5^24 = 2^0.5^12 = 2^6 = 64.

ANDREW

Just before leaving for David's house, Andrew would set the clock to twelve, and start it. When he arrived at David's, he'd note the correct time from David's clock, and he'd do the same when he left to return home, so he knew how long he'd spent with David. Then when he arrived home, he'd have a record of precisely how long he'd been away in total. Subtracting the time he'd spent at David's from this would tell him how long his journey there and back had been. Adding one half of this amount to the time when he left David's house then gave him the correct time now.

ROCK PAPER SCISSORS

Wiggins won, 7–3. Since there were no draws, Wiggins's 6 scissors met Alice's 4 paper and 2 rock, giving Wiggins 4 out of 6. The other games must have been Alice's scissors, which met Wiggins' rock three times, and paper once, giving Wiggins 3 out of 4. So he won 7 out of 10.

OLD HOOK

10 and 5/41sts hours. If Ted rides for x miles at 8 mph, then his journey time = (x/8) + (40–x)/1. Hob walks for y miles, so his journey time is y/2 + (40–y)/8. This means that Ern's journey time is x/8 + (x–y)/8 + (40–y)/8. Now all these total times are equal. So (x/8) + 40 – x = y/2 + (40–y)/8, which means 7x + 3y = 280. Also, by multiplying the second and third equation by 8, 4y + 40 – y = x + x – y + 40 – y, and 2x – 5y = 0. So now we have two simple equations for x and y. Solve, and we'll find that x=1400/41, and y=560/41. Note that leaving it in terms of 1/41 is simplest for this solution. Substitute x into Ted's time or y into Hob's time, and you'll find that the total is 10 and 5/41 hours.

ART

He lost £10 over all. £75 at 25% profit means that painting cost £60 originally. £75 at 25% loss means that the other painting cost £100. So he paid £160 for paintings that fetched in £150.

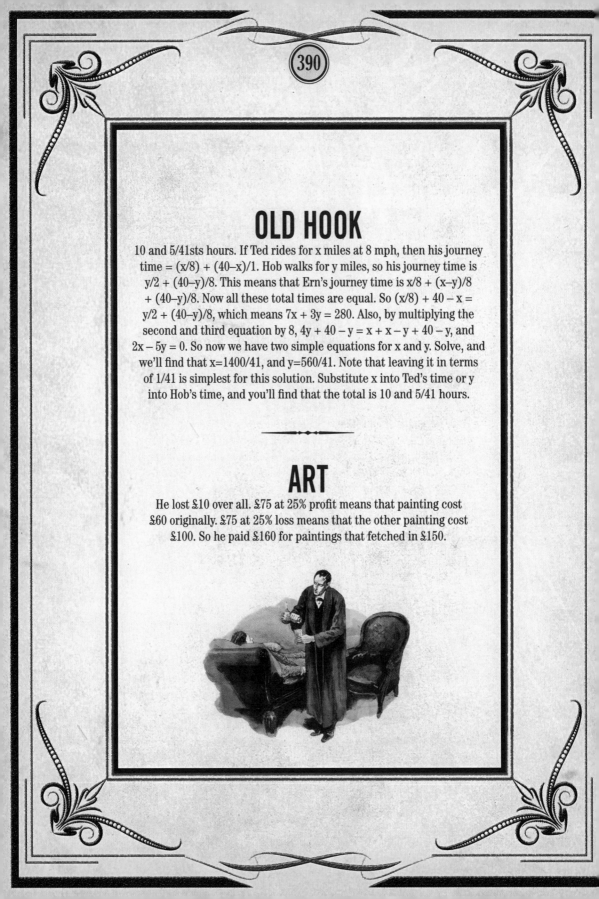

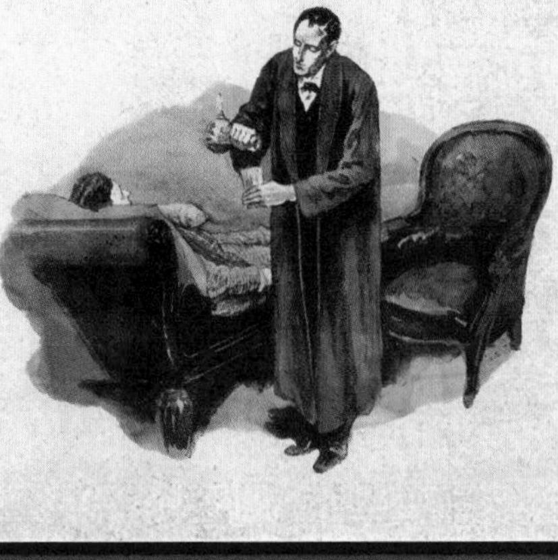

THE NINTH WORDKNOT

The words were *trebuchets*, *musketeers* and *broadswords*.

THE SEVEN

1 in 7, or about 14%. It turns out that the total number of ways the children could sit is 5,040, or 7!, which is 7*6*5*4*3*2*1. Since there are 3 girls, you can assign them into pairs to sit at the ends in 6 ways. For any given arrangement of two girls at the ends, there are 5 different ways the children in between could sit, so 5! = 120 options. Six different arrangements of 120 options gives 720 ways there could be a girl at each end. So the chance is 720 in 5,040, or 1 in 7.

BRIDGE

Absolutely none. The actual chance of a perfect deal occurring in bridge is 2,235,197,406,985,633,368,301,599,999 to 1. If the entire population of the planet played 60 hands of bridge every day, newborns included, you'd expect one naturally occurring perfect deal to occur slightly more often than once every 125,000,000,000 years. In practice, shuffling a deck of cards is often done ineffectively, and most occurrences of a perfect deal come down to poor randomization. The rest are the result of deliberate tampering.

THE FIFTH CAMOUFLAGE

The theme was dining out, and the words were *lay*, *sit*, *eat* and *tip*.

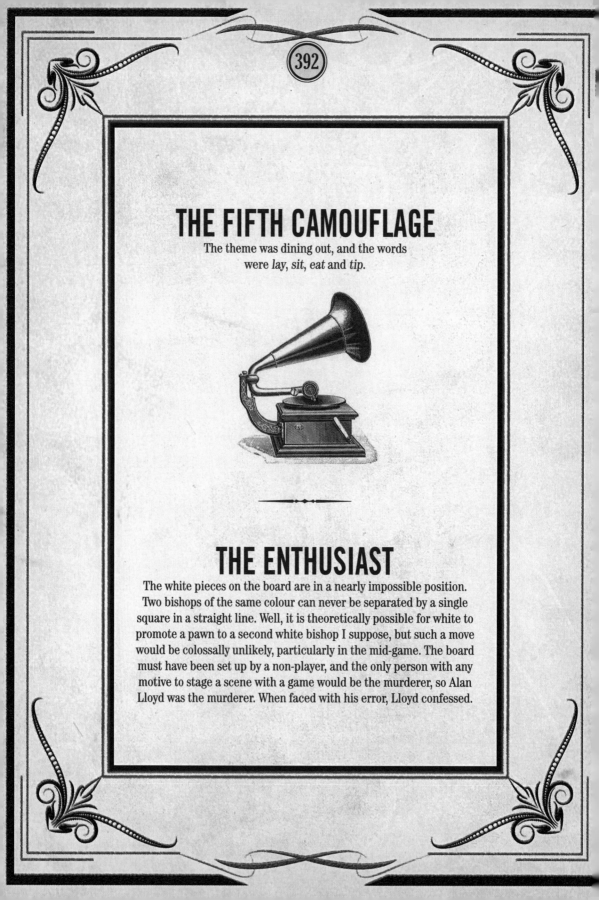

THE ENTHUSIAST

The white pieces on the board are in a nearly impossible position. Two bishops of the same colour can never be separated by a single square in a straight line. Well, it is theoretically possible for white to promote a pawn to a second white bishop I suppose, but such a move would be colossally unlikely, particularly in the mid-game. The board must have been set up by a non-player, and the only person with any motive to stage a scene with a game would be the murderer, so Alan Lloyd was the murderer. When faced with his error, Lloyd confessed.

THE RIBBONS

Mrs White. Remembering that each amount spent must be a square number, each mother's length of ribbon must be even, and working through the logic, Daisy bought 4y for 16 pence, and her mother Mrs Green 8y for 64 pence. Rose bought 6y for 36 pence, and her mother Mrs Brown bought 12y for 144 pence. Lily bought 9y for 81 pence and her mother Mrs Black bought 18y for 324 pence. And Heather bought 10y for 100 pence and her mother Mrs White bought 20y for 400 pence.

TROUT

72 ounces. If the tail weighs 9, the head must weigh 9+x/2, and the body, x = 18+x/2. So half x = 18, and x=36, which means the head = 27, and the total is 9+27+36.

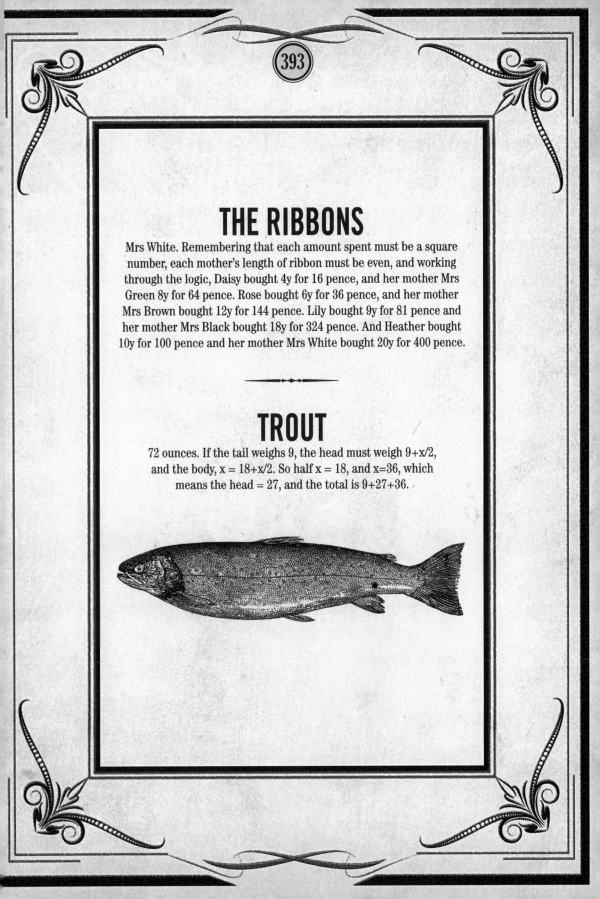

GETTING TO MARKET

10 miles. After 20 minutes, we had travelled half as far as the distance from that spot to Doglick, so it took an hour to Doglick. Then, five miles past Doglick, we had half that 5-mile distance still to go, and that took one hour. So we did 5 miles in 2 hours, our total journey time was 4 hours, and the full distance was 10 miles.

THE TENTH WORDKNOT

The words are *abacterial*, *biocenosis* and *halophytes*, and their broad theme is biology.

PENCILS

By arranging them in alternating rows of 19 and 20, as it turns out. By putting the second row in the hollows of the first, and then the third in the hollows of the second, you save enough space to get a ninth row in place. So you would have 180 pencils if all the rows were 20 pencils long, but four of them are one short, giving you 176 – 16 more than 160.

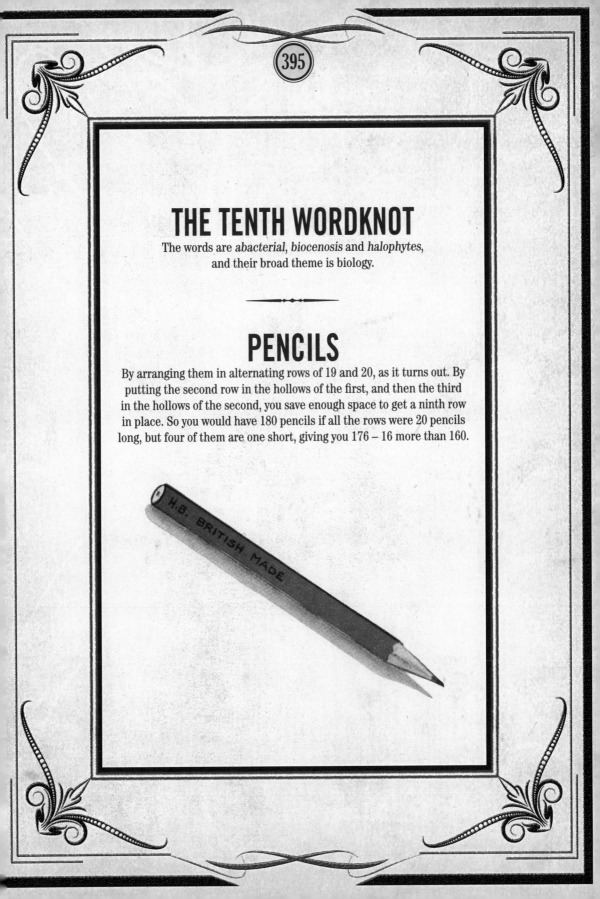

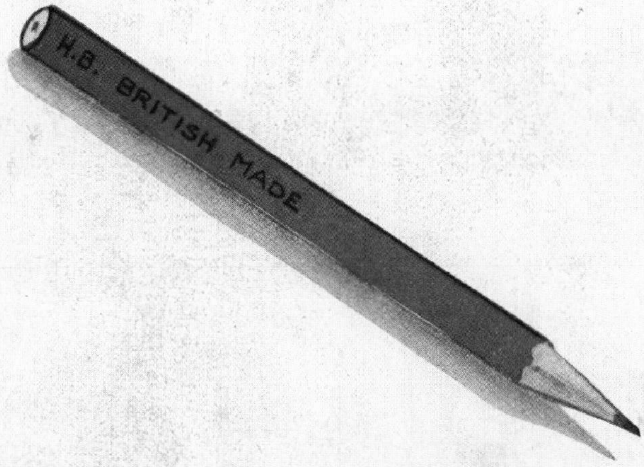

EASTER SPIRIT

1.5". Volumes of solids that are the same shape vary according to the cube of their relative lengths. So the largest egg has a comparative volume of 27, being 3" in length. So the volumes of the other three eggs have to add to $27 = x^3 + (x+0.5)^3 + (x+1)^3$. *Regula falsi* is probably simpler here than trying to simplify the equation, so try x=1, for 12.375 (or 2.3^3), and x=2 for 50.625 (or 3.7^3), and you'll see that 1 and 2 put you the same distance from the correct answer, so the midpoint between 1 and 2 must be where the volumes sum to 3^3. In other words, x = 1.5 inches.

RUFUS

16 mph. The overall distance to the end of the road in feet is $625 = 5^4$, and the end of the dog's running time is when the distance in feet is $81 = 3^4$. These quad roots are obviously in the ratio 5:3, so the sum of the two speeds and the difference between the two speeds must be in the ratio of 5:3, and thus the two speeds in the ratio of 4:1. Wiggins walks at 4 mph, so the dog runs at 16 mph.

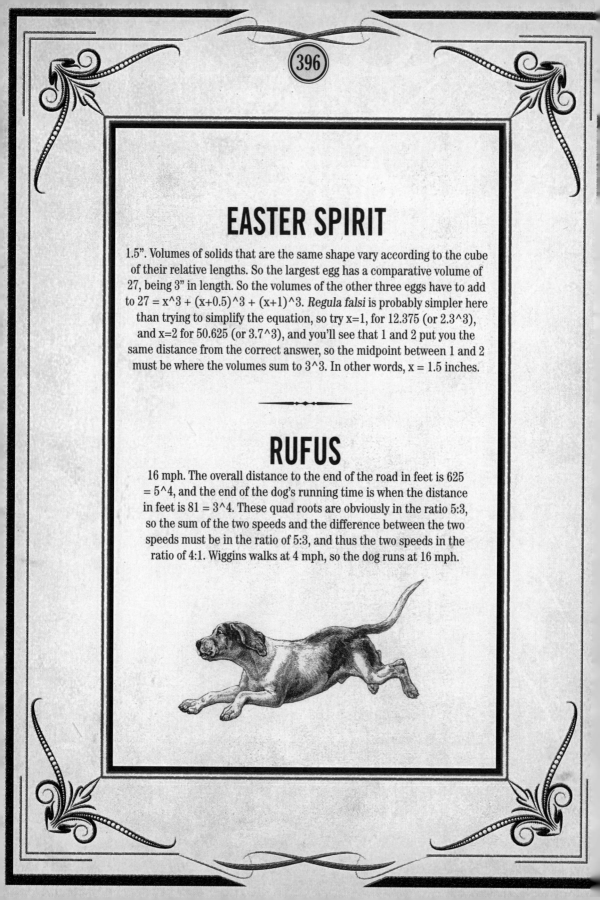

THREE MEN

The driver is called Smith. To find the answer, it is useful to keep a grid of possible (and impossible) associations to help make the facts clearer. From (1), Mr Robinson lives in Brixton and, associating (5), is not the professor. From (2), Mr Jones is not the professor either, so the professor is Mr Smith. From (5), Mr Smith lives near the conductor, so Mr Smith also lives in Chelsea. That means Mr Jones must live in Tottenham, and from (4), the conductor is called Jones. So from (3), the ticket inspector can only be Robinson, which means that the driver is called Smith.

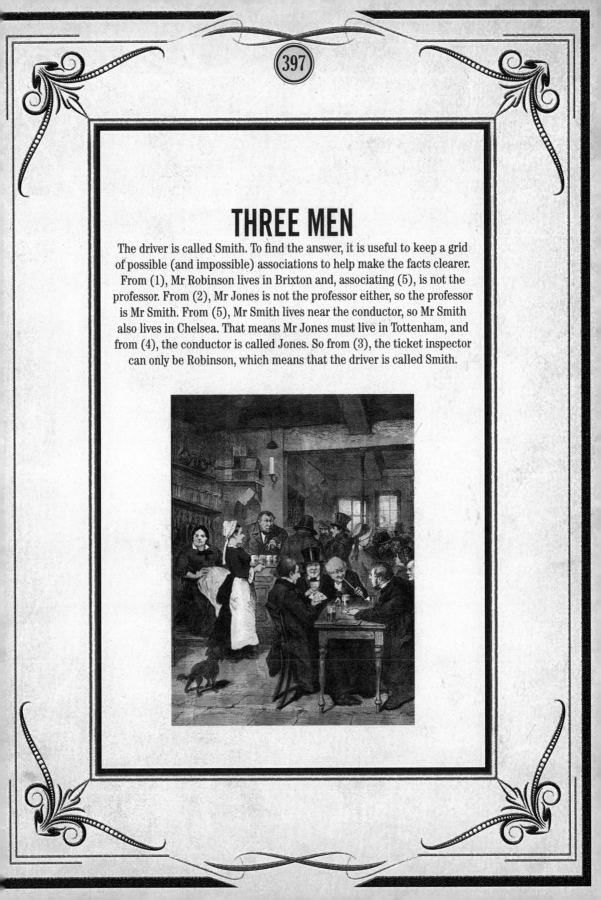

THE TYRANT

If I were to split my marbles evenly, 50 in each jar, then the 50/50 chance of getting either jar would keep my odds of survival at precisely 50%. However, if I place one white marble in one jar, and the other 99 marbles in the other, my chances go up to 1/2*1 + 1/2*49/99, or 74%. This is as good as it gets. Still not a chance I'd take willingly without significant duress, but a lot better than 50%!

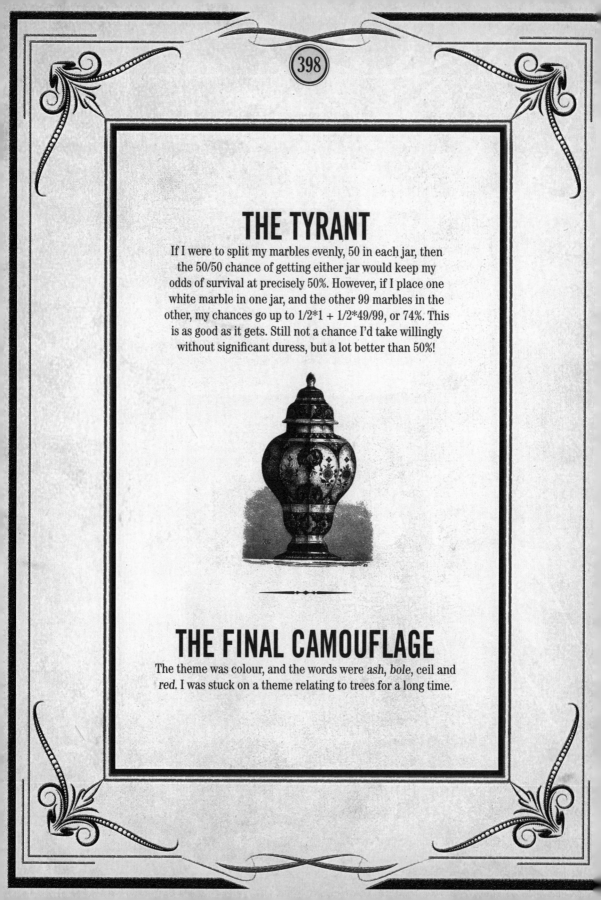

THE FINAL CAMOUFLAGE

The theme was colour, and the words were *ash*, *bole*, ceil and *red*. I was stuck on a theme relating to trees for a long time.

SEVEN APPLEWOMEN

One pricing scheme is 7 apples per penny, until less than 7 remain, at which point the apples become 3 pence per apple. The fact that there are seven women with a maximum number of 140 apples ought to point you towards the divisive break. So the first woman gets 2 pence from 14 apples, plus 18 pence from her remaining 6, whilst the last gets 140/7=20 pence all from batches of 7 apples per penny. The general solution for this sort of puzzle says that for x people with amounts of produce equal to y(x+0z) + x–1, y(x+1z) + x–2, y(x+2z) + x–3, ..., then these can be sold at x for 1 penny and then z for each remaining odd item, and all will receive y + z(x–1) pennies. In our case, y, an indeterminate factor in the equation, is equal to 2, giving us a z of 3 for the x of 7.

TERMINUS

The victim's jumper was back to front as well as inside out. One would only have seen the label if standing in front of the man. Bligh claims to have seen the label as the victim ran away, which is impossible, and marks him as the killer.